JOHN KNOX

AND OTHER PLAYS

AMATEUR RIGHTS

PROFESSIONAL RIGHTS

JOHN KNOX

AND OTHER PLAYS BY

JAMES BRIDIE

John Knox

Dr. Angelus

It Depends What You Mean

The Forrigan Reel

LONDON

CONSTABLE & CO LTD

LONDON
PUBLISHED BY
Constable and Company Ltd
10–12 ORANGE STREET, W.C.2

INDIA *and* PAKISTAN
Orient Longmans Ltd
BOMBAY   CALCUTTA   MADRAS

CANADA
Longmans, Green and Company
TORONTO

First published 1949

PRINTED IN GREAT BRITAIN
BY W. & J. MACKAY & CO., LTD., CHATHAM

JOHN KNOX

A Play
in Three Acts

This play was first performed at the Glasgow Citizens' Theatre on 18th August, 1947, with the following cast :

NORA	Lennox Milne.
HECTOR	Denis Pullein-Thompson.
JERRY	Laurence Hardy.
KNOX	John Laurie.
GEORGE DOUGLAS	Fred Law.
FRANCIS DOUGLAS	George McLean.
ALEXANDER COCKBURN	James Cameron.
HEW	Jane Lang.
MARY OF GUISE	Valerie Lush.
MARY STUART, AS A CHILD	Hilary Paterson.
LADY BOWES	Rosalie Westwater.
MARJORIE BOWES	Janet Drysdale.
LORD JAMES STUART	Duncan Macrae.
LETHINGTON	James Gibson.
CHORUS	John Casson.
BOTHWELL	Rupert Davies.
LENNOX	Graham Squire.
DARNLEY	Peter Macdonell.
MARY STUART	Mary McAlpine.
LIVINGSTONE	Anne Butchart.
BEATON	Maureen MacGregor.
SEATON	Gracie Dods.
FLEMING	Jacqueline Barnett.
RIZZIO	Daniel Thorndike.
PARIS	Andrew Buggy.
CHASTELARD	Denis Vaughan.
RUTHVEN	Kenneth Mackintosh.

The play was produced by John Casson ; the décor was by John Russell and the songs and incidental music were composed by Robert Irving.

CHARACTERS IN THE PLAY

NORA DONNELLY, A Leith Street walker.

HECTOR MACGILLIVRAY, A Divinity Student.

JERRY, A Street dancer.

JOHN KNOX.

GEORGE DOUGLAS.

FRANCIS DOUGLAS. ⎫

ALEXANDER COCKBURN. ⎭ Children.

Three other CHILDREN.

JAMES BALFOUR.

A LAY BROTHER.

ELIZABETH BOWES.

MARJORIE BOWES.

MARY OF GUISE.

LORD JAMES STUART.

MAITLAND OF LETHINGTON.

CHORUS.

HEPBURN OF BOTHWELL.

THE EARL OF LENNOX.

LORD HENRY DARNLEY.

A SINGER.

MARY STUART.

MARY LIVINGSTONE.

MARY BEATON.

MARY SEATON.

MARY FLEMING.

DAVID RIZZIO.

CHASTELARD.

THE EARL OF RUTHVEN.

NOTES ON THE CHARACTERS

KNOX :

   KNOX's appearance in the first two acts should conform to
the painting in the National Portrait Gallery. Rather below
the middle height ; broad shoulders ; black hair and beard,
the beard short and rather sparse ; narrowish forehead ;
grey-blue eyes, deep-set beneath ridged brows, and full
ruddyish cheeks ; long nose, long mouth, full lips, the upper
somewhat thicker than the lower ; a dour countenance but
not unkindly nor untouched by humour. Like a Lowland
farmer.

   In the last act his beard is long and grey, his face pinched,
but even then he should be liker the N.P.G. picture than the
Beza engraving. When he takes off his Geneva cap he should
be nearly bald. He moves with great energy and gesticulates
nervously when he is excited. His voice is very full, round
and rich.

MARY :

   A very tall woman. She was in fact six feet high. She was
a fine horsewoman and dancer, an archer and a golfer, and
her movements should suggest this. Another notable thing
about her was her extreme pallor. She should be made up
after the well known Clouet drawing, which is the only
picture that gives any idea of her character. Her clothes are
first white and then black. Chestnut hair. Rather sly expression
of the eyes, and slightly masculine bearing.

THE QUEEN REGENT :

   A mature woman exactly like the Duchess of Windsor, but
full of a rather sinister charm.

LORD JAMES STUART : (THE REGENT MORAY)

   A tall, alert young man with warm brown hair and beard
and heavy, weary eyes. Rather a long face with strong bones.
Black clothes.

A*   [1]

LETHINGTON :

A little man with a long, thin, peaked face and prominent bright red lips. Light brown beard and moustache and high, narrow forehead. There is something in him of a thorough-bred pony and something of a bird. His dress is dark in colour, but dandified. He played the part of Dr. Goebbels to the whole outfit, first to one side and then to the other and might slightly suggest that gentleman. He never appears to take anything seriously. But there is an undertow of strong political passion in him.

DARNLEY :

DARNLEY looked exactly like his descendant, Edward VIIIth., except that he was very tall.

BOTHWELL :

I don't think anybody knows exactly what Bothwell looked like. His skeleton showed him as a shortish, heavily built man. His hair was very dark red. He should certainly have a tremendous voice.

HECTOR :

His part should be played by an actor with a personality nearly as strong as Knox's and Bothwell's. He should be slightly dissolute, fairly young and should speak straight English.

NORA :

A chubby, sonsy woman of well under thirty, dressed in shabby finery. Her speech should be a mixture of Donegal and Glasgow, with a false gentility rubbed over it now and again.

THE MULATTO :

Has a hotch-potch of all the accents in the world, but his voice is that of a West Indian negro.

NOTE :—*I have said nothing of the speech of Mary Queen of Scots. She seems to have preferred to speak either French or broad Middle Scots ; but I think the safest way is for the actress to stick to fairly straight English and to allow her ear to guide her through the Scottish inflections of her speeches. The Queen Regent talks with a strong French accent.*

[2]

ACT I

*Before the Curtain rises the sound of bells and the singing
of " Auld Lang Syne " are heard, along with the confused
noises of a New Year celebration. These sounds fade as
the Curtain goes up slowly on the front of the National
Gallery of Scotland at the Mound, Edinburgh. A very
simple, stylised set should be used, with the Gallery
indicated by a row of Ionic pillars with darkness between
them and steps leading up to them. In this and succeeding
Scenes one or more spaces between the pillars may be lit
to show a Scene within the Scene. A back cloth shows
Edinburgh Castle with an angry sky behind it, lit by the
moon in its first quarter.*

The time is a little after midnight on 1st January, 19—.

A MULATTO *is asleep on the lowest step of the rostrum.
He is a West Indian of about 30 years old. He wears a
scarlet uniform jacket, a panama hat and striped
pyjama trousers. These things are covered by a bright
tartan blanket. Near him is a gramophone mounted on
a perambulator. The* MULATTO *is a clog dancer by
profession.*

A woman called NORA, *still young and personable, but
not too sober, passes and stops.*

NORA. Hello, Jerry.

JERRY (*half asleep*). Hello.

NORA. I thought it was you by the pram. Not dancing the
night ?

JERRY. No good me dancing. Everybody dancing. Maybe
I dance sometime. Now I take forty winks.

NORA. A Happy New Year, then.

JERRY. The same to you.

NORA. You'll be cold, lying there.

[3]

JERRY. Aye. I'm cold.

NORA. A Happy New Year to you then.

JERRY. A Happy New Year.

> NORA *suddenly becomes professional.* A DIVINITY
> STUDENT *is approaching. He is tipsy, but forging
> ahead, grimly. He has a dead cigarette in his mouth.
> When he speaks, he speaks like an Englishman. Only
> an occasional inflection or turn of phrase betrays the
> Highlander.*

NORA. Hello, big boy.

HECTOR. Hello.

> *He stops.*

NORA. A Happy New Year to you.

HECTOR. And a most prosperous New Year to you, indeed.

NORA. Going home, handsome ?

HECTOR. Indeed, I had that notion.

NORA. It's early yet.

HECTOR. Is it indeed ? For some reason or other my sense
of time has gone by the board. For all I know, it may be early.

NORA. Have you a home to go to ?

HECTOR. I hope so. I hope so. Though I speak more out
of blind faith than out of any fixed persuasion . . . Who is
that on the steps ?

NORA. That's Jerry. The dancing fellow. Everybody
knows Jerry.

HECTOR. Will he dance ?

NORA. He will if you give him a tanner.

HECTOR. I haven't got a tanner in the world.

NORA. Dear me. That's a pity. Good night, then.

HECTOR. Good night.

> *He mounts the steps.*

NORA. Hi, you don't live there. That's the National
Gallery, they keep pictures there. Not the right Pictures.
Paintings and that.

HECTOR. Paintings, eh ?

> *He sits down on the top step.*

NORA. Listen, where do you stay?

HECTOR. Here.

NORA. Have it your own way. Jerry.

JERRY. Yes?

NORA. Have you a corner of your plaidie for a bonnie wee lady,

> JERRY *rouses himself and they sit down together with the plaid over their shoulders.*

NORA. That's better. You're as warm as a wee pudding. Have you any hootch?

JERRY. No. Ma'am, no.

NORA. I wonder will the King of Siam up there have any hootch. Hey, Mister. Have you a drop of something at your hip?

> HECTOR *stands up.*

HECTOR. Ye men of Athens, I perceive that in all things ye are too superstitious. For, as I passed by and beheld your devotions, I found an altar with this inscription, "TO THE UNKNOWN GOD." Whom therefore ye ignorantly worship, him declare I unto you.

NORA. Here . . . You cley up or you'll get lifted.

HECTOR. God that made the world and all things therein, seeing that he is Lord of heaven and earth, dwelleth not in temples made with hands; neither is worshipped with men's hands, as though he needed anything, seeing he giveth to all life, and breath, and all things; and hath made of one blood all nations of men for to dwell on all the face of the earth, and hath determined the times before appointed and the bounds of their habitation.

NORA. See us a tambourine, Jerry. We'll be getting saved, the two of us.

HECTOR (*looks at her as if he had only half wakened from a trance*). What did you say?

NORA. What do I say? It's you that's doing the talking. All I have to say is you go on that gait and the polis'll get you, Hogmanay or no Hogmanay.

HECTOR. Be quiet. Something's going to happen. I don't know what it is, but something's going to happen.

After a short pause the voice of JOHN KNOX *comes strongly out of the dark entrance to the Gallery.*

KNOX. The sun keepeth his ordinary course and starteth not back from the west to the south. And so it is with the light of the Gospel. Most evident it is that where the light of God's word for the unthankfulness of men has been taken away, that there it is not to this day restored again.

NORA. Holy Mother of God ! What was that ?

HECTOR. I don't know.

NORA. There's some fellow in there taking a rise out of us.

HECTOR *goes into the dark entry and comes out again.*

HECTOR. There's nobody there.

He comes down the steps in a puzzled sort of way and sits down beside the other two.

HECTOR. I've heard those words before somewhere. Or read them. Let me think.

NORA. High time and nobody stopping you. Go on and think. Are you one of these ventriloquists, or what ? You might have given us a better turn than that. Would you like Jerry to give us a bit wallop with the clogs ? Go on, Jerry. Give us a bit wallop with the clogs. I'm feeling funny up and down the spine.

JERRY *gets up wearily, lays down his dancing board and turns on his cracked gramophone. He dances a few steps.*

HECTOR. Stop !

NORA. On you go, hen ! Don't mind him.

HECTOR. No, no, stop ! It was John Knox.

JERRY *stops his instrument and stands listening.*

NORA. It was who ?

HECTOR. It was John Knox.

[6]

NORA. You don't mean that blasphemious old blether, him that's deid long syne?

HECTOR. It was John Knox.

NORA. Do you mean it's a ghost?

She gets up and clutches JERRY.

HECTOR. Yes.

NORA. He used to live here. Maybe it *is* a ghost.

She crosses herself and mutters something under her breath, and suddenly screams.

Oh, look at the door! Look at the door!

She crouches down on the dancing board and JERRY *sits down beside her.* HECTOR *comes round behind them. All three face the doorway of the gallery, which becomes slowly illuminated to show a little bare chapel. There is a table littered with books, a rocking horse and a ladder leading to a little window high up. Four little boys are dancing round the rocking horse, quite solemnly and in silence. Another little boy is sitting on the table with two huge books clasped to his breast. He is* GEORGE DOUGLAS, *Younger of Longniddry. He is looking towards the roof like a dying duck. The dance goes on for a little, till* JOHN KNOX *enters. He is a square-faced man in his forties, with a black spade beard. He resembles the picture in the National Portrait Gallery. The children stop suddenly and turn towards him sheepishly.*

KNOX. What's all this?

GEORGE. It was Hughie, Maister Knox.

He points at one of the children.

It was Hughie, Maister Knox; it was Hughie's notion.

KNOX. What idiot beasts are you? I left ye ten minutes syne at the Gospel according to Saint John in the tongue of the Greeks and on my return I find ye leaping and staggering like sturdied tups or the swine of Gadara.

GEORGE. It was Hughie.

HEW. You're a clype.

GEORGE. Hughie said we should do the thirty second chapter of the Book of Exodus. He said it would find favour in the sicht of the Lord. He made the ithers be the children of Israel setting up the Gowden Calf and he made me be Moses.

KNOX. He made you what?

GEORGE. Moses, Sir John.

KNOX. You're a bonny-like Moses.

GEORGE. The rocking horse is the Gowden Calf. I'm Moses.

KNOX. Think ye the Children of Israel defied the Lord God of Hosts after a wabbit fashion like that? You're an object of pity and not of wrath. Let me see ye leap and dance and shout. Join hands. Spring in the air, Skirl till your lungs burst. Stop . . . Moses, you're up on an unco wee Sinai. The Lord will be hard put to it to roar at you from the lift. Up the ladder with you.

> *The children join hands half-heartedly but later enter into the spirit of the thing, lashed on by* KNOX'S *tongue.* GEORGE *begins to climb the ladder.*

KNOX. Up with ye. It's a sair trauchle to the top of Mount Sinai . . . And now, Israelites. You're gey taken up with your cawf. Show it, boys, show it. Sing now . . .

> " Here we go by jingoring
> Jingoring, jingoring.
> Here we go by jingoring
> Round about Mary Matanzie."

You're possessit by the de'il. The de'il's no' an auld wife in a mutch. He's lashing you with scorpions with henbane in the tails of them. There's a byke of the de'il's ain hornets in your hair. Prance, boys, prance. Sing, boys, sing. Is it no a bonny wee stot? See the sun of the desert sklent aff his gowden flanks.

> " Here we go by jingoring . . ."

Yell yourselves into a lather. Go on. Go on. The pipes are playing. The drums are playing ratatat, ratatat. Dance, my billies, dance. You've gotten yoursels a brand new God.

The BOYS *go into a wild dance.*

KNOX. The cat's away, the mice will play. Here's nae word of power to rend your spirit. Here's nae fear of the Lord to shake your banes apart. Here's nae straucht and narrow pathway. Riot round the mulberry bush. Eat drink and be merry, for it may weel be that the morrow never come. Sing my billies, dance till ye drap . . . " Ring a ring a roses and ye all fa' doon." Fa' doon. Wallow in the mire. Doon wi' ye.

The BOYS *collapse.*

KNOX. Moses. Look out the window into Eternity. What do you see ?

GEORGE. Rain.

A silence.

KNOX (*soberly*). Come doon, Moses.

GEORGE *comes down the ladder. He and the other* BOYS *silently join* JOHN KNOX *on the steps of the Gallery. They group themselves on the top three steps as the Chapel Scene slowly fades.*

KNOX. Lads, if I'd anything to give I would give it to be you at this hour. You were born to harsh times, but the storm will clear and you will spend your manhood in the Promised Land when John Knox is a deid old sinner below the yerd. In this town of Sanct Andrew you have seen sights that were not seemly for bairns to see. You have smelt the reek of George Wishart burning at the stake. The greatest deed I ever did or ever will do was to carry a twa-handed sword before that meek and godly man as Peter carried the sword at Gethsemane. Boys, I'd have been sair pitten to it to do so much as cut off a guardsman's lug. A bonny-like figure was I to carry a sword, and me a greeting, chittering man of peace. It was Dauvid Beaton, the Scarlet Cardinal, that burnt George Wishart as he burnt Pat Hamilton before him ; and not many

[9]

days syne you saw that same Beaton hung by a sheet from his chaumer window still dripping from his dagger wounds. Harsh times ! But these times are bye, and a new generation will enter the Promised Land.

He stands up.

You are to be the men, my lads. John Knox is an old havering priest, with the gravel aye yerk-yerking at his kidneys ; but when you march into the land of Canaan with your banners flying, remember what he told you and walk soberly. There is a young Queen over tha water in France. When you are men and she is a woman she will come to you and be ruler and magistrate over you under the hand of God. See to it that she takes joy in the palàce you have preparit for her. It is thus you shall prepare it :—This land shall be ruled by the Lord God alone with nae pardoners and nae damned dogs of bishops between his people and himself. And that the men of Scotland may be fit for this empiry every bairn and girl bairn in the Realm shall be taught to read, write and cypher withouten charge. Neither body nor soul shall starve in this land, nay, not even the humblest. When their bellies are full of meat and their heids are full of knowledge, then will they say who is to bear rule and governance over them, and no man shall rule them but by their ain consent. They will cause their Queen to punish wrongdoers, to keep the peace and to sustain the law of the land. In that peace and in that law there will rise up a nation of men living like brothers in Christ's true kingdom. This you will mak ready or the Queen come, and this you will tend and sustain when she dwells with you. Your deeds and your governance will warm auld John Knox when he lies cold in his grave, ten short years from now.

Sound of gunfire.

What was that ?

GEORGE. It sounded like guns, Mr. Knox.

KNOX. Away up the ladder, Moses, and see what you can see.

> *Gunfire continues as* GEORGE *mounts the ladder to the window. A short silence.*

[10]

GEORGE. Oooooooooooo ! St. Andrew's Bay is crowded with ships ! I think they're warships.

KNOX. The French fleet ! Maybe I spoke ower soon.

> *The porch slowly blacks out, until nothing is seen of it but the intermittent flash of gunfire through the little window.*

NORA. It'll be a dream, I wouldn't wonder.

HECTOR. Can two people dream the same dream ?

NORA. Who said there were two people ? You're maybe only a bit of the dream yourself. I had haggis for my dinner, and maybe a gill, and maybe more.

> KNOX *appears on the steps lit by a single spot.*

KNOX. In 1547, in the castle of St. Andrews, then becoming encompassed about by the enemies of the Faith with no help anywhere to be found, I was called suddenly to the ministry of that place to my great astonishment and to the perturbation of my spirit. At that call I burst forth in most abundant tears and withdrew myself to my chamber. All my mirth was dead in me and I saw the face of no man till the next Lord's Day when I preached on the seventh chapter of Daniel.

> KNOX *disappears.*

HECTOR. They said that where others lopped the branches he struck at the root. Never had such a sermon been heard. They said George Wishart never spoke so plainly and yet he was burnt, and so would John Knox be. But the great men of Scotland crowded into his sermons under the guns of the French fleet, until one summer day the French took the town and Knox was thrown into the galleys.

> *One of the lesser alcoves lights up and shows the naked backs of* JOHN KNOX *and* JAMES BALFOUR *as they pull at the oar. The marks of the lash are on their backs. They rest on their oars as a* LAY BROTHER *appears with a small rude image of the Virgin.*

KNOX. *Qu'est ce que c'est que ça?*

LAY BROTHER (*casually*). *La Sainte Vierge ! Commandements du capitaine !*

KNOX. And what have I to do with it ?

LAY BROTHER. Kiss it.

KNOX. Kiss a painted board ? D'ye take me for a bairn ?

> *He takes the image from the* LAY BROTHER.

Aye, she looks licht enough. We'll see can she swim.

> *He throws the image through the port. The light fades quickly. The last thing to be seen is the* LAY BROTHER'S *horrified face.*

NORA. I never saw blasphemy the like of that.

HECTOR. You never served in the galleys.

NORA. I have served in the Leith Walk on a Saturday night and I'm telling you I never heard blasphemy the like of that.

HECTOR. Look ! Where the devil are we now ? Oh yes. France. It must be France.

> *The alcove lights up to show a little summer house at Versailles in front of a sunny garden backing.* MARY OF GUISE, *the* QUEEN REGENT, *is hearing a little girl her lessons. The* CARDINAL OF LORRAINE *stands behind without speaking.*

That's the Queen Regent of Scotland. That's Mary of Guise. I think I know the little girl.

NORA. But . . .

HECTOR. Be quiet !

LITTLE GIRL. *Amo . . . J'aime . . .* I love. *Amas . . . tu aimes . . .* thou lovest. *Amat . . . il aime . . .* he loves. *Amamus . . . nous aimons . . .* we love. Oh, I'm wearied with this ! I want to ride my pony.

> MARY OF GUISE *is a tall, good-looking woman in deep black. She has an odd resemblance to the Duchess of Windsor. She speaks with a strong French accent and an overflowing charm.*

THE QUEEN. Ah, little one! My sweet rabbit! My heart's joy! You must not speak like that.

LITTLE GIRL. I do not like the words " must " and " must not."

THE QUEEN. But that is terrible. Your good uncle the Cardinal looks horrified. (*To the* CARDINAL.) Look horrified, my dear. (*To the* GIRL.) Nevertheless, they are works you must learn. You have a great destiny.

LITTLE GIRL. What is destiny?

THE QUEEN. Destiny is another word for must.

LITTLE GIRL. But who says I must? Who makes my destiny?

THE QUEEN. God, my little one, and His Blessed Mother.

LITTLE GIRL. What is my destiny?

The QUEEN *becomes sibylline.*

THE QUEEN. Ah-h-h-h-h-h-h! . . . Your destiny is to be a Queen.

LITTLE GIRL. But I am a Queen. I am the Queen of Scotland.

THE QUEEN. When you are big and tall you will be the Queen of England and of France and of Ireland. And who knows how many more? You will be the most powerful Princess in all the world. You will glorify the true Church and stamp the heretics under your foot. That is your destiny. And because of that you must be diligent and learn your grammar.

LITTLE GIRL. Shall I have soldiers?

THE QUEEN. Yes.

LITTLE GIRL. Will they die for me?

THE QUEEN. It will not be necessary that they should die for you. No one will dare to attack them, so mighty a Princess will you be. But you will not be a great Princess unless you learn your grammar.

LITTLE GIRL. And must I learn music and dancing and shooting and riding to be a great Princess?

THE QUEEN. These things too.

[13]

LITTLE GIRL. Very well. I will learn my grammar, but I should like to ride my pony first.

THE QUEEN (*laughs*). Come my bonny, my love, my precious lamb ! You shall ride your pony.

The three go out as the light fades.

HECTOR. Damn the old woman ! She fought like a wolf-bitch for her daughter's destiny. Throats were cut and bodies burned, and John Knox fled to Berwick and preached there. Sir Richard Bowes was the Governor of Berwick and his wife was called Elizabeth. And his daughter was called Marjorie. This was in 1553.

> *The centre-piece lights up. It is now the chamber of* LADY BOWES *at Berwick Castle. It is a dreary, stony little room, but there are some touches of style about it.* KNOX, ELIZABETH *and* MARJORIE *have just finished a three o'clock meal. The sun is shining.*

KNOX. Bountiful Jehovah, we thank you for these mercies in the name of Jesus Christ Our Lord, Amen.

LADY BOWES. Amen. Clear away, Marjorie. We'll not bother the servants. It will save time.

MARJORIE *begins to clear.*

LADY BOWES. Ah, Mr. Knox, if I could but find refreshment to the spirit as I have found in these mercies refreshment for the carnal belly.

KNOX. There are those, ma'am, who cannot take their fleshly victuals without rumblings and belchings. So it is with many when we essay to feed their spirits with the rich ambrosia of the Word.

LADY BOWES. I fear you find me a dyspeptic guest at the goodly table.

KNOX. We will cure that, ma'am, by the Lord His mercy. Where is the pain that irks you the nicht ?

LADY BOWES. The Devil will not let me be. At times I think I shall go mad ... Leave the wine, Marjorie. Mr. Knox has been over-eloquent to do it justice. . . It is as if all the imps of Hell took it in turn to assail me. They question me and I have no answer but " Get thee behind me, Satan," and they are behind me and over me and around me as it is.

EXIT MARJORIE *with dishes*.

KNOX. What do they spier at you?

LADY BOWES. Spier at me? Oh, you mean ask me? They say " Go back. Go back and be happy again." They say, " Was it not fine, when your head and your heart ached to go into the dim cool church and to hear the sweet monotonous voices of the singers and the priest? To smell the incense and hear the tinkle of the bell? That was peace," they say. " You are never more to have peace. You have taken back on your-self the burden of your sins and they are too heavy to bear. Lay them again on the broad back of Holy Kirk and you will be well." That is what they say and my head aches too much to answer them.

KNOX. The dronings and the stinks and the eenty-teenty-halisolum were witchcraft. You ken that? You were made drunken with their witchcraft till you didna ken whether you had sinned or no. How could a lecherous priest tak your sins on him? He was ower burdened with his ain sins.

LADY BOWES. I know that. I know that.

KNOX. You ken wha can tak your sins on him?

LADY BOWES. He stands away from me.

KNOX. Seek him, then. Seek him then in the crowd. Clutch the hem of his garment as it brushes the edge of Hell. Clutch it weel and haud on like grim death.

RE-ENTER MARJORIE.

MARJORIE. Mother.

LADY BOWES. What is it, dear?

MARJORIE. Father wants to speak to you.

LADY BOWES. Did you tell him I was with Mr. Knox?

MARJORIE. Yes, mother.

LADY BOWES. What does he want?

MARJORIE. I think it is something about the hens, mother.

LADY BOWES. Hens ? Hens ? Can hens give forth the pure milk of the Gospel.

KNOX. It would be a merry thing gin they gave forth milk ava.

MARJORIE *giggles.*

LADY BOWES. You are mocking me, Mr. Knox.

KNOX. Indeed, ma'am, not I. I mock at none of God's creatures ; least of all at one who planted my feet on the dry land when the dark waves had wellnigh swallowed me quick.

He takes her hand.

Go to your guid man. I will abide your return.

LADY BOWES. Do so, Mr. Knox.

EXIT LADY BOWES.

MARJORIE. I don't know what we should do without you, Mr. Knox. Since my mother took to the new religion she sits and weeps for hours at a time. You are the only one who can give her any comfort.

KNOX. It is no new religion, Miss Marjorie. It is the old religion breaking its bonds.

MARJORIE. It doesn't seem to make my mother very happy.

KNOX. Your mother was not very happy when you were being born. But when she held you in her arms you were a joy to her.

MARJORIE. You are not very happy yourself, Mr. Knox.

KNOX. Why should I be happy ? There is less room for happiness in my soul than there was room in the confessor for your mother's sins. My dolour answers to her dolour. I am wrestling with the black Devil and the very joints of my backbone are cracking and my hands are behind my back. I must stand on my narrow foothold and bide till the Devil tires. The ground behind me gives way. Mary Tudor has come to the throne of England and the De'il has given a great skelloch for very joy. Your King Harry was an inordinate man, but he sustained the Brethren. What will they do now ? What will come of my dream for Scotland ?

MARJORIE. What dream?

KNOX. Eleven years syne I earned my bread as teacher to a handful of bubbly-nosed brats. I told them that in ten years they would be shaping in Scotland the perfect regimen. The people would rule and the people would be instructed and worthy to rule. I told them the true kingdom of God was at hand. I told them that when it was in the making poor John Knox would be under the mools and taking nae art nor part in it. Would God that I had spoken truly.

MARJORIE. But why need you take art nor part in it? You are the parson of Berwick and my father protects you. Why should you concern yourself with these things?

KNOX (*simply*). Because I have been called.

A short silence.

But I made one error then and there is no need to repeat it. It was ill done to deave those callants with my daft notions. You are young and bonny and the black days for you are still to come. I'll not deave you.

MARJORIE. I want to be deaved. You can see deep into people, but you can't see into me. Go on deaving me, Mr. Knox.

KNOX. What you say is true. It is hard to read the heart of a child.

MARJORIE. I am not a child.

KNOX. How old are you?

MARJORIE. I am eighteen.

KNOX. And I am forty-eight. Forbye, when I pulled on an oar in the French galley an early winter brought the frost to my soul and to my beard. There's a wilderness of years between, us, my lassie.

MARJORIE. Wildernesses can be crossed if we have wings.

KNOX. What could give wings to a broken dotard the like of me? I am a moudiewarp burrowing deep in the yard. It isna often I get a glint of the natural sky.

MARJORIE. I suppose if you did see the sky it would be full of solemn men in white nightgowns playing harps.

KNOX. No, it would be blue. Plain blue. The Lord gives gifts to the eyes of the body as well as to the eyes of the spirit. You canna better that blue.

MARJORIE. Why are you looking at me like that?

KNOX. Because I see it reflectit in your eyes and I thank God for it and go back to my digging with a merrier heart. *O beaux yeux, qui m'estiez si cruels et si doux! Je ne me puis lasser de repenser en vous . . .*

MARJORIE. Who wrote that?

KNOX. An unregenerate Frenchman by the name of Peter de Ronsard.

MARJORIE. It is strange to hear you repeating a Frenchman's verses.

KNOX. There is some good even in Frenchmen. I read their verses as I listen to the mavis. Their souls are another matter, but God gave them a singing voice. There was good in this Ronsard too. He is maybe not so far from the Kingdom of Heaven. I have mind of a verse he wrote on the bishops and prelates of France. It fits our own dumb dogs not so badly.

" If good Sanct Paul came back to see his farm
   He'd find his shepherd lads an unco crew.
   The men he charged to keep his sheep from harm
   Have stawn their wool and rived their skin aff too.
   High do they live, these herds, nor preach nor pray.
   Scented and prinked, they hunt in coats so gay
   Wildfowl and women. God's good gifts are shed
   While hungry flocks look up and are not fed."

The weary truth, is, Marjorie, that the Devil holds all the castles and keeps the strong places in this sorrowful world today. Above all he sits armed in the heart of the Vicar of Rome while the faithful are driven to the bushes and the rocks. It is for that reason I maun tunnel and dig and dig and never behold the blue lift or the sweet flowers on the lawn.

MARJORIE. If you dig and do nothing but dig you will die.

KNOX. It's a queer thing how Peter de Ronsard keeps

edging in his neb. Profitable death, he called it. I would be
blithe to die.

MARJORIE. You mustn't die.

KNOX. Why should I not die?

MARJORIE. Because I love you.

KNOX. We are enjoined to love all God's creatures. But
that is no reason why death should not take them in God's
good time.

MARJORIE. That is not the way I love you.

KNOX. Whather you mean it or not that is ill talk. You are
young and I am old; but I am not old enough to be safe from
that madness.

MARJORIE. What do I care if you are old? Of all the men
I ever saw you are the kindest and the cleverest and the best.
Do you love me?

KNOX. To look on you is to love you.

MARJORIE. Don't talk like that. Do you love me?

KNOX. Yes.

> MARJORIE *suddenly throws herself at* KNOX *and slides
> down to his feet with her head on his knees, sobbing loudly.*

MARJORIE. If I had an alabaster box I would break it and
anoint your feet. If you go away I shall throw myself from
the walls. There is no meaning in the world without you.
You are everything. You are my God.

KNOX (*distressed*). No. No. No. No. No!

> *The scene fades.*

NORA. Did she marry that ugly old rat?

HECTOR. Yes.

NORA. What a fool.

HECTOR. They had to wait three years for their honeymoon,
but when it came they were happy together.

NORA. A young one like her with a dry old stick like him?

HECTOR. He wasn't such a dry old stick. And dry old
sticks sometimes burn best. It's said that a more remarkable
woman than Marjorie Bowes took a notion to him. Perhaps
we'll see. Anyhow, he went to London but had to fly to

France. He went to Geneva and was there for two years
while the fires were burning at Smithfield. He came back to
Scotland in '55 to visit the wife and to visit somebody else.
Have you ever heard of James Stuart, The Earl of Moray ?

NORA. Yes.

HECTOR. He was James Vth's Bastard.

NORA. Here, mind your language in the presence of a lady.

HECTOR. So he was half-brother to Mary Queen of Scots.
As he could read and write, and they couldn't, the gangsters
played him off against Mary of Guise, the Queen Regent. He
had no objection, and neither had she. Anyhow, Knox came
to see Lord James, and the Reformed Church was glad to
welcome Knox. He had a way with him in the pulpit.

The alcove on the extreme left lights up dimly, to show
KNOX *in the pulpit.*

KNOX. I admit to you now that I, John Knox, have long
been guilty of slothful coldness. But now my eyes have seen
in the midst of Sodom that God has more Lots than one and
more faithful daughters than two. Against my stubborn will
God has shown me the fervent thirst of the brethren, nicht
and day, sobbing and groaning for the Bread of Life. If I
had not seen it with my own eyes, in my own country, I could
not have believed it.

But now let the trumpet blow the old Psalm. It is for me
to expound to you, the richt use of the Lord's Table. For the
Son of God, who is the Wisdom of the Father, hath commanded us to assemble.

While he is speaking the centre scene lights up and
shows MARY OF GUISE *with a bishop and a lady-in-*
waiting in whispered conference. The light in KNOX'S
compartment dims gradually and his voice fades. A
LORD-IN-WAITING ENTERS *the centre scene, pauses*
for a moment and then announces.

LORD. Madam, My Lord James Stuart and Mr. Maitland of
Lethington.

KNOX'S VOICE (*becoming loud and strong in the darkness*). But first and above all things I tell you that it is not lawful for the men of Scotland to give their bodily presence to the Mass nor yet offer their children to the Papistical Baptism. These things are damnable idolatry and all plantation that our Heavenly Father hath not planted shall be rooted out.

> KNOX'S *scene has disappeared.* STUART *and* LETHINGTON *enter the* QUEEN REGENT'S *scene.* LORD JAMES *is a tall, saturnine man in black, with a thin, dark beard. He is twenty-seven years old. He takes little part in the dialogue of the succeeding scene ; but he should be placed so as to give some effect of silent domination.* MAITLAND OF LETHINGTON *is about the same age. He is a thin, horse-faced little man, with a full pointed beard, a low, sweet voice and an ingratiating manner. He is perfectly at his ease.*

THE QUEEN. Ah, my dear Jamie, my heart's joy ! It is long since I have seen you. You have, no doubt, come from going to and fro in the earth and from walking up and down in it ?

LORD JAMES. Yes Madam.

THE QUEEN. Have you enjoyed your little walk ?

LORD JAMES. No, Madam. There are over-many cut-throats and robbers in this realm, even amang the Lords nearest to your Majesty's person.

LETHINGTON. Lord James said these words in the knowledge that the thing nearest your Majesty's heart is peace and order in this kingdom.

THE QUEEN. It is near to all our hearts, Willie. But my dear Jamie knows that it is not I or my Lords who shake the peace of this kingdom. If indeed there is such a Lord, let him be named and we shall take order against him.

LORD JAMES. There are over-many to name.

LETHINGTON. May I be permitted to speak ? As my Lord has said, there are many names that have an ill repute and not all of your Majesty's lieges have yet learned that it is to their advantage to keep your Majesty's peace. I think my Lord has in his mind, for one, young James Hepburn of Bothwell, whose manners in the Borders are more those of a heathen Pict than of a Magistrate to your Majesty in this year of grace.

THE QUEEN. His father was a good friend to me.

LETHINGTON. And so will the son be but he needs tutoring. If it is your gracious pleasure I shall arrange a small slight gentle course of instruction for my young Lord of Bothwell.

THE QUEEN. Do what you wish. My Scotsmen must live together in amity and there is none so great that he need not fear our mild discipline. Do you think that well spoken, Jamie?

LORD JAMES. Yes, Madam.

THE QUEEN. I do not speak well your language but here in my head the intention is plain. You will remember that, my heart and my joy?

LORD JAMES. I will remember, Madam.

THE QUEEN (*to* LETHINGTON). What is it said of justice? That it has an even hand? Are there not others who do not wear the belt and the golden spurs who disturb the peace of this Kingdom and sow hatred among our lieges? It is in my mind that there are.

LETHINGTON. It is true that in spiritual matters there are those who differ from your Majesty in certain points of doctrine. Yet it is not too much to hope that a certain prophecy, with which your Majesty may or may not be familiar, is about to be fulfilled.

THE QUEEN. What prophecy?

LETHINGTON. The prophecy of the Hebrew Isaiah. If I may recall it to your Majesty it goes somewhat like this. " And the wolf shall dwell with the lamb, and the leopard shall lie down with the kid; and the calf and the young lion and the fatling together; and a little child shall lead them."

THE QUEEN. That is very beautiful. Please God it may be true. *C'est bien charmant*, Milord Bishop, is it not? . . . Willie, you shall write it down.

LETHINGTON. With pleasure, *Madame*.

THE QUEEN. You shall write it in Latin. I shall send it to

my little girl. It will be two lessons for her in one. That will save time and money. It is very good to save time and money. You think, perhaps, I have learned something, Jamie, since I come to Scotland ?

LORD JAMES. I hope so, Ma'am.

THE QUEEN. "And a little child shall lead them." *C'est tout à fait parfait.*

LORD JAMES. We shall be ready for her, Ma'am.

THE QUEEN. You make me happy. But will you tell to your wolves that they MUST lie down with the lambs. If they do not, I shall hamstring them. It is the correct expression, *M. le Secrétaire ?*

LETHINGTON. It is, *Madame.*

THE QUEEN. It must be very painful to be hamstrung. You will say what I have said to . . . to—what is his name ? To that Priest who so passionately adores the sound of his own voice.

LETHINGTON. *Madame* no doubt refers to Mr. Knox.

THE QUEEN. *Oui,* Knox. *C'est un nom assez drôle. Nox impenetrabile : Nox sempiterna.* You will tell him, Jamie ?

LORD JAMES. I will tell him.

THE QUEEN. We wish this poor man no evil ; but he must lie down as the Prophet Isaiah bide him. He must lie down. My weaned child must put her hand into the basilisk's den and take no hurt. They shall not hurt or destroy in all my holy mountain.

> *It grows suddenly dark. A nasty, sharp voice speaks out of the darkness.*

VOICE. Baal is confounded ; Merodach is dismayed. Her idols are confounded, her images broken.

KNOX'S VOICE. . . . Because they ministered unto them before their idols and became a stumbling block of iniquity unto the house of Israel ; therefore have I lifted up my hand against them, saith the Lord God . . .

VOICE. Baal is confounded. Merodach is dismayed. Baal is confounded ; Merodach is dismayed. Baal is confounded. . .

The light goes up on the centre scene. It is the same as before, but contains now, KNOX, LORD JAMES *and* LETHINGTON. LORD JAMES *is sitting where* MARY OF GUISE *sat before.* KNOX *and* LETHINGTON *are standing.*

LORD JAMES. Be seated, Maister Knox.

KNOX (*sitting*). I thank you, my Lord.

HECTOR. On the 16th of April, 1917, Vladimir Ilyich, who was called Lenin, arrived in St. Petersburg. But he did not go back to Switzerland.

NORA. Ach, sneck up, you !

In the meantime the three characters on the rostrum have been looking at each other in silence.

LORD JAMES. Well, Maister Knox ?

KNOX. Well, my Lord.

LORD JAMES. You find us in a happy hour. The Lords of the Congregation have reconciled their interests with what pass for their consciences and the Realm stands firm like a strong rock in an ocean of enemies. We can now proceed to build on that rock.

KNOX. I pray God you may be richt when you speak of a rock. There are ower many shifting sands in its composition, but we maun build. Let us look to our foundations. In the first place. . .

LETHINGTON. By your leave, Mister Knox, we ken very well what comes first. But there are sundry temporal matters that can be settled in a breath so that room may be left for our talk of things spiritual. I hope that is your will.

KNOX. Say your say.

LETHINGTON. The Queen has resiled from her notion to tax the shires for an army of mercenaries. I will not say that it was done without pressure, but we have had our way. The defence of the country will go on in the old fashion. The Lords will arm and maintain their own men. These Lords, as our friend has told us, are now weel affected. They held their loyalty to the Queen Mother but they hold faster to the Kirk.

[24]

Within these four walls we can put it this way. The Clergy hold the siller and the Lords of the Congregation hold the pikes. It seems a situation very capable of arrangement . . . of arrangement not unsatisfactory to the Lords of the Congregation. I can leave out unnecessary matters of detail; but when the siller has passed, as it naturally will, from the Clergy to the Congregation . . .

KNOX. If your matters of unnecessary detail include the breaking of heads and the cutting of throats, I am for nane of it. I am with that honey-tongued Jezebel in the thocht that there has been enough of murder and rope in Scotland. We shall not tak up the sword.

LETHINGTON. The sword has more than one function, Mr. Knox. My Lord here and I have swords on our hips. I will not say that from time to time in our argument you would not be moved in your wrath to punch us on the neb. But these twa irons in their scabbards would gar you think twice. The sword can be a very potent instrument of peace, Mr. Knox. A very potent instrument. Speaking for my ain, it is more potent in its scabbard for I have little skill in sword-play.

LORD JAMES. There will be no fighting. There is nothing to fight about.

KNOX. That is as it may be. But gin I have the assurance of you twa young men that Mr. Secretary's matters of detail will be doucely and honourably conducted I am willing to pass to the event.

LETHINGTON. Douce and quiet it will be, Mr. Knox, and with such honour as we can muster in this land. With the sword and the siller in our hands we can gang gimply and easily. It is for you to tell us the road we should gang. What is in your mind?

KNOX. There is in my mind a new Kirk and a new Realm. Under God Almighty there will be twa estates; on the one hand the Prince and Council of the Realm, and on the other hand God's Kirk. It will be for the Prince and the Council to uphold the Law and to nourish the Kirk. It will be for the Kirk to relieve the poor and the sick and to instruct the people. The Congregations of the Kirk will elect their own Elders and Deacons and appoint their own ministers, subject to the approval of learned ministers appointed for their examination. To haud together the Kirk Sessions there will be ten Superintendents who will travel from place to place like Apostles of old, each in his ain diocese. The Sessions will haud charge of the poor and the sick and will be bound by the sacred duty that every bairn in their parish can read, write and cypher. The siller for this will be the first charge on the Prince and his Council. These are the bones of it.

LETHINGTON. Is it your suggestion that I present these proposals to the Queen Regent? They are formidable proposals.

KNOX. Present them where you like.

LETHINGTON. But, Mr. Knox . . . I am a child in these matters and, indeed, almost a child in years. You will perhaps correct me if I am wrong, but it appears to me that the happy issue towards which our minds are bent is that so well described by the Prophet Isaiah when he foresees " that the wolf also shall dwell with the lamb, and the leopard shall lie with the kid, and the calf and the lion and the fat beast together, and a little child shall lead them."

KNOX. It is justly said, Mr. Maitland, but we maun first tame the wolf.

LETHINGTON. The wolf, Mr. Knox?

KNOX. Aye, sir, the she-wolf that issued from that nest of cockatrices and saps that burrow in the depths of the seven hells.

LETHINGTON. Within these four walls, I take it that you are referring to Her Majesty the Queen Regent?

KNOX. Nane other.

LETHINGTON. I had occasion to quote that passage of the Holy Scriptures to Her Majesty the other day. While she agreed that the consummation was one very near to her heart she did not cast herself in the part of the wolf. That is by the way. Whichever is the wolf and whichever is the lamb, it is highly expedient that they should be bedded together. In

Her Majesty's own words, her will is the bringing of a young people into a new subjection to those who desire to see justice reign. A young people, Mr. Knox. Justice, Mr. Knox.

KNOX. If she said that she said well. But she said ower little. In Scotland there is a universal defection as well in religion as in manners. We maun mend their manners. There maun be a justice inflexible against murderers and common oppressors. If Her Majesty will tak' that on hand I thank God for it. But my duty is plain. Vain is it to crave reformation in manners where the religion is corrupted. To this truth I have been called to testify. Let her deal justice and my voice will be loud in her honour. And let her not withhold the hand of justice from the rotten, dumb bishops as weel as from the false judges. Let her do that and my bonnet will be in my hand. For my part, I will hew down the groves and tak the idols from the Kirks as the Lord my God commanded.

LETHINGTON. It appears to me that the wolf and the lamb will be uneasy bed-fellows, if the lamb persists in kicking out the teeth of the wolf. Have you heard of the principle of give and take, Mr. Knox ? Under the Lord's good mercy we shall take a good deal. It would surely be magnanimous to give a little.

KNOX. We will give them the benefits of an orderly and Godly State. We will not give them licence to devour the immortal souls of our children.

LETHINGTON. Mr. Knox, Mr. Knox, you will coup the whole tattie barrow ! You say you are a man of peace and that you will have no blows or bloodshed, and here you are like Friar John in the story swinging the Cross like a bludgeon. Can you no' be douce and politic, man ? We have the game in our hands. Let us play it cannily.

KNOX. Mr. Maitland of Lethington, it may be in your constitution to blow hot and cold out of the same mouth like the Sadducees, but it is not in mine. You have not seen your friends disembowelled and hanged and burnt at the stake. You have not felt the galley-master's whip on your naked back. It is long syne, but I still feel the lash curling round my bones and I cannae walk delicately or gang warily.

LETHINGTON *gives a despairing gesture.* LORD JAMES
rises from his seat and comes forward out of the picture.
He leans against the pillar and begins to manicure
himself with his dagger. Both look at him intently.

LORD JAMES. You two men have fathers and mothers. You
are men with the habits of men and the passions of men. I am
a King's bastard. I am a by-blow. I did not grow in the field
with the rest of you. Yet I am a King's son with the blood
of William the Lion and Robert the Bruce. Though I stand
aside and see the sowing and the growing and the hairst I save
still the itch in me to order the comings and goings of mankind without prejudice and maybe without conscience. If I
had felt the lash on my back, Mr. Knox, it would be the same,
for that is the way of the sons of Kings. Lethington is right,
Mr. Knox, I know my father's wife and better still I know the
bairn in the palace of France. She is a bonny bairn with the
grace of God shining around her, and a fair body warm with
the blood of kings. Let us be, and we shall prepare for her
a realm she can rule honourably and justly with the head of a
great prince and the heart of a child.

If you cannot master yourself, Mr. Knox, you must go
back to Geneva to your wife and possess your soul in patience.
Lethington and I are of like mind with you, but our acts need
not be in your hands nor our deeds on your conscience. We
will send you word when the time is ripe for you to return
and that will be when the wolf is bound and dare not bite.

KNOX. My Lord, it is known to you that I came to Scotland
most contrarious to my own judgment. The mother of my
wife, a godly but afflicted woman, drew me to Scotland for
that my wife was great with child. I found the brethren ill at
ease and spoke to them what comfortable words I could. I
found too a task at which I shall labour to the day of my death.

LETHINGTON. Your task is to remove mountains or, if I
may so put it, to blow down the walls of Jericho with your
trumpet. Have patience a little while till the sappers and
miners have performed their part of the task. They will not

be idle, those sappers and miners. They will make sure that the walls of Jericho come down with a sair dunt.

KNOX. It is ill to return to the den of mine own ease when such great things are afoot. They will say. . .

LORD JAMES. They will say? What will they say? Let them say. In matters political you are for the rule to be held by the rightful princes. I am nearest to a prince in this presence and you will do as I bid you. Go back to Geneva. Take your wife with you. We shall send for you.

KNOX (*after a pause*). I will obey you, sir. I have trust in you though I have little in your whippet dog there. But on one thing more I must have your word. In your sapping and mining let no man's blood be shed.

LORD JAMES. On my honour no man's blood will be shed.

KNOX. And so I take my leave of your Lordship, asking God's blessing on your enterprise.

LORD JAMES. And God's blessing on you, sir. You are to Scotland as the Prophet Samuel was to Israel.

> KNOX *bows, descends the steps and passes into dark alcove on the* L. LETHINGTON *and* MORAY *retire into the porch.* LETHINGTON *laughs. They begin to study papers as the light dims out.*

NORA. So they got rid of him all right.

HECTOR. Not quite. He wrote to the Queen. He said that maybe God had moved her to save her country as he had moved Rahab the harlot.

NORA. That wasna very polite.

HECTOR. John Knox was not a very polite man. But he wasn't so rough as his followers. He had hardly crossed the Channel when the mob attacked the church at Perth and burned the images of the saints and tore down the altar. The Queen Regent restored order there with a regiment of French soldiers. But the fire was alight. Look at that.

> *The glow of fires and the silhouettes of churches are seen between the pillars of the Gallery, and the distant shouts of the mobs are heard.*

NORA. The Gallery's on fire!

HECTOR. No. It's only the dream. It's St. Giles' Day in Edinburgh and Knox is safe in Geneva.

> KNOX *comes rushing down the steps in a great state of excitement and addresses the three onlookers directly for the first time.*

A VOICE FROM THE FLAMES. Baal is confounded! Merodach is dismayed! Ding down Baal!

KNOX. Saw you ever sic a lowe! The people that walked in darkness have seen a great light: they that dwelled in the land of the shadow of death, upon them hath the light shined. Every battle of the warrior is with noise and with tumbling of garments and blood; but this shall be with burning and devouring of fire. Did ever you hear tell of the burning of Old St. Giles, that wooden image the idolaters had set up? In Edinburgh was that great idol called St. Giles, first drowned in the North Loch and after burnt; which raisit no small trouble in the town; for the friars ran rouping like ravens upon the bishops and the bishops ran upon the Queen, who was favourable enough but that she thocht it could not stand with her advantage to offend such a multitude. Yet on St. Giles' Day she led them down the High Street her ain sel before a little marmoset idol they had borrowed from the Grey Friars fast fixed with iron nails to a barrow, with tabors and trumpets, banners and bagpipes following after. West about goes it and comes down the High Street and down to the common cross. But syne the Queen being empty in the stomach turned into Sandy Carpenter's house betwixt the Bows and so when the idol returned back again she left it and went in to her dinner.

> *The* MULATTO *wakes and sets his gramophone going. As the climax of the speech approaches, he dances an accompaniment, solemnly, but affected by the savagery of the words.*

The hearts of the brethren were wonderously inflamed at seeing sic abomination so manifestly maintained. So when the

Queen had left the rout a band of them drew nigh to the idol as willing to help to carry him ; and getting the barrow on their shoulders began to shudder and shake, thinking thereby that the idol would fall, but it was nailed to the barrow. Then began a man to cry " Down with the idol ! Down with it ! " And it was pulled down. At first the priests made some outcry, but they soon saw the feebleness of their God when the young fellows were dadding his head on the causeway. They soon left Dagon without heid or hands and the papists fled faster than they did at Pinkie Cleugh. Down goes the crosses, off goes the surplices, the round caps, the cornet with the crowns ; the grey friars gaped, the black friars blew, the priests panted and fled and happy was he that first gat to his house. Such a sudden fray came never amongst the generation of Anti-Christ before.

For once that Baal had broken his neck there was no more comfort in his confusit army.

> *He goes out laughing on the O.P. side of the forestage.*
> NORA *and* HECTOR *are dumbfounded by this speech and stand staring after him. The* MULATTO *continues to dance, snapping his fingers and uttering low cries.*

CURTAIN

END OF ACT I

ACT II

The setting is the same, but this time the Act opens in silence. A cloud has passed over the moon and there is a slight flurry of snow. The three raisonnaires are sitting huddled together on the lower step with the MULATTO'S *blanket over their shoulders.*

NORA. You can say what you like, but Knox was a devil. He was a pure devil, you can say what you like. You'd think that at least he would have some respect for the priests. He was a bloody communist, if you ask me.

HECTOR. Oh, hell, have I got to go over all that again ? He was down on the priests because they weren't doing their job. The Queen Regent was down on them. The Pope himself was down on them.

NORA. But there must be something sacred. Fancy wrecking the churches ! That was an awful-like thing.

HECTOR. I tell you Knox wasn't there. He was in Geneva.

NORA. He was at the bottom of it. Besides you heard him laughing. He was laughing like a devil. He wanted them to wreck the churches. You call that keeping peace and order ? They set the churches on fire. That's a bonny-like peace.

HECTOR. The bishops set the match to the fire themselves. In April, 1558, they burnt a decent old chap for heresy. In September a spark from his ashes set the kirks ablaze.

NORA. I didna come here for a lecture in history. It's all lies, anyway. And it's all queer. Anyways, we're daft . . . ghosts and bogles skipping about the Mound in fancy dress and talking each others heads off. I never heard the like of it. We'll be in Morningside luny-bin before we know where we are. I'm for no more of it. I'm away to my bed.

She gets up. At the same moment a CHORUS *appears. He is a tall, fantastic figure in a ragged heraldic costume. He has a very powerful voice.*

CHORUS. From fifteen hundred and fifty-three to fifteen hundred and fifty-eight, Queen Mary Tudor reigned in England.

In fifteen hundred and fifty-five Latimer, Ridley and Hooper were burned at Smithfield.

From fifteen hundred and fifty-four to fifteen hundred and sixty, Mary of Guise reigned in Scotland. In fifteen hundred and fifty-seven, The Lords of the Congregation met.

NORA (*to* HECTOR). He's worse nor what you are.

HECTOR. Be quiet.

CHORUS. The Lords of the Congregation met and put their case to the Queen.

The case was the case of Mr. Knox, the child of his brain and soul.

The arguments for the case were strong.

They wore steel caps upon their heads and broad swords in their fists.

So the Queen Regent opened the yett and the path was straight for the model state.

Till the Bishop of Moray burnt Walter Mill and the fat was in the fire again.

In that season of April showers and flowers,

The bonny young Queen had known sixteen summers.

She married the son of the King of France.

From April to November heads were broken and churches burnt and holy men ducked in the lochs.

In November the Queen of England died and Gloriana came to the throne.

In May, fifteen hundred and fifty-nine, Knox came back.

Knox preached here and Knox preached there.

He preached in St. Andrews under the Bishop's guns.

A year went by and he had his way.

Mary of Guise was dead and gone.

Francis of France was dead and gone.

Mary Stuart was widow and orphan.

The Lords of the Congregation were set in the saddle.

And Knox in the ring with his whip showed them the way
to ride.

> CHORUS *withdraws.* KNOX *appears in his pulpit, in an*
> *alcove to the left.*

KNOX. Thus speaketh the Lord of Hosts, saying, "This
people say, the time is not yet come that the Lord's House
should be builded." Then came the Word of the Lord by the
Ministry of the Prophet Haggai, saying, "It is time for yourselves to dwell in your ceiled houses and this house lieth
waste." Now therefore thus sayeth the Lord of Hosts,
"Consider your own ways in your hearts. Ye have sowen
much and bring in little; ye eat but ye have not enough;
ye drink but ye are not filled; ye clothe you but ye be not
warm; and he that earneth wages putteth the wages into a
bag full of holes." Thus saith the Lord of Hosts, "Consider
your own ways in your hearts. Go up into the mountain and
bring wood and build this house, and I will be favourable in
it and I will be glorified," saith the Lord.

"Ye looked for much, and lo, it came to little; and when
ye brought it home I did blow upon it and why," saith the
Lord of Hosts, "because of mine house that is waste and ye
run every man to his own house."

Then spake Haggai the Lord's Messenger in the Lord's
Message unto the People, saying, "I am with you," saith the
Lord. And the Lord stirred up the spirit of Zerubabel, the
son of Shealtiel and the spirit of Jehoshua, the son of Jehoza-
dak, and the spirit of the remnant of the people. And they
came and did the work in the House of the Lord of Hosts
their God.

> KNOX *descends from the pulpit and sits down in an easy*
> *attitude on the top step of the rostrum. The scene is*
> *suffused with a rosy light.* LADY BOWES *and* MARJORIE
> *come out of an alcove on the right and join him.*

KNOX. Well, my heart's own lambs, the Lord has greatly
blessed us. As I stood in His pulpit but now I had a gliff of
the land of Canaan.

MARJORIE. I am happy for that, Mr. Knox.

LADY BOWES. I wish my heart were as light as yours. It sits heavy on my liver like a granite rock in a swamp, and my mind travails with all manner of fearful thoughts.

KNOX. There was a callant I met in Dieppe thought a lot of Hog's Fennel sniffed up the nostrils for that, and another fellow came near blows in standing up for the Melancholy Thistle. He would make a decoction of the roots and drink it a few days and in a week he would be as merry as a cricket.

LADY BOWES. You have sadly changed, John. A year back you would have said that the only cure was the Grace of God and we would have wrestled for it in prayer and fasting.

KNOX. There is much of the Grace of God in the thistle. It's birky and prickled but it's a handsome upstanding plant. There's virtue in the thistle. Away you go, Marjorie, and get some. Make a decoction for your mother. I'll pray with you, my Lady, at the evening diet of worship. Leave me for a wee.

The two women go. The scene darkens.

I need nae fumitory or thistle to keep my heart merry. The Lord has been pleased to smite the wabbit wee French King with a tetter in his lug and the French widow is a bonny and kind lass. John Knox and his dogs have their virtues, but they arena bonny. We will be better of some gracefulness in our grim crew.

EXIT KNOX *into the porch. The* CHORUS *reappears on the roof.*

CHORUS. On what passes in Edinburgh for a summer day
The Lords of the Congregation meet.
It is a happy meeting, for the fighting is over
And the Queen will come to a land of order and quiet.
Open the doors and let out the Lords of the Congregation.

KNOX'S VOICE. . . . and the Communion of the Holy Ghost be with you and remain with you. Amen.

MANY VOICES. Amen.

[35]

The whole stage is lit up, showing the porch closed by two great doors. A step or two down a sinister looking brute called PARIS *is standing with a long rapier in a sheath waiting for his master,* JAMES HEPBURN OF BOTHWELL. *The doors swing open and* LENNOX, BOTHWELL *and* LETHINGTON *come out and two or three other Lords run down the steps past them and* EXIT. BOTHWELL *takes the sword from* PARIS *and buckles it on. He is a tall, reckless looking young man with a powerful voice.* LETHINGTON *and* LENNOX *come down the stairs to the forestage, where the rest of the scene is played.* BOTHWELL *presently joins them. As he does so a dandified youth attended by a page* ENTERS *from the prompt side, nods to* LETHINGTON *and* LENNOX *and stands slightly apart, looking curiously at* BOTHWELL. PARIS *remains on the upper step.*

LETHINGTON. Well, my Lord of Bothwell, what do you think of it ?

BOTHWELL. Good day to you, Lord Lennox . . . Were ye speaking to me, Lethington ?

LETHINGTON. I wondered to what extent you were inspired by these good and Godly proceedings.

BOTHWELL. I was inspired to this extent, that I am going round to Sandy Carpenter's for a jug of Hollands gin to wash the dronings of these old crows out of my lugs. After that I'll bid Paris rake Edinburgh for an accommodating slut . . . D'ye hear that, Paris ? . . . And what happens then is my own affair . . . I notice ye had a good sleep, Lennox. Like myself.

LENNOX. I may have closed my eyes. I may have closed my eyes. You will be acquainted with my son Henry, James. Lord Henry Darnley, the Earl of Bothwell.

BOTHWELL. You're an upstanding lad, sir. I hear they have a thought to make you the Queen's bed-fellow.

LENNOX. Well . . . There has been some talk . . . But it's hardly at the stage. . .

BOTHWELL. Well, why not ? He's got royal blood in him, though it's maybe as thin as the swipes in the Calton alehouses.

Forbye, you have a kindly and generous face. I doubt not you'll be pleased to share that same bed with a hundred other mettlesome lads ; for I doubt that'll be the way of it.

> *This throws* DARNLEY *into a fit of irresolute anger. He thumbs the hilt of his sword.* LETHINGTON *and* LENNOX *close in on him.*

DARNLEY. My Lord Bothwell. . .

BOTHWELL. My Lord Harry. When you ken me better you'll know I'm a man that speaks his mind. If you are for drawing iron on a word like that you have a lot of fighting before you. You'll find I am not the only callant with that in his mind. But I'll meet you when and where you like. Paris, you dog, come in to heel ! Good day, My Lords ! Good day, Mr. Politician !

> EXEUNT BOTHWELL *and* PARIS.

DARNLEY. The filthy hound. Oh, the filthy hound. I'll cut his heart out. By God, I will.

LENNOX. Now, now, Harry. He has a rough tongue, but he is no' such a bad fellow. Besides we need him.

LETHINGTON. He is as bad a fellow as the Lord ever put breeks on ; but, as you say, my Lord, we need him. Moreover, in the matter of cutting out hearts, he is not inexperienced. You would be wise to pay no more heed to his ill talk than you would to a pig grunting.

DARNLEY. That's what he is. A pig. I'll cut his throat and hang him up and salt him and . . . and . . .

LETHINGTON. All in good time . . . I think it went well, my Lord.

LENNOX. Ye-e-es.

LETHINGTON. It will go better when the young Queen comes. The Congregation is loosely held. What has gone so far is a great sussurrus of buzzing. When the Queen comes they will swarm and we can get them hived. Are you an apiarist, Lord Henry ?

DARNLEY. My brother and I had a pet monkey once. He was killed by a sheepdog.

[37]

LENNOX. As you say, there was much buzzing. I could not help from feeling that much of it was little to the point. Many of the Lords said as much to me.

LETHINGTON. What point, my Lord?

LENNOX. Oh, the main point. What is there in it for us? Oh, I know we can go back to our castles without the fear that our neighbours will be at our throats. But we'll go back poor men. It seems to me that the labourer is worthy of his hire.

LETHINGTON. You should be the last to take that tone. The Crown of Scotland is in it for you, when Lord Henry marries the Queen.

LENNOX. Aye. Maybe. I hope so. But will the Congregation permit it?

LETHINGTON. He is of the Blood Royal and he is a Protestant. Very high qualifications for a young bridegroom.

LENNOX. I wish I were certain of it all. And of the dowry. My lands yield little and will yield less, what with these new-fangled ideas of government.

LETHINGTON. Leave the dowry to me. A kingdom is not a bad security; and the market value of Scotland has gone very high in the past two years.

DARNLEY. There's another matter. I don't pretend to be a religious man. Nobody can say I'm not broadminded in these things. But there are those in the country who are not broadminded, and the girl is a Papist.

LETHINGTON. You're a Papist yourself.

DARNLEY. In a way, yes. But I have always held that religious matters and temporal matters should be kept apart. It isn't the fashion to be a Papist.

LETHINGTON. You're turning philosopher. I must tell the Queen that. It will please her. She will talk philosophy to you in the long winter evenings.

DARNLEY. To Hell with that. I've more to do with my time.

LENNOX. Nay, but there is another doubt. Have you talked to Knox of this marriage?

LETHINGTON. My Lord Lennox, I suspect that you think me a knave ; but I am surprised to find that you think me a fool. My Lord Henry, put your mind at rest. Her Majesty will thriep no religion down your throat. She is a modern woman. She has had her upbringing in Paris. Her mind is on the new sciences and on verses and dancing and pictures. She will not catechise you or us. She is no Mary Tudor with her silver bells and cockle shells and pretty nuns all in a row. She rides to hounds and rakes the town with the maskers. I'd wager on her against you at boxing or wrestling or the small sword. She's for Peter Ronsard and Chastelard before any pocky old Friar. You'll find her a lass of mettle.

DARNLEY. I hope so.

LORD JAMES *and* KNOX ENTER *from the doorway.*

KNOX. Ah, my Lord Lennox. I am glad to see you.

LENNOX. I am glad to see you, Mr. Knox. Do you know my son ?

KNOX. I am honoured. Well, young sir, you are fortunate in your years. The sun has risen this day, but we old rickles of bones will not see it in the glory of noon. I hope you thank the Lord God daily for being a Scotsman and for being young. You will see great days, sir. You will enter into the lands of Canaan with shouts and rejoicing.

DARNLEY. Very kind of you to say so.

KNOX. The South Wind of the Spirit has blown over the hard hearts of the great ones of this land. They will melt and blossom like a garden. Today, no man was for himself, but every one was for his Country and the regimen of the Holy Ghost therein. The golden streams of loving kindness flowed bountifully beneath a cloudless sky. Vile self was forgotten. A happy day indeed and a pleasant augury for the days to come.

LORD JAMES. Amen to that. It went well.

LENNOX. Amen to that indeed.

KNOX *takes* DARNLEY *affectionately by the arm as the* PLAYERS *move out left.*

KNOX. We must get you a good wife, young man. You must rear workers for the Lord's plentiful harvest.

> KNOX *and* DARNLEY *go out, followed by* LENNOX. LORD JAMES *and* LETHINGTON *pause for an instant.*

LORD JAMES. God send that the young fool keeps his mouth shut.

LETHINGTON. When Mr. Knox has embarked on a monologue it would take a stronger wit than Master Chucklehead to interrupt him.

> EXEUNT LORD JAMES *and* LETHINGTON. *The stage has gradually darkened. It is now lit by a dim, sulphurous light. The three* MODERNS, *who have been grouped unobtrusively round the perambulator, come back to the lower step.* NORA *huddles up to* JERRY.

NORA. It's cold. I'll wake up and find the blanket's off the bed and the sleet blowing in.

HECTOR. It's colder on the North Sea in the late August with the fog drifting down. " The nineteenth day of August, 1561 years, between seven and eight hours before noon, arrived Marie, Queen of Scotland, then widow, with two galleys furth of France."

> KNOX *is seen dimly in one of the alcoves.*

KNOX. The very face of Heaven, the time of her arrival, did manifestly speak what comfort was brought into this country with her, to wit, sorrow, darkness, dolour all all impiety ; for, in the memory of man that day of the year was never seen a more dolorous face of the Heaven than was at her arrival, which two days after did so continue. For, beside the surface wet and corruption of the air, the mist was so thick that scarce might any man espy another the length of two pair of butts. The sun was not seen to shine two days before nor two days after. That forewarning God gave to us ; but, alas, the most part were blind.

> KNOX *fades and the rest of the stage goes into complete darkness. The porch is slowly lit to show a tableau of*

> MARY STUART, *resting on a bed on the deck of her galley.*
> *The* FOUR MARIES *are grouped round the bed, and a*
> MAN IN ARMOUR *stands apart.* RIZZIO, *in a sea-cloak,*
> *sits on the rail, singing. Over the rail, nothing but mist*
> *is seen. Before the light does more than outline the*
> *figures on the deck, a* VOICE *is heard singing.*

SONG (*ex* RONSARD) :

RIZZIO. " As we behold, half rosy and half white
           The Birth of Dawn ; and the late evening star
           Hangs in the Heavens, supreme, serene, afar,
           The Queen of Scotland rises on our sight."

> *The guitar accompaniment of the song continues through*
> *the first line or two of* MARY'S *speech and then dies away.*

MARY. *Et jam prima novo spargebat lumine terras,*
      Tithoni croceum linquens, Aurora, cubile :
      Regina e speculis ut primum albescere lucem
      Vidit, et aequatis classem procedere velis,
      Litora et vacuos sensit sine remige portus . . .
What is that ?

MARY LIVINGSTONE. It's from Virgil, is it not, my Lady ?

MARY BEATON. Yes. Where Dido looks out at dawn and
sees the fleet of Aeneas sailing away.

MARY. Sailing away. Dido looked out to sea, but my eyes
look always to the land. The curtain has fallen now. The
happy play is ended. Dear France I shall never see you again.

MARY SEATON. They will miss you, my Lady. Their sun
has gone out too.

> *During the second song, the scene fades and the stage*
> *is dark again.*

SONG :

RIZZIO. " Like a sad meadow, ravished of its flowers
           Like a parched wood forsaken of its showers
           Like a gay picture with its colours gone
           Like a black sky where once the bright stars
              shone ;

[41]

> A waveless ocean, a leafless tree,
> A cavern empty of its mystery,
> A dusty Palace, empty of its King,
> Or the torn setting of a gemless ring ;
> So is our France, losing her sweet Princess
> Who was all flowers, colour and loveliness."

The forestage is lit suddenly with a watery light as the FOUR MARIES *come fluttering out of the dark entry and quickly descend the steps.* MARY FLEMING *is the first to reach the ground and she gives a little scream as she finds that the causeway is thick with mud.*

FLEMING. Help me. I shall drown in the mud.

> *The others help her to the lower step.*

FLEMING. My good shoes ! Where shall I see another pair ? Oh, what a city of clartiness and rags and filth. Oh, the barbarous land !

SEATON. It is not Paris.

BEATON. It is not Paris. *Ah Ciel*, I could laugh if my heart were not so heavy.

LIVINGSTONE. O, that little tumbledown house on the quay side that stank of herring !

FLEMING. " Wull your Leddyship be pleased to partake of a cogie of brose ? "

SEATON. The hours we sat there, awaiting the Nobility and Gentry, and choking with the haar.

BEATON. And when the Nobility and Gentry arrived ! That long, sour Jamie Stuart like a blackened kail runt. And old, dirty Ruthven, new risen from the mortuary.

FLEMING. And old, greeting Lennox with his popinjay brat.

LIVINGSTONE. And the daft Earl of Arran, with the slavers running down his fat chops.

BEATON. Such faces. Such greasy ruffs. Such illset bonnets. It was like a masque of the seven deadly sins attended by the plagues of Egypt. And the hoody crow ministers, sore vexed that there was so little flesh on the bones of that clamjamfray of disjaskit corps.

LIVINGSTONE. Never shall I forget the ponies they brought us to ride. The pelts of them matted like brambles and their legs like four wee feather dusters. Those of them that had four legs. I think mine had one leg missing. They must have robbed all the tinkers' carts in the Lothians.

SEATON. The poor beasts. They did well enough. Mine picked his way among the fishguts and sharn as if he were carrying a mosstrooper through a bog. Indeed, am sure that was his daily vocation.

LIVINGSTONE. The heart's a'. The ragged folk on the way to Holyrood were glad to see us.

BEATON. Well they might be. But I wish they thought less of themselves as serenaders. I didn't sleep a wink last night.

SEATON. No more did I.

FLEMING. Nor I.

LIVINGSTONE. It was a pandemonium of fiddles and rebecs, screeching like animals in pain. And the thumping of tabors and the clanging of old iron buckets. And the songs they sang!

FLEMING. Yes. Psalms.
> "As precious ointment down the beard
> Even Aaron's beard did flow
> And running down did to the skirts
> Even of his garments go."

Hideous!

SEATON. What a country! What people!

BEATON. Black atheists, too.

LIVINGSTONE. I don't mind their being atheists, if they would wash occasionally. The Queen will cure their atheism, but it would take the North Sea to wash them.

SEATON. The Queen is a Saint. She waved to them from the window and called to them to play on.

LIVINGSTONE. The Queen warms to kindliness. She said they meant it all kindly. I hope she may not be mistaken . . . *Pardieu*, we must go in. She is giving audience to one of their witch doctors this morning. Hurry.

As they mount the steps, KNOX *comes out of one of the alcoves and is about to cross, but stands aside to let them pass.*

FLEMING. Are you Mr. Knox?

KNOX. Yes.

FLEMING. I think the Queen expects you.

KNOX. You will be her Four Maries?

FLEMING. Yes. We are.

KNOX. She is a bold woman who surrounds herself with four such bonny creatures.

LIVINGSTONE. Oh? Why?

KNOX. It is the way of woman to set off her beauty by surrounding herself with ill-faured visages. The four of you are like to marry monkey-faced men, from the vanity of your spirits.

LIVINGSTONE. They did not tell us you were so gallant, Mr. Knox.

KNOX. The truth bides in queer places, and maybe in gallantry too.

FLEMING. We must come to your sermons.

KNOX. I hope you may. I have great compassion on the silly hedge roses. O fair ladies, how pleasing were this life of yours, if it would abide forever and you could float up to Heaven at last in all your gay gear! But fie upon the knave Death, that will come, whether ye will or not. And when he has laid his arrest, the foul worms will be busy with this flesh be it never so fair and tender. And as for the silly Soul, I fear it will be over feeble to carry up the gold and garnishing and targeting and precious stones.

SEATON. Will you let us pass, please?

KNOX. You must not take my merry jests ill.

He bows in courtly fashion as they enter the porch; and then follows them.

KNOX *and the* LADIES *enter the porch and disappear.*

NORA. This was three or four hundred years ago, wasn't it?

HECTOR. Yes.

NORA. Round about the time of Henry the Eighth and his seventeen wives.

HECTOR. A bit after that.

NORA. But not so very long after?

HECTOR. No, twenty years or so. I forget.

NORA. And Mary Queen of Scots was the Queen of all the land? . . . All the same as Henry the Eighth?

HECTOR. Yes.

NORA. I know the first thing I'd have done if I'd been Queen of all the land.

HECTOR. What would you have done?

NORA. I would have chopped off that old basket's head.

HECTOR. Mary Stuart wasn't that kind of girl, to do her justice. In some ways she was four hundred years before her time. Be quiet!

> ENTER MARY *and* KNOX *from the porch. They are followed by* LETHINGTON, LORD JAMES *and the* FOUR MARIES.

MARY. Come, Mr. Knox, there's a bonny stranger in the Heavens who has come to visit us. It is not so often that Phoebus Apollo does Scotland this honour. Let us do him a little courtesy in return. Bring two chairs to the bowling alley. Mr. Knox and I will have our crack in the sunshine . . . Or is the blessed sun an over-pagan institution for you, Mr. Knox?

KNOX. Pagan or no pagan, I hope it will ever shine on your Majesty and on this land.

MARY. Come along then, Mr. Knox. Let it shine on both of us.

> *She takes his arm affectionately and they descend the steps. The three* MORTALS *retire backstage. Attendants place chairs for* MARY *and* KNOX *on the left.* LORD JAMES, LETHINGTON *and the* MARIES *form a respectful group on the right.* MARY *sits down and motions* KNOX *to be seated after her. He bows and sits down.*

Well, Mr. Knox, what shall we talk about?

KNOX. It is at your Majesty's pleasure.

MARY. Very well, Mr. Knox, I think I shall scold you.

KNOX. To scold, Madam, is a perquisite of your sex.

MARY. I have been told, Mr. Knox, that you have raised a part of my subjects against my mother and against myself.

KNOX. They did you no service who told you that, Ma'am.

MARY. Allow me to go on. It is true, I think, that you have written a book.

KNOX. I have, Madam.

MARY. That was very clever of you. It is called, I think . . . correct me if I am wrong . . . *The Monstrous Regiment of Women*.

KNOX. That was its name, Madam.

MARY. It was not a very good book. I have put certain literary gentlemen to the trouble of answering it.

KNOX. I shall abide their questionings.

MARY. You hate women, Mr. Knox?

KNOX. No, Madam, I do not.

MARY. We shall talk of that presently. It has been further told to me that you have been the cause of great slaughter and sedition in England, and it is the common talk in that land that you did this by necromancy. Now, there is no smoke without fire, Mr. Knox, although it seems strange to me that such things should be said of a douce, respectable looking man like yourself.

KNOX. Madam, it may please your Majesty patiently to hear my simple answers. First of all, if to teach the truth of God in sincerity, if to rebuke idolatry and will a people to worship God according to His Word be to raise subjects against the Princes, then I cannot be excused. It has pleased God of His Mercy to make me one among many to show this Realm the vanity of the Papistical religion and the deceit, pride and tyranny of that Roman Anti-Christ. But surely, Madam, the true knowledge of God and His richt worshipping must move the hearts of men to obey their just and lawful Princes . . . as it is most certain that you are . . . and not to disobey them. I think and am fully persuaded that your

Majesty has as much unfeigned obedience from the Godly in this Realm as ever your father had from the Bishops.

MARY. That is as may be. But they will obey me none the better if you turn their heads with wicked, foolish and impertinent books.

KNOX. As touching that book which seems so highly to offend your Majesty it is most certain that I wrote it and I am content that all the learned men in the world should judge it. I hear an Englishman has written against it but I have not read him. If he has established his contrary propositions and disapproved my reasons I shall not be obstinate. I shall confess my error and my ignorance. But to this hour I have thought and yet think that I myself alone am more able to sustain the things affirmed in that work than any ten scholars in Europe will be able to confute it.

MARY. You think, then, that I have no just authority?

KNOX. All through the ages, your Majesty, learned men have been allowed to have their judgments free, whether or no they differed from the common judgment of the world. Plato and his book of the Commonwealth damned many things that were maintained in the world and required that many things should be reformed; yet notwithstanding he lived a peaceful citizen under those politics and did nothing to trouble the State. Even so, Madam, I am content to do in uprightness of heart and with the testimony of a good conscience. I have communicated my judgment to the world. If the Realm finds no inconveniency in the Regiment of a Woman that which they approve I shall not further disallow other than in my own breast, so long as you defile not your hands with the blood of the saints of God. But to tell you the truth, Madam, I did not write that book against you, but against that wicked Jezebel Mary Tudor of England.

MARY. That is all very well. But the book is about women in general.

KNOX. That is most true, Madam. Yet it appears to me that wisdom should persuade your Grace never to raise trouble for that. I think you have the wit to discern the difference between philosophy and sedition. If I had intended to have troubled your estate because you are a woman I could have chosen a time more convenient for that purpose then when your own gracious presence is in the Realm.

MARY. These are very beautiful words, Mr. Knox ; and I perceive that you are a courtier. But there are things that you have done beyond the walls of my court, and these things were a little less polite.

KNOX. Yes, Madam, I incited to slaughter and I practised necromancy. My incitements maun ha'e been feeble indeed for no man has lost his life because of them.

Madam, I have been in England for five years. The places were Berwick, Newcastle and London. While I was in these places there was neither battle, sedition, nor mutiny. In Berwick, all fighting and brawls between the soldiers ceased and there was peace and quiet as there is in Edinburgh at this day.

MARY. That may well be. I care nothing for what you did in Berwick, and your reputation as a conjuror may be ill-deserved. But you have taught my people to receive another religion than their Princes can allow. How can that doctrine be of God ? God commands subjects to obey their Princes.

KNOX. Madam, right religion takes neither origin or authority from worldly Princes but from the Eternal God alone : so are not subjects bound to frame their religion according to the appetite of their Princes. Where would be your religion and mine if the Children of Israel had conformed to the religion of Pharaoh, of Nebuchadonasor and Darius ? Or if the twelve Apostles had taken their religion from the Emperor of Rome ?

MARY. None of those men raised the sword against their Princes.

KNOX. Ah, but, Madam, you cannot deny that they resisted. To disobey commands is to resist.

MARY. But the sword, man, the sword. They did not resist by the sword.

KNOX. God had not given them the power and the means.

MARY. Very good. If they have the power and the means, then subjects may fight against their Princes?

KNOX. If the Princes exceed their bounds and if . . .

MARY. If a subject dislikes what is done by his Prince, he may take up his sword and strike at his Prince? Why Princes, then? Why subjects? And what has become of your solemn injunction of Scripture?

KNOX. Madam, if my father is mad or drunk, I may seize him and bind him till his frenzy is past. If, in his frenzy, he attacks my brothers and sisters, I may take his weapons from him by force. Madam, will God . . . or for that matter, my father in his sane senses . . . be offended that I hindered him from committing murder? That is not rebellion, but true and just obedience.

> The QUEEN *has a sudden flush of rage. She beats the arm of her chair.*

MARY. *Sacré nom de Dieu*, Mr. Knox, remember to whom you are speaking.

> LORD JAMES *leaves the group and hurries towards her.*

LORD JAMES. Has he offended you, Madam?

MARY. No. Leave us alone.

> LORD JAMES *withdraws.* MARY *controls herself and looks at* KNOX *keenly for a few minutes.*

MARY. Well, then, Mr. Knox, I see how it is: that my subjects shall obey you and not me; that they shall do what they like and not what I command; and that so I shall be subject to them and not they to me.

KNOX. God forbid that anyone should obey me, or that subjects should be free to do whatever pleases them. But my argument is that both Princes and subjects obey God. It is God who subjects the people to their Princes and decrees that obedience shall be given to them. And to the Kings he says that they will be foster-fathers to his Church; and to Queens that they shall be nurses to his people. And this subjection, Madam, is the greatest dignity that flesh can get upon the face of the earth, for it shall carry them to everlasting glory.

MARY. That is true ; but it is not your Kirk that I shall nurse and nourish. I will nourish and defend the Kirk in which I was born ; because I think and believe that it is the true Kirk of God.

KNOX. Your will, Madam, is no reason. Neither does your thinking make that Roman harlot to be the true and immaculate spouse of Jesus Christ. Madam, the Church of the Jews that crucified Jesus Christ was not so far degenerated from the ordinances that God gave to Moses and Aaron as the Church of Rome has declined and more than five hundred years has declined from the purity of the Religion the Apostles taught and planted.

MARY. My conscience is not so.

KNOX. Conscience, Madam, requires knowledge. And I fear that richt knowledge ye have none.

MARY. Knowledge ? Since I could read, I have heard and read and talked about religion.

KNOX. So had the crucifying Jews. They read the Law and the Prophets and heard them interpreted after the manner of the Pharisees. Have you heard anyone teach apart from such as the Pope and his Cardinals have allowed ? They will teach you nothing that will offend their own estate.

MARY. You interpret Scripture in one manner. They interpret it in another. Whom shall I believe ? And who is to be the judge ?

KNOX. You shall believe God, that plainly speaks in His Word. And further then that word teaches you, you shall believe neither the one nor the other. To take one matter of controversy between the Papists and us : The Papists allege and boldly affirm that the Mass is an ordinance of God and a sacrifice for the sins of the quick and the dead. We deny both the one and the other and affirm that the Mass, as it is now used, is nothing but the invention of man ; and, therefore, is an abomination before God and no sacrifice that He ever commanded. You ask who is to be the judge between the two of us contending? There is no reason to believe either further than they are able to prove. Let them lay down the Book of God before them and by the plain words prove their affirmation and we will give them the plea. But so long as they are bold to affirm and yet prove nothing, we are bound to say that even if the whole world believe them, yet they believe not God but the lies of men. What Christ did, we know from His Evangelists. What the priest does at his Mass, the world sees. Now, are we not assured from the word of God that Christ Jesus neither said nor commanded Mass to be said at His last supper, seeing that no such thing is mentioned in the whole Scripture?

MARY. Ye are ower sair for me. But if there were some men here that I have heard, they would answer you.

KNOX. Madam, I would to God that the learnedest Papist in Europe were here present with your Grace to sustain the argument.

MARY. Well, well. You may perhaps be answered sooner than you expect.

KNOX. If I am answered in my life, it will be sooner than I expect; for the ignorant Papists will not reason patiently, and the learned and crafty Papists will not come to the forum to have the ground of their religion searched out. Their only judges are their own laws and their only arguments are fire and sword.

MARY (*rising*). So you say. And I can believe that it may have been so to this day. But we live in other times and with other manners, Mr. Knox.

KNOX (*also rising*). I pray God it may be so, Madam. And if you can show to me that your priests can argue openly like men, I will confess myself to have been deceived.

MARY. That will be indeed a memorable occasion. But I see from the impatience of my ladies that their dinner is getting cold.

KNOX. I thank your Grace for having heard me so patiently. I pray God that ye may be as blessed within the Commonwealth of Scotland as ever Deborah was in Israel.

The QUEEN *and her* LADIES, *attended by* LORD JAMES,
ENTER *the porch.* LETHINGTON *lingers behind and
approaches* KNOX.

LETHINGTON. What do you think?

KNOX. If there be not in her a proud mind, a crafty wit
and an indurate heart against God and His truth, my judgment
faileth me.

LETHINGTON. Well, well. We shall see. We shall see.

The lights fade as LETHINGTON *and* KNOX *EXEUNT
through the porch. When it is almost completely dark,
the porch is illuminated to show the figures of* MARY
and LORD JAMES.

MARY. Jamie.

LORD JAMES. Madam?

MARY. I shall hear Mass and my friends shall hear it, when
I wish and where I wish and you will silence the braying of
that old mule.

LORD JAMES. As to silencing him, I cannot work miracles.
As to the Mass, if there is to be freedom of religion in Scotland,
you have as much right to it as any of your subjects. Hear
Mass if you will. I shall keep the door.

MARY. Thank you, Jamie.

LORD JAMES. I am ever your faithful servitor.

MARY. I shall be a benign and gentle prince, but they must
not vex me. My arms are quartered on the arms of England
and France. I shall be Queen of France, of Scotland, of
England, of Ireland; and you shall help me. But first thing
of all you must stamp that wicked atheist Knox into the dust.

LORD JAMES. As to the Kingdom I will do what it is in the
power of an outlier and a bye-blow to perform. But I counsel
you to forget what you said of John Knox.

MARY. Why? I hate him.

LORD JAMES. He doesn't hate you, Madam. A comely
woman can always catch him by the heel.

MARY. You are pleased to be merry.

LORD JAMES. Not I. I am never merry. He is a strange

man. Superstition is not part of my nature, but I know in my
bones that it is unchancy to meddle with Mr. Knox. He is
the Prophet Samuel, who set the Kings of Israel on the
throne and dinged them down from it. It is not wise to cross
a Prophet.

MARY. I will cross him. He made me weep and shed nae
tears himself. We will see if I can make him weep.

LORD JAMES. You and Knox stand on a precipice, Madam.
You can only bring him down by falling yourself and falling
terribly.

MARY. It seems that you yourself are a Prophet, Jamie.

LORD JAMES. No, Madam.

MARY. *He* would take up the sword! That decrepit old
goat. You were right. I saw his eyes flowing with desire,
like phosphorus on a dead skate. Well, we shall see. There
are rougher men who will desire me . . . men with swords
and daggers. Let the old warlock take heed. I have magic of
my own. If I use my magic on your Scots brutes we may yet
smell goats' flesh roasting at the Mercat Cross . . . Sweetheart,
am I talking like my dear cousin of England? I must not be
Elizabethan. I shall show that wizened, foul-mouthed, little
English bastard how to be a Queen. That old heretic angered
me. I was not myself. I shall be a good Queen and a credit
to my grave brother. You know that I trust you, James.
Trust you me.

LORD JAMES. Do you trust me, Madam?

MARY. You know I do.

LORD JAMES. Then trust me alone. Maitland of Lethington
is cunning and a good servant; but do not be ruled by him.

MARY. I will be ruled by nobody.

LORD JAMES. Has he told you that he will get you a husband?

MARY. The whole world is busying itself in getting me a
husband. I will get me a husband for myself.

LORD JAMES. God send you choose wisely, Madam.

MARY (*dropping into broad Scots*). Jamie, lad, were it no' a
deidly sin I would mairry *you*.

> *She gives him a hand to kiss and disappears laughing into
> the back of the porch.* ENTER below BOTHWELL *and*
> DARNLEY *carrying lanterns. They come into a spot-
> light.*

LORD JAMES. Who is that?

BOTHWELL. The King of Scotland and a friend of his.

LORD JAMES. It's you, Bothwell, is it? What kind of talk is that?

BOTHWELL. Speak up to him, Harry boy. You are as good as he is.

DARNLEY. I know I am as good as he is. And both of us are better than you. We have the Blood Royal and you haven't the Blood Royal. So don't you interfere between my cousin Jamie and me.

BOTHWELL. I am not interfering. I am an extra pair of legs for you, and God's wounds! You need them. Your Royal Cousin is no' very steady on his pins, Lord James.

LORD JAMES. What is all this talk about Royalty?

BOTHWELL. The object I am supporting to the best of my ability is the future King of Scotland. The future consort of the Queen's Most Gracious Majesty.

LORD JAMES. Be silent! That is no sort of talk.

BOTHWELL. It's the talk of the town. Does nobody tell you anything?

LORD JAMES. You're drunk, Bothwell. Take that wretched young man home and try to keep your unruly tongue between your teeth.

DARNLEY. You must not speak like that to my friend.

LORD JAMES. He's your friend, is he? The last I heard you were ruffling down the Cannongate and swearing to cut off his ears.

DARNLEY. That's all forgotten. That's all forgotten, do you hear?

BOTHWELL. Haud up, ye lang leggit stirk ... Aye, it's all forgotten. We have put away envy, malice, hatred and all uncharitableness. God, that's good! Ye cannae say I don't listen to sermons. I'll be a praying jack in a pulpit before I know where I am.

DARNLEY. When I am King, Jamie, I'll give you an abbey. I'll make you a good fat rousting fornicketing cardinal.

BOTHWELL. You make me a cardinal and leave the fornicketing to me.

DARNLEY. You're a skulduddery old toad, Jamie, and I love you.   *He embraces* BOTHWELL.

BOTHWELL. Keep your wantoning for the French widow. Come, we'll split a bottle in my lodging. Good night to you, my very good Sir James. Good night to you, Holy Sir. You'll be hard put to it to recognise your Scotland when Harry and I have done with it.

> *The two stagger out into the darkness singing " Todlin'*
> *Hame." The light fades on* LORD JAMES *looking after*
> *them sullenly. For a moment there is complete darkness*
> *and then dawn music is heard and dawn lights grow. A*
> *shaft of light strikes the* CHORUS *above the portico.*

CHORUS. Time has passed and Mary has gone to Loch Leven.
Hawking in the dawn and hunting in the day and dancing in the night.
The iconoclastic John had his sport at the same time.
Roaring maledictions, raging against the Mass.
The Queen sent for John to come to her where she lay at Loch Leven.
For two hours she earnestly besought him to make peace in the land ;
To persuade the people and the gentry of the West to hold their hands ;
To allow all men to practise their several religions in peace.
To her he answered that she should enforce the law.
At the end she went angered to her supper and John satisfied, to his bed.

> CHORUS *retires. The dawn light is now full.* MARY
> FLEMING *comes in rapidly from the Left and approaches*
> *one of the alcoves.*

FLEMING. Mr. Knox! Mr. Knox! Are you awake?

ENTER KNOX *from the alcove, buttoning himself and arranging his gown.*

KNOX. I have been waking these two hours. I beat the cock by ten minutes.

FLEMING. Did you hear him crow three times?

KNOX. Young woman, gin ye studied the Scriptures with more reverence ye would see that there was nae similarity between the cases. What is your pleasure?

FLEMING. You are to see the Queen before you ride for Edinburgh.

KNOX. I had thought she would have had enough of me yestre'en. Is Her Majesty stirring?

FLEMING. She has beaten both you and chanticleer. She was out with the hawks before daybreak.

KNOX. Is she still angered?

FLEMING. No. The morning winds have blown away her anger.

MARY (*calling without*). Fleming: Where is he?

FLEMING. He is here, Madam.

ENTER MARY *in riding costume. She carries a hooded hawk on her wrist and looks flushed and gay.*

MARY. Ah! You are there, Mr. Knox. Fleming, my darling, take you this clumsy bird. She stooped at the heron like a paralytic old vulture. You cannot train hawks in Scotland . . . Don't be afraid. Take her, glove and all. Her wings are brailed. She won't hurt you. I doubt if she can hurt anything. Can you, sweetheart?

She kisses the hawk, which is now on FLEMING'S *wrist.*

MARY. Now, Mr. Knox.

KNOX. Now, Madam. So I am to be your quarry.

MARY. You are strong on the wing, Mr. Knox. I cannot get above you. But we shall not fight on this merry morning. I need your help. Let us be friends.

KNOX. Your Majesty does me too great honour.

MARY. You go to Dumfries tomorrow?

KNOX. Yes, Madam.

MARY. It is to instal a Superintendent of your Kirk, is it not?

KNOX. It is, Madam.

MARY. It is Alec Gordon, the Bishop of Galloway?

KNOX. Yes, Madam.

MARY. He is a false villain. He will corrupt your people.

KNOX. It is true that he was a Prince of the false Kirk, but that was in the days of darkness. We canna hold it against him now that it is daylight. He has the election.

MARY. He has the election by bribes. The man is bad. In a new Kirk, you must have men you can trust. Is it not so?

KNOX. It is so.

MARY. Remember what I told you, then.

KNOX. I will remember.

MARY. Oh, God! I would I knew where I could put my trust.

KNOX. There is the Providence of Almighty God, Ma'am.

MARY (*walking up and down*). I know. But you must not preach to me. You know very well what I mean. I am ringed round with rogues. Lord Arran, Lord Lennox, Lord Morton, Lord Ruthven . . . Do you know Lord Ruthven?

KNOX. Yes, Ma'am.

MARY. When he speaks to me I shiver below my skin from my head to my heels.

KNOX. He is an old man and a sick man and three parts mad.

MARY. And four parts bad. They say he is a sorcerer.

KNOX. They say so.

MARY (*taking him by the arm and walking with him*). And Lethington. What do you think of Lethington?

KNOX. What I have to say of the Secretary, I will say to his face.

MARY. I am young. I was a child only yesterday. I need help. I think that you are the only honest man in my Kingdom and you are my enemy.

KNOX. Nay, Madam. It is true that I reason with you respectfully, for the good of your immortal soul. It is true that I am a hard man and whiles speak harsh words. But I am in

C   [57]

no way your enemy. Indeed, I am enjoined by the Scriptures not only to reverence you as my lawful sovereign, but to love you as a fellow creature.

> *He has gently disengaged himself and they stand facing each other.*

MARY. Is that a word you use very often?

KNOX. What word, my Lady?

MARY. Love.

KNOX. I have no very bonny face to be talking about love ... But I am sure that was not the subject on which you wished to speak to me. So, if your Grace pleases to dismiss me, I will get on my journey.

MARY. No. Not yet. I am troubled about my half-sister, the Countess of Argyle. Her husband treats her very ill.

KNOX. I have been troubled about that matter before, Madam. The fault is not all with her husband. Before your Majesty's coming, I admonished them both gravely and it seemed that, for a time, they were at ease one with the other.

MARY. They are not so now. Will you go to them?

KNOX. I will, Madam.

MARY. I am grateful, Mr. Knox.

KNOX (*bowing to kiss her hand*). I will do what I may. I am your Grace's humble and obedient servant.

MARY. You may go now. But come to me again.

> EXIT MARY, *into the Gallery,* KNOX *looks after her for a moment and then comes downstage brooding.*

KNOX. We call her not a hoor, though she was brought up in the company of the wildest hoormongers. We call her not a hoor. There is no grace forbye the Grace of God and it maun surely be the Grace of God that shines in her countenance. But there are devils at her heart. We maun cast out the devils. We maun wrestle and pray. We maun wrestle with her. It cannot be that she is a hoor.

> EXIT KNOX. *As he goes the day grows sunny. A sound of chatter and laughter is heard and loud music comes from the building. The* FOUR MARIES, *pursued by*

> DARNLEY, *blindfolded, run across the stage.* DARNLEY
> *catches* MARY LIVINGSTONE *and embraces her before
> all go off.* KNOX *appears in the alcove where the* CHORUS
> *stood before.   The* MUSIC *grows louder and wild
> laughter comes from the building.*

Is this the blessed land of Canaan ; the safe refuge for the
brotherhood of the Godly ? The haill Court is entirely gaen
ower to skippers and dancers and dallyers with dames, and
amang it a' the abomination of the Mass flourishes in the dark
like an evil and secret weed.

> *The* QUEEN *and the* FOUR MARIES *run laughing down the
> steps. They are followed by* DARNLEY, CHASTELARD,
> RIZZIO *and two or three other ladies and gentlemen, all
> in masking clothes.* RIZZIO *is a little dwarfish Italian
> with an air of deformity about him. He carries a lute
> and sits on a step to play it.*

MARY. The Purpose, Davie, we will have the Purpose !
RIZZIO. *Presto, Madame ! Subito !*

> *They take their places for the dance called the Purpose,
> which begins.* RIZZIO *and the unseen orchestra playing.
> There is much laughter and rather startling displays of
> affection between the* QUEEN *and some of the gentlemen.*
> CHASTELARD *is particularly favoured.   The dance
> includes frequent change of partners, and when* DARNLEY
> *becomes the* QUEEN'S *partner* KNOX *begins to speak,
> topping the music and laughter with his voice.   Just
> before this the* MULATTO *places his board close to the
> proscenium arch and begins a stately clog dance in time
> to the music.*

KNOX. Henry Darnley, have you for the pleasure of that
dainty dame cast the Psalm book into the fire ? The Lord
shall strike you both head and tail.

> *At the last sentence there is a sudden silence and the
> dancers look up at* KNOX *as the Curtain falls.*

END OF ACT II

ACT III

The Curtain rises on a scene supposed to be taking place a few moments after the end of Act II. The dancers have gone and the stage is left to NORA, HECTOR *and the* MULATTO. *It is moonlight again. The* MULATTO *is picking up his dancing board in a disconsolate fashion.* HECTOR *is lighting a cigarette.* NORA *has half crossed the stage and is looking up towards the porch.*

NORA. Your dance didna last very long, Jerry.

HECTOR. Nobody's dance lasted very long.

NORA. What was the auld yin narking about? They can surely dance if they want to dance. And why should she not marry the lad if she wanted him? He was a poor fish, but he was bonny. I'd have married him myself, if it was only to keep him in order.

She crosses back to the Group.

NORA. Have you a fag, handsome?

HECTOR *gives cigarettes to* NORA *and the* MULATTO *and lights them.*

HECTOR. The clouds are crossing the moon.

The stage darkens till only the three cigarettes show. The porch lights up to show a room in KNOX'S *house. He sits at a table, reading a book. To him,* LORD JAMES.

LORD JAMES. There was no one to announce me.

KNOX. Forbye myself and the two bairns sleeping ben the house there is nobody here but mysel'. I am blythe to see your Lordship.

LORD JAMES. It was a grief to us all when Mrs. Knox died.

KNOX. It was a strange thing in the Lord to tak' one so young and bonny and leave a withered auld runt like me.

LORD JAMES. It was in His purpose.

KNOX. It is not from me only that the Lord has turned the light of His face. Man, but my heart is heavy : I see nocht but avarice, oppression of the poor and riotous cheer. How is it at the Court ? Are they aye fiddling and flinging ?

LORD JAMES. Aye.

KNOX. I danced a spring or two mysel when I was a callant. There is kindliness in dancing. But there is a time for dancing and a time for prayer and fasting. I fear me they will get the reward of dancers and that will be drunk in Hell.

LORD JAMES. Mary Livingstone is with child by John Sempill and Chastelard has lost his head.

KNOX. Poor lad. It was a sore business yon. He made a good enough end, for a Frenchman.

LORD JAMES. Even Frenchmen are ill-placed under the Queen's bed. She was for me killing him on the spot.

KNOX. He was a stranger. She was honest enough, I think, and only showing gentleness to a stranger. But it's not to be expected but a young fellow will make a mistake when he finds in the Court the manners of a brothel.

LORD JAMES. He said : " *Adieu*, the most beautiful and the most cruel Princess of the world," and then the axe fell.

KNOX. That was the reward of his dancing.

LORD JAMES. He will not be the last.

KNOX. I fear it.

LORD JAMES. If this marriage comes to pass there are other necks that will itch in their collars. Her spies heard your sermon against the marriage.

KNOX. I think they did. She has sent for me.

LORD JAMES. Will you go ?

KNOX. I will go.

LORD JAMES. She will be angry.

KNOX. I do not fear her anger.

LORD JAMES. She will marry him whatever we do. She is besotted with him. And our worthy brethren the Lords of the Congregation will not raise a finger to save his enemies. They look godly enough in St. Giles ; but the devils we bound in them are loose again. We have lost our labour, John.

KNOX. No.

LORD JAMES. My hope is near gone. It was high when we rode stirrup to stirrup at Corrichie, she and I. Her eyes were shining through the rain that whitened the buff coats of the pikemen. On that day we killed Huntly together and broke the power of the Pope in the north. I thanked God that we had a Princess who put justice before all. Now I am not so sure.

KNOX. I will tell you why you are not so sure. If your time of decay has come upon you . . . as I begin to fear that it has . . . then call to mind by what means God exalted you. It was not by bearing with impiety nor yet by the maintaining of pestilent Papists.

LORD JAMES. You speak with a proud tongue.

KNOX. God forbid.

LORD JAMES. I have tried to make peace and order and freedom in this land. And when I had it in the palm of my hand, who broke it ? What harm was it to you that a poor lassie should worship God as her fathers did before her ?

KNOX. You kept the gates of the temple of Baal. You countenanced idolatry. See where it has brought you. Where is now your place and order ? With this whelp on the right hand of the throne, all the ill-begotten tykes in the land will rise and bay at us with their jaws slavering for murder.

LORD JAMES. Aye, talk, talk, talk ! You can talk your fill. But God help us poor souls who are charged with the doing. Farewell, to you, Master Knox ; and I hope you find the Queen's Grace in a mood for your talk.

> *He flings angrily out of the room. After a moment's pause* ENTER LETHINGTON.

LETHINGTON. Good evening to you, Mr. Knox.

KNOX. I am honoured, my Lord Secretary.

LETHINGTON. You have distinguished visitors tonight. I passed my Lord of Moray on the stair.

KNOX. No doubt you did, sir.

LETHINGTON. He seemed ill-pleased with his reception. I hope I may be more fortunate.

KNOX. I hope you may.

LETHINGTON. I have a proposal to make to you, Mr. Knox.

KNOX. And what may that be?

LETHINGTON. That you should put on your cloak and bonnet and take the air with me.

> *Two* MEN-AT-ARMS *appear in the wings.*

KNOX. For what destination?

LETHINGTON. Not the Tolbooth, my dear sir. This is not an arrest. I had thought of Holyrood house.

KNOX. I have two bairns in their beds and none to watch them.

LETHINGTON. I'll post a man at the door. You will return home soon. To tell you the truth, her Majesty is impatient to see you.

KNOX. Once more I am honoured.

LETHINGTON. Very much so, Mr. Knox. Very much so. Her Majesty is, as you know, deeply interested in matters of religion. She wishes to discuss with you a certain sermon. In case you forget it, the subject was, I think, Holy Matrimony.

> KNOX *puts on his cloak and cap and the two begin to descend the stairs. As* KNOX *puts out a candle, the porch darkens.*

LETHINGTON. Ah, Gibbie. Will you go round to the close mouth and mount guard over Mr. Knox's lodging. And if his bairns greet, give them some pap.

MAN. Very good, my Lord.

> EXIT MAN-AT-ARMS.

LETHINGTON. Wat, you will follow us at a respectful distance ... It is long since we have met, Mr. Knox, but it has been in my heart to have a word with you.

> *He punctuates each sentence by descending another step.*

I have wondered if it might not be possible for you to be more circumspect ... even in the matter of your very loyal prayers for the Queen as well as in the occasional reflections you indulge in as touching her estate and obedience. This is not in any manner meant as a reproach; but your example may encourage others to take the like liberty, perhaps without the modesty and foresight that you invariably show. And, if that happens, a wise man like you will have no difficulty in imagining what may be engendered in people's heads as a result of it. Forgive me for being so plain and blunt; but it was ever my habit.

> EXEUNT *to Right of stage. The porch is now covered by a heavy curtain with a brilliant light shining behind it.*
>
> *A* PAGE *comes out and meets a* LORD-IN-WAITING *in full armour, with a drawn sword, entering from one of the alcoves, which is dimly lit to show him. The* PAGE *whispers to him, laughs, and goes out* R. *He returns almost at once, leading on* KNOX.

PAGE. Mr. Knox to see the Queen.

LORD. Pass, Mr. Knox.

> KNOX *ascends two or three steps. The* PAGE *and the* LORD *draw back the curtain, showing* MARY *standing. She is very still, but very furious. The* PAGE *and the* LORD *disappear into separate alcoves.*

MARY. You have come at last, Mr. Knox.

KNOX. I do not apprehend what your Grace means by " at last." It was to be my pleasure to attend your Grace to-morrow morning and it was . . .

MARY. I can listen no more to your argle bargle. God's Death, was ever a Prince handled as I have been? I have borne with your flyting and barking and blowing against me and against my uncle, the Cardinal. I have tried to please you by every possible means. I offered you my presence and audience whenever it pleased you to advise and admonish me. And yet I cannot be quit of you. I avow to God I shall be revenged . . . Marnock! Bring me my handkerchief.

> PAGE *appears with a handkerchief, and the* QUEEN *falls back on a chair in a fit of angry weeping.*

KNOX (*after a patient pause*). Madam, it is true that your Grace and I have had divers controversies, though I never perceived your Grace to be offended at them. If I have offended, I must bide till the Lord has delivered you from the bondage of darkness and error. I think you will not then find the liberty of my tongue offensive. Outside the pulpit, Madam, I am known as a quiet, genial man. In the pulpit I am not my own master. I must obey Him who commands me to speak plain and to flatter no flesh upon the face of the earth.

MARY. What have you to do with my marriage?

KNOX. If it please your Majesty to hear me patiently, I shall show the truth in plain words. I grant that your Grace has offered me more courtesy and kindness than I ever required; but God did not send me to wait upon the courts of Princesses nor in ladies' chambers, I am sent to preach the evangel of Jesus Christ to such as please to hear it. That evangel hath two parts, repentance and faith. It is not possible, Madam, to speak of repentance without speaking of sin that man may know wherein they offend. The magic of your person, Madam, has so worked on the nobility that they heed neither God His word nor yet their duty to the Commonwealth. It becomes me to remind them of these things.

MARY. I ask you again, what have you to do with my marriage? What are you within this Commonwealth?

KNOX. A subject born within the same. I am neither Earl, Lord nor Baron, and to your eyes I may appear of small account. But both my vocation and my conscience crave plainness of me. And therefore, Madam, to yourself I say that which I speak in a public place: whensoever the nobility of this Realm shall consent that you be subject to an unfaithful and renegade husband, on that day they shall do as much as in them lies to renounce Christ, to banish His truth, to betray the freedom of the Realm and, perhaps, in the end, to do small comfort to yourself.

> *Once more the* QUEEN *bursts into tears and* LETHINGTON
> *comes hurrying from behind a curtain to comfort her.*
> KNOX *stands immobile on the lower step.*

LETHINGTON. Madam, Madam! This is unlike your Grace

. . . One with the speech and appearance of a goddess should have a goddess's composure . . . If this man offends your Grace he will be dealt with . . . what would the Princes of Europe say if they saw the object of their worship in such a guise . . . Shall I send for your ladies ?

MARY. No, no, no, no, no, no !

> LETHINGTON'S *speeches are broken and mostly drowned by the* QUEEN'S *sobbing.*

LETHINGTON. Your Majesty is not well . . . You must call on the resources of your princely will . . . Take hold on yourself, Madam . . . The servants will hear you.

MARY. Go away. Go away.

> KNOX *speaks again in a gentle, reasonable voice which has the curious effect of stopping her tears without mitigating her anger.*

KNOX. Madam, I never delighted in the weeping of any of God's creatures. I can scarcely weel abide the tears of my own boys when I am driven to correct them. Much less can I rejoice in your Majesty's weeping. But seeing I have offered to you nothing but the truth I must sustain however unwillingly your Majesty's tears rather than hurt my conscience and betray my Commonwealth through my silence.

> *The* QUEEN *starts up trembling with rage.*

MARY. Leave my presence. You have had much to say about discipline but you seem loath to apply discipline to yourself. I will take order to show you discipline. Now take yourself out of my sight.

> *The light fades on the* QUEEN *as* KNOX *comes down the steps. On his* EXIT *the porch is again dark. The* CHORUS *appears. Trumpets are heard. The sky is lit as with sunset.*

CHORUS. Forasmuch as at the will and pleasure of Almighty God, the Queen has taken to her as husband the Right Excellent and Illustrious Prince Harry, Duke of Rothesay, Earl of Ross, Lord Darnley ; therefore it is her will that he shall be holden and obeyed and reverenced as King: and she further commands all letters and proclamations to be made in the names of Henry and Mary in times coming.

> *The* CHORUS *withdraws. The alcoves light up to show lighted windows and the sound of music and laughter comes out of the building.* KNOX *appears on the fore-stage close to the three* MORTALS.

KNOX. See how God sets in that room for the offences and the ingratitude of the people, boys and women.

> *The central porch lights up once more as the Queen's Chamber.* DARNLEY *is lolling in the chair playing at cup and ball. He looks rather sulky. The* QUEEN *is walking to and fro like a caged tigress in a confined space.*

DARNLEY. Why do you walk to and fro like a leopard in a cage? Come sit on my knee.

MARY. I am in a cage. If you had the heart of a man you would break the bars for me.

DARNLEY. I cannot understand why you don't send for the French Army to knock some sense into their thick heads.

MARY. If they offered us an army I should not take it. This is my country, yours and mine. By God's Death, we shall rule it for ourselves!

DARNLEY. We shall have poor assistance in ruling now you have banished Lord James. If we forget that stinking fox Lethington, which I should be glad to do, there never was such a parcel of knavish dolts as those who rally round our person, crown and dignity. They are cowards too. They will not punish Knox.

MARY. They will punish Knox all in good time. I know what I shall do. I shall send for Bothwell.

DARNLEY. Bothwell? I don't like him.

MARY. Bothwell is a man. I must have a man at my elbow.

DARNLEY. And I am not a man?

MARY. You are my love and my dear and the only king of my heart.

> *She sits on his knee and the scene fades on their embrace.*

KNOX. Think you I am a false prophet? Think you the Lord is mocked? Suffer me a moment and I will show you the terrible anger of God. I will show you the mandrakes and the tares torn screaming from the earth and the growth of the good corn torn up with them. I will show you my silly prayers turned to dust and ashes in my mouth because I bore not hardly enough on the workers of iniquity. Have patience a while. Have patience. You will see in a stage how Davie Rizzio was stuck full of daggers and a foolish king was blown from his bed. You will see the adulteries of the Queen and how Hell rose up against her to meet her at her coming. Hush! Be patient. You shall see.

> *The clouds grow red again and the forestage is lit by an*
> *unearthly half light. The windows in the alcoves appear*
> *in an amber light. The faint tinkle of a guitar comes*
> *from the building.*

KNOX. You will mind . . . you that looks a lettered king of lad . . . that rebellion lifted its heid in Scotland at this ungodly marriage. Lord James, who was neither to haud nor bind, made to take Edinboro with his men, but he couldna for the rock held fast. The Queen hersel' raised twenty thousand men and scoured Lord James across the Border. She rode in the rain like a trooper with a steel hat on her head and slept we kenna where. My Lord, her husband, rode with her, though he had rather abode by the fireside with his puppies and his puppets, and schemed with the Lords to make him King indeed.

You will have heard of Davie Rizzio, that was a black-avised and foul knave but a man with his head on his shoulders? He kenned that gin my Lord was King indeed what would be the upshot of that. On a black night in March, the Queen being seven months gone with child, Davie went to his account.

> *The following scene is played in the porch in Pantomime.*
> *Two small thrones are set.* RIZZIO *is playing to the*
> QUEEN. *Presently* DARNLEY ENTERS *and sits on the*
> *vacant throne. He kisses the* QUEEN, *who takes his*
> *kiss absently.*

KNOX. Judas, ye'll observe. Young Lord Judas Iscariot.

Suddenly four or five LORDS *burst into the room. The* QUEEN *rises to meet them.* RUTHVEN, *a villainous old man, with armour over his nightshirt, throws over a table and* RIZZIO *runs behind the* QUEEN *and cowers, clutching her skirts. One* LORD *holds a pistol to the* QUEEN'S *belly while the others dispatch* RIZZIO *with sword and dagger.*

They throw his body down the steps and tear him like hounds. The light fades on the silent QUEEN, *with* DARNLEY *behind her, as the* LORDS *pick up* RIZZIO *and carry him away.*

The Curtain closes on the Queen's Chamber and RUTHVEN *is left standing alone on the rostrum, leaning heavily on his sword and grinning like a fiend. To him,* DARNLEY.

DARNLEY. Who's that ? O, it's you, Lord Ruthven.

RUTHVEN. Yes.

DARNLEY. Is it done ? Is he dead ?

RUTHVEN. He's deid.

DARNLEY. They told me you were sick. They said you were at death's door.

RUTHVEN. I have been at death's door for long enough. Death'll no' let me in.

DARNLEY. You're like a corpse. You should be in your bed.

RUTHVEN. I'm obliged to your Majesty for your considera-tion. But it would ha'e been an ill thing if this good deed had been done, and naebody here to represent the Old Laws.

DARNLEY. I fear the Queen will take it badly. You were over rough.

RUTHVEN. The Old Laws were aye rough.

DARNLEY. What did you say ?

RUTHVEN. Under the Old Laws a man took what he had the strength to take and kept it till a stronger man came. They were clean laws, the old ones. There was nae place in them for white slugs of priests with their Paters and their Aves. We

[69]

called in the crows to peck the slugs to death and will shoot the crows when the time comes.

DARNLEY. The Queen will not forgive this night's work.

RUTHVEN. The Old Laws took nae text of the howling and greeting of dames. You'll never be a King till you can master women . . . Oxter me in, Hairry; I'm feared I'm gey faur through. But, man, this night has been the grandest medicine I've ta'en in a twalmonth.

DARNLEY helps him off.

The tocsin begins to clang and torches glimmer as the Gallery blacks out.

KNOX. The Queen said to the King: " You have done me such wrong that neither the recollection of our early friendship, nor all the hope you can give me of the future can ever make me forget it." And from that hour her heart was as hard as the granite stane and for a time her heid was cool and crafty. She sent for the Lord James and pardoned him : and, indeed, she was wise; for better a den of wild beasts than the Lords of her Court. And she gave to Lord Bothwell the rule of the east, middle and west, and in that she was not so wise. On June the nineteenth of fifteen hundred and sixty six, her son, King James was born. You shall hear her speak of that.

The porch shows the QUEEN in bed, with her son in her arms. Two MARIES stand at the head of the bed and DARNLEY and LETHINGTON at the side.

MARY. My Lord, God has given you and me a son, begotten by none but you.

DARNLEY stoops and kisses the child.

MARY. No. It is a grave matter. As I shall answer to God on the great day of judgment, this is your son and no other man's son. Let all here bear witness. He is so much your own son, that I fear it will be the worse for him hereafter . . . Lethington.

LETHINGTON. Madam.

MARY. You have come from England. Is our Cousin as wise as they say.

LETHINGTON. She has great wisdom, Madam.

MARY. I think not. The wisest among us women is only a little less foolish than the rest. Is she wise enough to know that this is the first King of England and Scotland ?

LETHINGTON. Why, Madam, should he succeed before your Majesty and his father ?

MARY. Because his father has broken with me.

DARNLEY. Sweetheart, is this your promise that you made to forgive and to forget ?

MARY. I have forgiven ; but I cannot forget.

DARNLEY. Madam, these things are all past.

MARY. Then let them go.

The light fades.

KNOX. That brute knave Bothwell was now Lieutenant General of the east, middle and west Marches and Lord High Admiral of Scotland and in honour above all her subjects. She spoke with him and she rode with him and she sailed with him in a little ship manned by his pirates, frae Newhaven to Alloa . . . for she joyed to handle the boisterous cables. When he was hurted in a tuilzie in the Borders, she rode frae Jedburgh, thirty miles and back on horseback to his castle. She had given reign to the Devil in her Realm and now Beelzebub had entered her daft, reckless body and was to be her master from that time forth. What came of it, you shall learn.

PARIS *appears in the darkness in one of the alcoves and stands waiting.*

KNOX. It is on a nicht of February in 1567 . . . The nicht when John Knox's Utopia blew up sky-high in the cold air. The place is the Kirk o' Field. In a lone house between twa ruins the King lies sick of the small-pox. The man ye see there is Paris, a black villain in Bothwell's hire, and blacker the nicht with the gunpowder he laid in for the King's taking off. Watch and listen.

[71]

ENTER BOTHWELL *from the opposite side to* PARIS.

BOTHWELL. Paris?

PARIS. Aye, my Lord.

BOTHWELL. Is it ready?

PARIS. Aye.

BOTHWELL. Is he sleeping?

PARIS. He is not. He keeps calling for the Queen. I'm not sure he hasna' got wind of it.

BOTHWELL. Stand by. Dinna let him out o' your sicht. If he breaks cover choke him with your two hands. Ye mauna use the knife. Hae ye seen a clock?

PARIS. Aye.

BOTHWELL. What time is't?

PARIS. It wants hauf an oor to the time.

BOTHWELL. God's nails, I maun ride. I maun be seen in the toon afore it goes up. Good night.

PARIS. Good night, my Lord.

EXEUNT *severally. A distant rumble of thunder.*

KNOX. We'll to Holyrood now. Bastien the Queen's page has been wedded and bedded and the Queen has withdrawn her from the dance. You shall see her.

The porch lights up. The Queen's room contains a dressing table and a prie-dieu at the back. MARY BEATON *is preparing the* QUEEN *for bed. They appear to be talking but no words are heard. The* QUEEN *looks excited and restless. There is very distant music.*

KNOX. It will be soon now. Speak up, woman, and let them hear you.

MARY. Are they dancing still?

BEATON. Yes, Madam. It is a gay wedding.

MARY. I saw a picture once of people dancing at a wedding. There was a great door in the picture and beyond the door the house was in ruins. And in the ruins the dead rotted and the crows picked out their eyes. In the picture death, like a skeleton, was prising and prising at the door.

BEATON. That was an awful picture.

MARY. I saw it again tonight. Tonight I left the King's bedside at the Kirk o' Field and rode to Bastien's wedding. The King lay on a little purple bed with a taffety mask over his face. His vanity holds, Mary. Even by me he would not be seen with his face ruined by the small-pox. There was tapestry on the walls that we looted at Corrichie. There was a red carpet on the floor and a red velvet cushion or two. There was a tall chair and a wee table covered with green velvet. There was a bath with a door of the house for a lid. There was no air stirring and the stink of pestilence in the room. There were two guttering candles and sometimes I wrote and sometimes I talked to him.

BEATON. Is he better?

MARY. I think so. I could not go near him or touch him. I sat at his bed's foot and listened. He asked me to forgive him. He said he had been chastised by experience. He said I was the cause of his follies, for he had no one to talk to but me, and, since I held him aloof, he had perforce to keep his passion and his anger buried in his breast.

BEATON. Poor soul!

MARY. I know that his heart is of wax and that mine is as hard as a diamond. No shot can breach it now. But I almost had pity on him.

A short silence.

He was not for me leaving him. He begged me to stay . . . I think with tears, but I could not see them for the taffety mask. He was lucky to be able to weep . . . I met my Lord Bothwell's man Paris at the door. He was begrimed with dirt and as black as the Devil. What he had been about I know not.

Sound of a distant explosion.

Jesu, what was that?

BEATON. A thunder-clap, Madam.

MARY. Thunder? It may be that. Have you seen the Lord Bothwell tonight?

BEATON. He rode from the Palace two hours ago.

MARY. Did you see him? Did he look merry?

BEATON. He threw a jest over his shoulder as he rode off.

MARY. What did he say?

BEATON. If I heard him aright, Madam, it was no jest for a lady to repeat.

MARY. Give me my bed-gown. Leave me now. I shall read a little and say my prayers. I am very weary. I wish that I could die.

> BEATON *is about to speak, but curtsies and goes out,
> leaving* MARY *alone. The* QUEEN *now betrays agitation.
> She goes to the prie-dieu but cannot pray. She returns
> to her chair and sits staring in front of her, gnawing her
> finger. The clock strikes one.* ENTER BOTHWELL.

MARY (*without looking up*). Is it you?

BOTHWELL. Yes.

MARY. What has happened?

BOTHWELL. The Kirk o' Field has been struck by lightning. Your husband is dead.

MARY. How do you know that he is dead?

BOTHWELL. They have seen the body. He was blown yards away from the house. There wasn't a scratch on him.

MARY. Oh, God!

> *She suddenly throws herself on* BOTHWELL'S *breast in a
> wild fit of weeping.* BOTHWELL *laughs. As the porch
> blacks out* BOTHWELL'S *laugh is drowned by the
> clanging of bells and shouting. Some shots are fired and
> flashes appear at the back of the dark stage. Voices
> are heard, confused at first, but gathering into what is
> almost a chant.*

VOICES. Rout out the murderers! Who killed the King? Bothwell killed the King! Hang Bothwell! Rout out the murderers! . . . Burn the hoor! Burn the hoor! Burn the hoor!

> *The six alcoves light up and six dim figures are shown
> in silhouette.*

KNOX (*shouting*). The Kirk bids you hang the murderer!

FIRST FIGURE (LENNOX). The father and mother of the King bid you hang the murderer.

SECOND FIGURE (*a woman*). Your infant son bids you hang the murderer.

THIRD FIGURE. The Lords of the Congregation bid you hang the murderer.

FOURTH FIGURE (*a woman*). The Queen of England bids you hang the murderer.

FIFTH FIGURE (*a woman*). The Queen of France bids you hang the murderer.

SIXTH FIGURE. The Pope of Rome bids you hang the murderer.

> BOTHWELL *appears from the dark porch and stands on the step.*

BOTHWELL. I have tholed my assize. I had for witnesses two hundred arquebusiers, with their matches lit and two thousand stout gentlemen with whingers in their fists. The high and honourable court found me not guilty and dismissed me without a stain on my pure and noble character. And now if any man, gentle or simple, will raise his voice against that court of justice I will defend that court's honour with my sword. I will meet him foot to foot and cut his guts out at his good pleasure, and when I have done that I will marry the Queen.

> *He laughs. The lights fade.*

VOICES (*muttering*). Burn the hoor!

> *A sulphurous light comes up again as* KNOX *rushes up the steps and turns to the audience.*

KNOX. She married the bloody dog while his wife still lived. She married him under the ordinances of the Kirk I, John Knox, had laboured to build. Oh, foolish Scotland, that would not obey the voice of God when he had delivered that vile adulteress and cruel murderer of her own husband into their hands! Wherefore the great plague of God fell and will fall heavily on this whole country and nation. (*A pause.*) Lord, in thy hands I commend my spirit; for the terrible roaring of guns and the noise of armour do so pierce my heart that my soul thirsteth to depart. Lord Jesus, receive my spirit and put an end to this my miserable life, for justice and truth are not to be found among the sons of men.

He goes into the porch and disappears.

VOICES. Burn the hoor! Burn the hoor! Burn the hoor! Burn the hoor!

> MARY *appears above the portico; as nearly as possible she conforms to* BEATON'S *description of her appearance at the window of the Provost's house.* "She came to the said window sundry times in so miserable a state, her hair hanging about her lugs and her breast, yea, the most part of all her body from the waist up, bare and discovered, that no man could look upon her but she moved him to pity and compassion."

MARY (*screaming*). Look at me, men of Scotland! Is there not a man among you with a sword ye can use to kill me or set me free? They have betrayed me. I am a prisoner. The dogs have betrayed me. Look at me. I am your Queen. God made me your Queen. Help! Help! Help! James Stuart! Brother, come and save me!

> Two MEN-AT-ARMS *appear on either side of her, swing round before her, crossing their halberds, and force her down out of sight. It is as if she were pressed back by a great machine.*

They have all deserted me. All!

> *The light rapidly changes to that in which the play opened. The three* MORTALS *drift towards mid-stage,* HECTOR *first; then* NORA; *then the* MULATTO *with his perambulator.* HECTOR *speaks in a dazed sort of voice.*

HECTOR. I do not know what has happened or what will happen or whether the story is true; but it has been nearly told. Lord James drove the Queen and Roman Communion from Scotland and was shot in the street at Linlithgow. Lethington was the cleverest of them all and he died a broken

man. Knox died the year before him. Long years afterwards
his dream came true and it proved to be no great matter. Mary
laid her tired grey head on the block fifteen years after that
and reigns to this day with Helen of Troy and Cleopatra of
Egypt in the crazy imaginations of men. It will be all the same,
says the proverb, a hundred years hence. Three hundred
years hence it is all the same. What do they think of it now,
the beautiful Queen and the hard old man ?

NORA. I know what he thinks of it. My God, I know what
he thinks of it. He is roasting in Hell howling for the poor
beautiful lady to dip her handkerchief in her tears and moisten
his burning tongue.

HECTOR. Do you think so ?

NORA. I know so. Otherwise, what would be the meaning
of religion ?

HECTOR. Jerry, what do you think is the meaning of
religion ?

JERRY. I donno. Some says one thing and some says another. I learned a piece once in a Mission School. I got a
picture for that. It was a picture of the Lord Jesus jollying on
a lot of school kids. I still got it.

HECTOR. What was the piece you learned ?

JERRY. Lemme see. It's a long time since. Something like
where it said : The poor in spirit, they'se all right ; theirs is
the kingdom of Heaven. The sorrowful, they'se all right.
Somebody going to comfort them. The meek, they'se all
right. They going to get the whole earth. Them that is
hungry for good, they'se all right. They get what they want.
The merciful, they'se all right. They get mercy when they
need it. The pure in heart, they'se all right. They'll see they
gat fust chance of seeing God, see ? The peacemakers, they'se
all right ; they're God's kids, see ? I forget the rest. I think
it said it was a good thing to be knocked about a bit, but *I*
donno.

HECTOR. Is that all ?

JERRY. That's all. Except one bit more I read on a tract
with ivy on it. Ivy, see, and robins. I think the Lord Jesus

say it himself. " O righteous Father, the world hath not known thee . . . " Sorry, I forget the rest. John XVII and 25. You find it there.

> KNOX *comes out of the alcove* R. *and sits easily and affably on the top step.*

KNOX. Aye. You'll find it there. " The world hath not known thee ; but I have known thee and these have known that thou has sent me." I got great comfort from that chapter. It sustained me ; but it misled me too.

JERRY. Sorry, Mister. I didn't know you was there.

KNOX. I'm not there. No, nor anywhere. I am a ghost.

JERRY. I never see a ghost before. But my ole mammy, she seen plenty. Pleased to meet you. All them other guys and dames ghosts too ?

KNOX. Yes.

JERRY. I thought so. I'd a told you two if you'd have asked me.

> *He collects his blanket and sits down on the bottom step, taking no further interest.*

KNOX. Ghosts, Ghosts. All Ghosts.

> ENTER *the* QUEEN *from alcove* L. *She is dressed in white as she was when she was first a widow. She walks over to* KNOX *and sits down beside him, taking his hand.*

MARY. Poor John.

KNOX. Oh, you're there are you ?

MARY. Yes. We were the best of them all. What went wrong with us ? Tell me. Not a sermon, but tell me.

KNOX. It's true that we were the best of them all, but not in the way we thought.

MARY. No. Not in the way we thought. Perhaps that was what was wrong. Was it our fault ?

KNOX. No. The crab is not to blame for his shell. He grows it to guard him against the brute world, Molly. And our shells were gey tough.

MARY. I was a King Crab. I thought I was born that.

KNOX. You were born a gasping screaming little morsel of female flesh with an immortal soul somewhere in you, and you were born nothing else.

MARY. That is true. And how were you born?

KNOX. I thought there was a man sent from Heaven whose name was John, but I took the ordinary road for getting here. It was ill luck that I got a voice that could talk Kings off their thrones and I thought too much of it.

MARY. I had an unchancy gift too, Johnny.

KNOX. By God, you had! You know, in many ways I was right. There was a strong core of truth in my folly. But you came with your gift, more terrible than an army with banners and swept my wisdom and my folly into dust.

MARY. But you won in the end.

KNOX. I won nothing. To this day I am half a pantaloon and half a villain. It's my own fault. While I lived I was not content to be a man.

MARY. I would have been a woman if they had let me.

KNOX. You would have been what God made you; and to what God made you would have added and added, for that is the way of all that are remarkable among God's creatures. And you would have held to words forms and to your own mad idea of yourself; but you would have come to grief at last; for you would have left yourself far behind.

MARY. As you did too?

KNOX. As I did too. We are poor creatures when all's said, but we are what we are. And that's better than to be a swaddled Queen with a hundred-weight of metal on her head or a bawling doctrinaire in a high pulpit. We're not gods yet, though we do our best to pretend it. Some of us.

MARY. We're lucky to be dead.

KNOX. Madam, I have had occasion in the past to rebuke you for blasphemous words and thoughts. We are NOT better to be dead. We must have life and have it more abundantly. We must glorify God in the flesh as in the spirit. We must . . .

MARY. Oh, sermons, sermons, sermons . . .

KNOX (*laughing*). Mary.

MARY. John, I love you. We didn't know what that meant did we ?

KNOX. We knew nothing.

CURTAIN

END OF THE PLAY

DR. ANGELUS

A PLAY IN THREE ACTS

*The play was presented at the Phoenix Theatre on 30th July, 1947,
with the following cast :*

JOHNSON	George Cole.
ANGELUS	Alastair Sim.
JEANIE	Molly Urquhart.
MRS. CORCORAN	Betty Marsden.
SIR GREGORY BUTT	Charles Carson.
MRS. ANGELUS	Jane Aird.
INSPECTOR MACIVOR . . .	Archie Duncan.
POLICEMAN	Rex Gardiner.

The play was produced by Alastair Sim.

The scenery was designed by Kathleen Ankers.

PERSONS IN THE PLAY

DR. ANGELUS
DR. JOHNSON
MRS. CORCORAN
MRS. ANGELUS
JEANIE
SIR GREGORY BUTT
INSPECTOR MACIVOR

TIME : 1920

PLACE : Glasgow

ACT I

*A dark Stage. A clock strikes nine. A door opens,
letting in a beam of light. A* YOUNG MAN *in a bowler hat,
carrying a small black bag, comes in. He opens the desk,
throws his hat, overcoat and bag on an examination couch and
sits down to the desk, making entries in a daybook from his
pocket diary. His back is to the audience.*

*The audience can now take in the dimly lit scene. It is a
rather cheaply furnished Doctor's Consulting Room. As the
detail is picked up, it adds up to something slightly sinister,
though it is an ordinary enough room of itself, with two doors—
one leading to a passage, the other to a little lavatory. Dark
green curtains cover the window. A number of heavy curios
show that the* DOCTOR *has travelled a bit. The Solomon
Islands, India, China and East Africa are all represented,
usually by something rather repulsive. Enlarged photographs are
mostly of a tall, not ill-looking man in various tropical cos-
tumes. In one of them, he has killed a hippopotamus. Over
the fireplace is a large oil painting of a formidable looking,
whiskered K.C. in his robes. There is a smallish bookcase
and a largish medicine cupboard. A microscope, a urine-
testing stand and a weighing machine are prominent. There is
also an indeterminate large object that is apparently some sort
of electrical machine. The periods of the furniture vary ; but
the time is, in fact,* 1920.

The YOUNG MAN *goes on working, whistling rather shrilly but
mournfully, " If you were the only girl in the world."*

The TALL MAN *of the photographs comes in without being
noticed. He is dressed in a velvet smoking jacket, striped
trousers and carpet slippers. His name is* DR. ANGELUS. *He
looks benevolently at the young man's back. He then speaks
suddenly :*

ANGELUS. Bauff! (*Laughs*) Hard at work, I see. Hard at work.

The YOUNG MAN, JOHNSON, *turns round quickly and then grins.*

JOHNSON. Oh, good evening, Dr. Angelus.

ANGELUS. Good evening to you, Johnson. You have just got in?

JOHNSON. Yes. Just a minute ago.

ANGELUS. Have you had a hard day?

JOHNSON. Pretty stiff, Doctor. Twenty-seven visits and two surgeries of about three hours each.

ANGELUS. We must do what we can for suffering humanity. We must do what we can. I am sorry that you have been kept so late. You might have joined us in family prayers.

JOHNSON. I'm afraid that's not much in my line.

ANGELUS. A pity. A pity. In a world like this it ought to be a case of all hands to the pumps. But I find most young men of our profession take rather a materialistic outlook, these days. It is their teaching. They are not to blame. They are ill-served by their teachers.

JOHNSON. Oh, I don't know. I wouldn't say that I was a materialist, exactly. More a sort of a rationalist, if you see what I mean.

ANGELUS. I see what you mean, my dear boy. I deplore it, naturally. Spiritual values are very real and living things to me; but I am well aware that to others they may mean very little . . . How is Lady Cohen?

JOHNSON. Much about the same.

ANGELUS. You explained, I hope, why I couldn't call today?

JOHNSON. Yes. She quite understood.

ANGELUS. Good. She is a stupid old bitch, but she has a very kind heart. Indeed, I don't know what I should do without her, in these hard times.

JOHNSON. How is Mrs. Taylor?

ANGELUS. Ah, poor Mrs. Taylor! I hope you never make foolish jokes about mothers-in-law, Johnson. My poor mother-in-law has taken the place of my own dear mother

[2]

for me. And now, I am very much afraid, I am going to lose her.

JOHNSON. I hope it's not so bad as that.

ANGELUS. It is, it is. I hope against hope. One must never give up hope. But I'm afraid her gastric condition is malignant. I greatly fear it.

JOHNSON. Wouldn't it be a good plan to have a second opinion?

ANGELUS. Do you think so? I have not learned to place any great reliance on the opinions of the physicians and surgeons of the Glasgow hospitals. But if you would feel happier in your mind . . .

JOHNSON. Oh, it's nothing to do with me . . . I mean to say, it might help to give Mrs. Angelus some confidence.

ANGELUS. Mrs. Angelus has every confidence in me.

JOHNSON. Of course. But you know yourself, sir . . .

ANGELUS. Don't call me, sir, please. We are colleagues and partners. There should be no formalities in our relationship.

JOHNSON. Sorry. I keep forgetting.

ANGELUS. Perhaps you are right about calling a consultant. In the meantime, I should be very glad of your opinion. I had some delicacy about asking you before; but, if you feel that way about it . . .

JOHNSON. I couldn't think of setting my opinion against yours.

ANGELUS. But I don't anticipate that you would, my dear boy. I'm afraid the case is all too plain. But you, with your more recent experience of the hospitals and the more modern gadgets, jimmy-fixings and whigmaleeries—your opinion might be of very great value to an old fogey like myself.

JOHNSON. Now you're pulling my leg.

ANGELUS. Not at all. Not at all. We shall meet tomorrow in consultation. Mrs. Taylor and Mrs. Angelus will be more than delighted. Tomorrow at nine o'clock, shall we say?

JOHNSON. Yes, of course, if you like.

ANGELUS. It will be your first experience as a consultant.

JOHNSON. Yes. In a way.

ANGELUS. I shall have two guineas ready in an envelope.

JOHNSON. I thought it was the custom—I mean etiquette—for one doctor to see another doctor's dependants for nothing.

ANGELUS. We shall snap our fingers at etiquette in this case. It is a sweet sensation to get a new kind of fee. The wind on the heath, brother, is nothing to it. You shall have your fee.

JOHNSON. It's very kind of you, Doctor. I don't like taking it.

ANGELUS. Then cultivate the principle of the Moral Holiday. It strengthens one's moral constitution for the other days of the year. And it is very agreeable.

An old-fashioned doorbell rings. JOHNSON *gets up.*

JOHNSON. I'd better answer that.

ANGELUS. Not at all.

He goes to the window, draws aside the curtain cautiously and peers out.

It is a lady. A patient, probably. She is fashionably dressed. Very likely a bad debt. You had better see her.

JOHNSON. She's a bit late.

ANGELUS. One of my reasons for diagnosing a bad debt.

The bell rings again.

She is very impatient . . . Yes. You had better see her. The unhappy domestic situation upstairs would distract my mind. I like to devote all my mind to my patients.

JOHNSON. I really think I'd better answer it.

ANGELUS. No. No. I'd rather you didn't. Perhaps you will ring the bell for Jeanie, however. It is our duty to train her to answer the bell at all hours of the day or night and it is not yet a quarter past nine.

JOHNSON rings the bell at the fireside.

Thank you. I am not a strict disciplinarian, but I have learned in my long and varied life the value of discipline. I am sure you realise its value do you not?

[4]

JOHNSON. Oh, yes. We'd have got nowhere in the war without it.

ANGELUS. It is very pleasant for me to have found a colleague with whom I am so completely in accord. Let me see. How long have you been with me ?

JOHNSON. Three weeks tomorrow.

ANGELUS. Strange. I feel as if we had been older friends than that.

> *A good-looking rather blowsy young* MAID *appears in the doorway.* ANGELUS *approaches her.*

JEANIE. What is't ?

ANGELUS. Did you hear the doorbell ?

> JEANIE *looks at him rather impudently.*

JEANIE. Aye, I did.

ANGELUS. Answer it, then.

> *As she turns to obey, he smacks her bottom playfully. She giggles.* EXIT JEANIE, *leaving the door open.*

ANGELUS. A child of Nature. A child of Nature. Unspoiled, it is true ; but uncouth. We must introduce a little discipline.

> *He closes the door behind her and turns with his hand still on the handle.*

If you should find yourself in any difficulty, let me know. But don't disturb me unless it is really necessary. Make my apologies to the patient. As you see, I am a little distressed and preoccupied.

> JEANIE *pushes the door open, bumping it against him.*

Do be careful.

JEANIE. Sorrow. It's a woman to see you. She's in the dining-room.

ANGELUS. A patient ?

JEANIE. Aye.

ANGELUS. Give me a few moments to get upstairs and then tell her that Dr. Johnson will see her.

JEANIE. Aye. It was him she wanted to see, anyway. A Mrs. Corcoran.

> ANGELUS *shakes his finger playfully at* JOHNSON

ANGELUS. They like the young Doctor best. I shall have t
get myself some beauty treatment. But I must go to Mr
Taylor. Good night, Johnson.

> *As he is going out, he surreptitiously unties the* MAID
> *apron. She does not notice what he has done, bu*
> *wriggles at his touch. She waits till he has gone, lookin*
> *curiously at* JOHNSON *and then goes out.* JOHNSO:
> *picks up his overcoat, hat and bag, bundles them into th*
> *lavatory, straightens his necktie and sits down at th*
> *desk, swinging the swivel chair round to face the door.*
>
> *During the foregoing scene,* JOHNSON *has been poli*
> *and correct with* ANGELUS. *Apart from a slight*
> *puzzled expression at some of his changes of mood*
> *there has been nothing to indicate what he thinks of h*
> *senior partner.*
>
> JEANIE *reappears, kicking the door open with her foo*
> *as she reties her apron.*
>
> *A tall, handsome woman of about thirty follows he*
> *into the room. She wears a fur coat.*

JEANIE. Here's your patient.

> *She shuts the door behind* MRS. CORCORAN

MRS. CORCORAN. Good evening. I'm glad it's you.

JOHNSON (*rising*). Good evening. Won't you sit down?

MRS. CORCORAN. Thank you. I'm *so* glad it's you. Isn't i
hot?

JOHNSON. Would you like to take off your coat?

MRS. CORCORAN. Yes. I think I would . . . O thank you

> JOHNSON *helps off her coat and lays it carefully on a chair*

MRS. CORCORAN. I'm so sorry to bother you at this hour
but I felt I was going to have another of my bad nights and
I thought I'd come round.

JOHNSON. Oh, that's quite all right, Mrs. Corcoran. Wha
is the trouble now?

MRS. CORCORAN. Well, you know that feeling of restless

ness and depression I told you about ? It's coming on again. Not very badly, but it's coming on again. And that nodule or patch of fibrositis or whatever you call it—it's here . . . (*she touches her back below the shoulder blade*) . . . It's perfectly agonising tonight. Wait, I'll show you.

> *She pulls off her jacket impulsively and then her silk blouse, throwing them both at a chair a few yards away. She turns her back on* JOHNSON *and edges her chair up to him.*

JOHNSON. Where is it ?

MRS. CORCORAN. Here.

JOHNSON. Sing out if I hurt you.

> *He examines her back.*

MRS. CORCORAN. Oh, I will. I will. I'll yell the house down . . . But you're so gentle. Not like Dr. Angelus . . . I'll tell you a secret, if you like . . . Yes, you're near it now . . . I peeked out of the window and saw you coming in. Otherwise I wouldn't have come. I can't *bear* Dr. Angelus.

JOHNSON. Have you any pain when I press there ?

MRS. CORCORAN. Not much. Not yet . . . Ough ! You're tickling ! . . . We only went to him at first because he was in some shady share-broking business with my husband. I don't think Doctors ought to be interested in shares, do you ? . . . But after Jack went to London a year ago, I wouldn't have him in the house. I just suffered or went to an osteopath. But I felt funny, taking off my clothes before an osteopath. It's not the same as a real Doctor, somehow. Is it ?

JOHNSON. No.

MRS. CORCORAN. Dr. Angelus is a bit of a quack too, isn't he ?

> JOHNSON *jabs a knuckle into her spine.*

MRS. CORCORAN. Wow ! You've found the spot . . . Oh, dear. I'm sorry I'm such a baby. I'll try to be brave . . . But I shouldn't be saying that to his assistant, should I ?

JOHNSON. Partner.

MRS. CORCORAN. What did you say ?

JOHNSON. Dr. Angelus and I are partners.

MRS. CORCORAN. Of course you are. I saw at once you were far too clever to be an assistant. That day you came round last week. You did me such a lot of good. So quiet and sensible.

JOHNSON. Raise your arms a little, please, and try to relax your muscles.

He holds her by the elbows and rotates her shoulders.

JOHNSON. Does that hurt you?

MRS. CORCORAN. No. I think you must have cured me. That time you jabbed me hard ... Angelus isn't very popular in the profession, is he?

JOHNSON. I wouldn't know. I qualified in England. I've only been here a few weeks. Do you mind if I mark the spot with a blue pencil?

MRS. CORCORAN. No, nobody's going to see it. Except you ... It must be very sad for you, being away from all your friends.

JOHNSON. No. It's all right when you're busy. Take a deep breath. Does it hurt you when you breathe?

MRS. CORCORAN. No. Not much. Do you want me to take off any more?

JOHNSON. No. I don't think so.

He percusses the area and then takes out his stethoscope.

MRS. CORCORAN. I never listen to gossip; but you know how it is. I hear them talking. Angelus has a very funny reputation.

JOHNSON. Please breathe normally ... Now say " One, two, three." Deep breath. Once more. Thank you.

MRS. CORCORAN. Have you found anything?

JOHNSON. No. I went over your chest pretty thoroughly on Thursday. It's all right.

MRS. CORCORAN turns round to face him.

MRS. CORCORAN. Thank the Lord for that. I'm not a coward; but one feels nervous sometimes, living all alone. Have you a cigarette? I left mine at home.

JOHNSON. Sorry.

He gives her a cigarette and lights it for her.

MRS. CORCORAN. Ta . . . What do you really think of Dr. Angelus?

JOHNSON. I'm terribly sorry, but I can't very well discuss Dr. Angelus with a patient.

MRS. CORCORAN. Oh, what a pity! But I'm not really an ordinary patient. My father was a Doctor. He died when I was a kid. But he used to talk to us quite freely about the other Doctors. I wanted to be a Doctor myself. I might be still. I'm not getting on very well with my husband. Is it difficult? To be a Doctor?

JOHNSON. It's fairly stiff.

*MRS. CORCORAN. Gets stiffer every year, I suppose?

JOHNSON. Yes, I think so.

MRS. CORCORAN. Won't you smoke too?

JOHNSON. Not in working hours.

MRS. CORCORAN. These aren't working hours. Be matey for once. You've no more to do tonight.

JOHNSON. I hope not.

MRS. CORCORAN *leans over and takes his cigarette case from his waistcoat pocket. She puts a cigarette in his mouth and lights it for him.*

MRS. CORCORAN. That's much better. You're awfully straight-laced, aren't you?

JOHNSON. I don't think so. Not specially.

MRS. CORCORAN. I suppose Doctors have to be. But you do relax sometimes, don't you? I mean, a Doctor's not a sort of parson, is he?

JOHNSON. No. But we have to be careful.

MRS. CORCORAN. I quite see that. I mean, people *trust* you, don't they?

JOHNSON. Yes. That's the point. We have to be a bit strict.

MRS. CORCORAN. I suppose a patient's just a sort of specimen to you.

93   [9]

JOHNSON. I hope not.

> *He is engagingly and youthfully pompous about it all*

MRS. CORCORAN. I think people like to think of the Doctor as their best friend.

JOHNSON. He often is.

MRS. CORCORAN. He couldn't be that if he looked on patients as *exactly* specimens, could he?

> *She gets up and wanders about*

JOHNSON. No. I suppose not.

> MRS. CORCORAN *studies a painted Juju on the wall*

MRS. CORCORAN. He's travelled a bit, Dr. Angelus.

JOHNSON. Yes. He was in the Navy and in the Mercantile Marine for a bit.

MRS. CORCORAN. Why did he leave the Navy?

JOHNSON. I don't know.

MRS. CORCORAN. He hasn't the cut of a naval man ... How old are you, Doctor?

JOHNSON. Well, as a matter of fact, practically twenty-four.

MRS. CORCORAN. You look younger. And yet, you're so solemn and responsible and reliable, you might be much older.

> *She throws herself down on the couch and blows smoke rings into the air.*

MRS. CORCORAN. I'm thirty. I must look like a wizened old hag to you.

JOHNSON. No, of course you don't.

MRS. CORCORAN. I feel deadly old. I haven't had a very happy life. Have you?

JOHNSON (*getting up and standing by the mantelpiece*). Well ... Not very, as a matter of fact. But I've been too busy to notice it. My people hadn't any money and I had to work myself through with scholarships and things.

MRS. CORCORAN. A drab sort of life.

JOHNSON. A bit drab.

MRS. CORCORAN. What kept you at it? ... Come over and sit down here ...

[10]

She makes room for him on the couch. He sits down gingerly.

JOHNSON. Oh, I don't know.

MRS. CORCORAN. I think you know very well. But you're inhibited, aren't you? You think people will laugh at you. I won't laugh at you. You know that, don't you?

JOHNSON. Yes. I don't think you would.

MRS. CORCORAN. It must have taken enormous will power to keep you hard at work when all sorts of amusing things were going on around you.

JOHNSON. It was a bit of a job.

MRS. CORCORAN. You must have had some sort of inspiration.

JOHNSON. I suppose I had, in a way.

MRS. CORCORAN. You're not religious are you?

JOHNSON. Oh, Lord, no. But there was something religious about it. I had a feeling . . . well, in a way, it was like what the religious blokes call a Call. I thought there was something terribly honourable about it. It was a sort of a—a holy quest. Like the Holy Grail. I mean, you were after something. It might even be a way of saving mankind. And although you didn't believe in God or any of that sort of rot, you were really a kind of a priest; with high standards and self-discipline and fine, simple rules and so on. Did you ever hear the Hippocratic Oath . . . but I'm boring you.

MRS. CORCORAN (*stroking his hand*). No, no. Go on.

JOHNSON. " So far as power and discernment shall be mine, I will carry out regimen for the benefit of the sick and will keep them from harm and wrong. To none will I give a deadly drug nor offer counsel to such an end; but guiltless and hallowed will I keep my life and my art . . . Into whatsoever house I shall enter, I will go for the benefit of the sick, holding aloof from all voluntary wrong and corruption, including the seduction of females and males, of freemen and slaves. Whatsoever I shall see or hear amid the lives of men, whether in my practice or not in my practice, I will not divulge as,

95   [11]

reckoning that all such things should be kept secret ... " And so on. It's rather fine, in a way, I sometimes think.

MRS. CORCORAN. Yes. It is rather fine. What's your first name?

JOHNSON. George, as a matter of fact.

MRS. CORCORAN. It suits you. I think. Mine's Irene, but I'm sometimes called Dodo ... Oh, dear! I haven't felt so happy for years and years. Do you think we could be friends, George?

JOHNSON. Yes, I think we could ...

> JOHNSON *He says this after due consideration and with any emotions he may be feeling well under control. He gets up.*

JOHNSON. At the same time, I don't think this is very professional, somehow.

MRS. CORCORAN. I'm sorry. I forgot I was a specimen for the moment.

JOHNSON. Oh, please don't take it that way. The only thing is that patients don't sometimes quite realise ...

MRS. CORCORAN. No. I didn't quite realise. I'm sorry. I just felt ... happy, for a minute or two. It doesn't matter. Where are my things?

> JOHNSON *hands her blouse. She begins to put it on. He begins to shuffle with papers in the desk.*

JOHNSON (*with his back to her*). Have you got any sulphonal? I think you should take five grains tonight.

MRS. CORCORAN. Yes, I will, Doctor, thank you ... Damn, I've lost my brooch ... It must have dropped on that vile woolly rug.

> JOHNSON *turns and begins to look at the rug. He picks up the brooch and gives it to her.*

Oh, thank you, Doctor. You are a darling ... I mean it. You are!

> *She suddenly throws her arms round his neck.*

MRS. CORCORAN. I do love you.

[*A knock at the door.*

JOHNSON. Mrs. Corcoran. Dodo. Please. Someone's coming.

> *The door opens as they break away.* MRS. ANGELUS, *a
> rather timid little Scotswoman in her late thirties
> insinuates herself round the edge of the door.* MRS.
> CORCORAN *and* JOHNSON *break away and*
> MRS. CORCORAN *rapidly buttons herself up.*

MRS. ANGELUS. Oh, I beg your pardon. I thought the patient had gone.

JOHNSON. No. As a matter of fact, not yet. She's just going. This is Mrs. Angelus ; Mrs. Corcoran.

MRS. ANGELUS. How do you do, the telephone's broken down upstairs. Cyril wants you to 'phone Sir Gregory Butt, will you please ? It's urgent or I wouldn't have bothered you. Mother's worse.

JOHNSON. Oh, yes, of course ; will you excuse me, Mrs. Corcoran ?

> *He picks up the telephone book and searches it.*

MRS. CORCORAN. That's quite all right. I'll call tomorrow at the consulting hour, or can you come to see me ?

JOHNSON. You'd better come here. Half-past five.

MRS. CORCORAN (*putting on her coat*). Righto.

MRS. ANGELUS. I'm awfully sorry. Were you quite finished ?

MRS. CORCORAN. Oh, yes. Quite. Good night, Mrs. Angelus.

JOHNSON (*at telephone*). Woodside 723.

MRS. CORCORAN. Good night, Doctor.

JOHNSON. Good night, Mrs. Corcoran. Five grains of sulphonal.

MRS. CORCORAN. I'll remember.

MRS. ANGELUS (*showing her out*). You see, we've got illness in the house. My mother is very seriously ill and the Doctor is most anxious about her . . .

> EXEUNT MESDAMES CORCORAN *and* ANGELUS.

JOHNSON. Hello. Hello. It is Sir Gregory Butt ? . . . May I speak to him, please. This is Doctor Johnson. He won't know me ; but it's rather urgent . . . Yes . . . Is that

Sir Gregory? . . . Oh, yes, sir. Dr. Johnson. Dr. Angelus's partner. Dr. Angelus . . . I wonder, sir, if you would mind coming round as quickly as possible.

> RE-ENTER MRS. ANGELUS. *She stands about in a tearful, helpless sort of way.*

JOHNSON.   It's a Mrs. Taylor.   Dr. Angelus's mother-in-law.   It's an acute gastro-intestinal condition.   Dr. Angelus is very anxious . . . Yes, I think he's afraid that . . . Yes, sir.   Very urgent.   You will?   Thank you very much indeed.   Thank you. (*To* MRS. ANGELUS.) He's coming. He won't be five minutes. Can I help? Shall I go up?

ANGELUS (*upstairs*). Margaret!

MRS. ANGELUS (*at door*). Yes, Cyril. Sir Gregory's coming round.

ANGELUS (*upstairs*).   Don't shout, then.   Come up here.

MRS. ANGELUS. Yes, Cyril.

> *She scurries out.   He stands irresolutely, wondering whether to go upstairs.   Blows his nose and notices lipstick on his handkerchief.   He wipes it away at the mirror.* ANGELUS ENTERS *in a very gorgeous dressing-gown.*

ANGELUS. Is he coming?

JOHNSON. Yes! Right away.

ANGELUS. What did he say?

JOHNSON. Nothing. Except that he would come.

ANGELUS. Please God he come quickly.

JOHNSON. Is she worse?

ANGELUS. Much worse. I think this is the end.

JOHNSON. Can I do anything?

ANGELUS. My dear boy, none of us can do anything. It is in higher hands than ours . . . I wish that blustering old pill-pedlar would hurry up.

JOHNSON. He isn't five minutes away.

ANGELUS. But he hurries like a paralysed plumber. Poor, poor Mama. I've seldom seen anyone suffer so much.

JOHNSON. Did you give her morphia?

ANGELUS. Morphia? Yes, of course. Why shouldn't I give her morphia?

JOHNSON. I didn't mean that. I meant, I thought it might ease things. I meant, I thought if you hadn't given it, it might be a good idea.

ANGELUS. I am most grateful for your valuable advice; but I have a certain amount of experience. A *certain* amount. And if you think I am the man to stand by and let my nearest and dearest suffer without raising a finger to aid them, you have misjudged me sadly. Sadly, sir.

JOHNSON. Of course I didn't mean that, sir. You took me up wrong. I'm sorry.

ANGELUS. Where is that dogmatic, incompetent old brute?

JOHNSON. Shall I ring again?

ANGELUS. Yes, do. This is killing me. I cannot imagine how after receiving a call of that nature, the man could delay an instant.

JOHNSON. Woodside 723.

ANGELUS. People have called me a hard man, but I could not find it in my heart to treat a professional colleague in that fashion. No. Not for a million pounds. It—it is men such as he who are entrusted with the instruction of the young—those tender shoots . . . No wonder they are so often blasted in the bud.

Front doorbell rings.

JOHNSON (*at telephone*). I think he's there now. Never mind.

He hangs up.

That was the doorbell, wasn't it?

ANGELUS. Yes. Why can't that infernal girl answer it?

JOHNSON. I'd better go.

ANGELUS. The rules of this household are not made to be broken; as she shall very soon find out.

He rings the room bell violently.

JOHNSON. I really think you'd better let me answer the door.

ANGELUS. No. What would Sir Gregory think of us?

99   [15]

These little points may not seem important ; but all life, my dear young friend, is made up of apparently unimportant details. You must remember that. If you are to be a good Doctor, you MUST remember that.

ENTER JEANIE.

ANGELUS. Ah, there you are. Who the Hell do you think you are ? Why the Hell do you think I pay you ? Go at once and answer the door and show the gentleman straight in here. I will have my orders obeyed, do you hear ?

JEANIE. Keep your hair on.

EXIT JEANIE.

ANGELUS. I wish I could keep my hair on. You will make a fortune Johnson, if you discover a method for making hair grow on bald scalps. You would hardly believe the sense of frustration it gives a man to be prematurely bald. Yet, to the philosophic mind comes the reflection that we are all more or less born bald. Even Lady Godiva was born bald . . . And to the practical mind, the condition has obvious advantages. A bald head and a grave expression are worth a great deal in the practise of our noble profession . . .

> JEANIE *shows in* SIR GREGORY BUTT, *an oldish, wise-looking grey man, with a forthright manner.*

JEANIE. This is the Professor.

EXIT JEANIE.

ANGELUS. My dear Sir Gregory, how good of you to come. This is my young colleague, Dr. Johnson. I do not know whether you have met.

BUTT. No. How do ? What's all this ?

ANGELUS. You don't mind Dr. Johnson being present ?

BUTT. No.

ANGELUS. We are partners, but very good friends in spite of that . . . Our patient is my wife's mother, Mrs. Taylor. I have been very anxious about her for a long time. Quite a year. (*He consults notes.*) She is sixty-four, and a widow. My wife is her only daughter. She is of a cheerful, lively dispo-

sition. Naturally, as she has no other family circle, she has
interested herself a good deal in her only daughter's welfare
and she is a frequent and very welcome visitor to my humble
abode. She lives in Edinburgh . . .

BUTT. Get on, man, get on. What's the matter with her ?

ANGELUS. About eighteen months ago, in December, 1918,
to be exact, she began to complain of a dull epigastric pain,
with occasional purging and vomiting after taking large
quantities of carbohydrates. I'm afraid she was rather a
devotee of High Tea, Sir Gregory.

BUTT. Turning her poor, tortured stomach into a starchy
midden of tannic acid and hog fat. Go on.

ANGELUS. Last spring she began to lose weight. Let me see.
Since April she has lost twenty-eight pounds. She now
weighs eight stone one. During the summer, I passed a
stomach tube and personally carried out a gastric analysis. I
found marked diminution of free acid and . . .

BUTT. Any blood ?

ANGELUS. A trace. A trace. The combined acid . . . let me
see, let me see.

BUTT. Never mind that. What's she like now ?

ANGELUS. Ah, dear me, I am afraid the poor woman's
condition is pretty desperate. She has been unable to touch
solid food for over a week. She has subsisted almost entirely
on egg albumen and iced water. Her pulse rate has been
rapid and irregular and she complains of practically contin-
uous pain.

BUTT. And when did these symptomatic manifestations
begin to make themselves apparent ?

ANGELUS. Within the past three weeks. At first I thought
it was a type of gastric influenza. Or that she had taken something that disagreed with her. Later I suspected para-
typhoid fever, but she has had no temperature. If anything,
it has been subnormal. I have here a record of her agglutina-
tion reactions . . .

BUTT. Let me see the patient.

ANGELUS. I beg your pardon ?

BUTT. Let me see the patient. I don't treat the sick on paper.

ANGELUS. Certainly. Certainly . . . I think everything is ready. Will you come this way ? . . . I have been unable to detect on abdominal examination any evidence of tumour or swelling, but no doubt your practised hand will be able to . . .

> ANGELUS *leads* BUTT *out, talking all the time. After a pause,* JEANIE *comes in.*

JEANIE. Oh, it's you, Doctor ?

JOHNSON. Yes. What is it ?

JEANIE. I thought the Doctor might be here.

JOHNSON. No. He's upstairs with Sir Gregory.

JEANIE. I thought the Professor might be seeing to Mrs. Taylor himself. She's in an awful state.

JOHNSON. So I hear.

JEANIE. I hope you don't mind me coming here, just for a wee minute. I got feared, down in the basement. It's an awful thing, a death in a house.

JOHNSON. It may not be so bad as that.

JEANIE. She'll die all right.

> JEANIE *reels.* JOHNSON *goes to help her.*

JOHNSON. What's the matter with you ? Here, sit down.

> *He helps her to a chair. She sits grinning foolishly.*

JEANIE. Thank you, Doctor. I don't know what came over me.

JOHNSON. Do you feel ill ?

JEANIE. A wee. It'll soon pass over.

JOHNSON. You haven't been . . . drinking, have you ?

JEANIE. Aye. I took a wee nip.

> *She begins to cry.*

JOHNSON. Stop that. Come along. Pull yourself together.

JEANIE. I wish it was Mrs. Angelus.

JOHNSON. What are you talking about ?

JEANIE. I wish it was her. I do. He doesna like her and he's quite right.

JOHNSON. Look here. You'd better get to your bed. Put your head under the cold tap.

JEANIE. I couldna help it, Doctor. I couldna really. Them turns comes over me. And it's dark and cold down there. And whiles he's so queer.

JOHNSON. Look, do you think you can manage by yourself? You can't wait here.

JEANIE (*getting up*). I'm all right now. It was something that came over me.

JOHNSON. You're sure you're all right?

JEANIE. Oh, aye, I didn't take much.

> *She goes over quite steadily and looks at one of the pictures of Angelus.*

JOHNSON. You'd better be getting along.

JEANIE. They last house they were in, they had an awful fire. They had gold and silver plates then and the melted gold was running down the stairs. They say there was a big insurance money to pay.

JOHNSON. Listen, Jeanie, do as you're told.

JEANIE. I aye do as I'm told... There was a servant lassie burned to death in that house. They said he had his reasons; but it was a lie. He's a good man, the Doctor. He's a kind man. He wouldna do a thing the like of that.

JOHNSON (*going to her and gripping her arms*). Stop that. You're hysterical. You're drunk. You must *not* say things like that, do you hear? You mustn't touch another drop. Not another drop, do you hear? Where's the bottle?

JEANIE. It's empty.

JOHNSON. Is that true?

JEANIE. Honest to God.

JOHNSON. Go and bring it up to me.

JEANIE (*on her way to the door*). All right, Doctor... Doctor, you wouldna come over what I said just now? Will you, Doctor?

JOHNSON. No. But fetch the bottle and be quick about it.

JEANIE. O.K.   EXIT JEANIE.

MRS. ANGELUS' VOICE (*upstairs*). Jeanie!

JEANIE'S VOICE. Yes, Mrs. Angelus?

MRS. ANGELUS' VOICE. Come up. Come up at once.

JEANIE'S VOICE. I'm getting something for the young Doctor.

MRS. ANGELUS' VOICE. Never mind that just now, come up, come up quickly.

JEANIE'S VOICE (*fading as she mounts the stairs*). I was getting something for the young Doctor. They expect you to be in two places at once in this house. It's sheer nonsense to expect a person to be in two places at once . . .

> JOHNSON *is walking up and down, deep in thought. He is about to go out, but changes his mind. He lights a cigarette and almost immediately stubs it out. He goes back to the Day Book on the desk. He has hardly sat down to it, when* SIR GREGORY BUTT *comes in, mopping his forehead with a large handkerchief.* JOHNSON *jumps up.*

JOHNSON. Is there anything I can get you, sir?

BUTT. Yes. A large whisky and soda.

> *He sits down.* JOHNSON *fusses round.*

JOHNSON. I don't know whether . . . Dr. Angelus is a teetotaller, I think. There may be something in the dining-room . . . No. There's a bit of luck. Here it is.

> *He finds a bottle and a syphon in the low cupboard below the Poison Cupboard. He pours out a drink for* SIR GREGORY.

BUTT. Thankee. Take one yourself?

JOHNSON. No, sir. I'm TT.

BUTT. That's right . . . The old lady's dead.

JOHNSON. Oh!

BUTT. I should say she'd been moribund for a couple of hours. He's an extraordinary fellow, your Chief, this fellow Angelus.

JOHNSON. He's . . . well, perhaps he's a little eccentric;

but that's only his manner. He's awfully good, sir, really. He'll feel this very badly. He was very fond of Mrs. Taylor.

BUTT. I never saw such an exhibition. He's like David howling for Absalom at the gates of Mahanaim. He was weeping like a cloudburst and praying and kissing the cadaver . . . It was too much for me. What sort of a being is he, at all?

JOHNSON. Most people seem to think he's a little eccentric . . .

BUTT. I know. You said so. Use not vain repetitions as the heathen do . . . You're not one of my students, are you?

JOHNSON. No, sir. I did part of my course at Durham and the rest in London. At Thomas's.

BUTT. God help you. Did you meet anyone like our lachrymose friend in Thomas's?

JOHNSON. No, sir. Not exactly. Of course, he's a little eccentric, but . . .

BUTT. *Ach Himmel!* You are like Lewis Carroll's Bellman. Whatever you say three times is true . . . His eccentricity does not greatly commend itself to the profession in this city.

JOHNSON. I've heard that, sir; but they're wrong. I couldn't wish for a better Chief. He's kind and he's helpful and he knows his work. And he's got a great sense of humour. I think he's a bit of a genius.

BUTT. Which bit?

JOHNSON. I'm afraid I don't quite follow you, sir.

BUTT. He was threatening just now to blow his brains out. I was wondering at what portion of his anatomy he was proposing to take aim.

JOHNSON. I don't know how you do here, sir; but I must say that in Thomas's we'd have thought that kind of talk pretty thick in the circumstances.

BUTT. *Donner und Blitzen*, do you know who you're talking to?

JOHNSON. Yes, sir. It's a pretty average cheek, I know. But I can't stand by and let you call down Angelus. He's been very decent to me and he's a damned good man. He

105   [21]

may be a bit ecc—unorthodox, but I've never seen him put a
foot wrong. Everybody yaps at him because he tries to cure
people instead of sticking to the book of words. And because
he's a General Practitioner who had the guts not to go on the
Panel. But everything he does is strictly professional and I've
never met anybody who knew his job better. If you treat him
like a pariah, it's your funeral. He could see the boots off any
of you. And I don't think much of what I've seen myself of
provincial medicine.

BUTT (*rising*). Provincial Medicine! Provincial Medicine!
Young man, if I were a man given to losing his temper, I
would not like to think of the apocalyptic vials of wrath that
would overwhelm you at this moment. You poor, doited
gomeral, you have little discretion. I will take my leave of you.

JOHNSON. Won't you wait for Dr. Angelus?

BUTT. I will not wait for Dr. Angelus!

> *He stumps towards the door ; then turns.*

By Heaven, sir, you don't deserve it ; but a wave of compassion for you overcomes me. I'll give you a bit of advice.
He'll ask you to sign the death certificate. Don't do it.

JOHNSON. I'll see you out.

BUTT. You shall *not* see me out. If there is one thing I can
do in this house, it is to find my way out.

> EXIT, *slamming the door behind him in* JOHNSON'S *face.*
> JOHNSON *opens the door and follows him. The stage is*
> *empty for a moment. The voices of* BUTT *and* JOHNSON
> *are heard at the front door.* ANGELUS *comes in. He*
> *takes out a damp pocket handkerchief to blow his nose ;*
> *notices how damp it is and replaces it with a clean one ;*
> *cocks an eye at the whisky bottle ; goes to the desk and*
> *takes out a book of certificates, shaking his head sadly ;*
> *turns round as* JOHNSON RE-ENTERS *immediately*
> *following the sound of a front door slamming.*

ANGELUS. Have you seen the Professor out?

JOHNSON. Yes.

ANGELUS. Not very courteous of him not to wait until I had composed myself. But the man is a boor.

JOHNSON. I'm terribly sorry about Mrs. Taylor.

ANGELUS. Thank you, my boy. Thank you. It was a heavy blow, but not unexpected. The Lord gave and the Lord taketh away. Sir Gregory, I am happy to say, confirmed my diagnosis. Gastric tuberculosis.

JOHNSON. But I thought you said it was a tumour.

ANGELUS. No, my dear boy, no. Gastric tuberculosis. Perhaps you will kindly fill in the certificate accordingly.

JOHNSON. But I haven't seen the patient.

ANGELUS. Yes, my dear boy, yes, you have. Repeatedly. In any case, all you are required to do is to certify that poor Mrs. Taylor is dead and, to the best of your belief what was the cause of death. If you wish to satisfy yourself that she is dead, you may go upstairs now and look at the body. It is not necessary that you should have been in professional attendance.

JOHNSON. Perhaps I had better go up.

ANGELUS. Yes. Certainly. You can perhaps say a word or two to Mrs. Angelus. She is inconsolable. Inconsolable. It is a great blow. A great blow. But we must have courage. Death is the common lot. Run upstairs now. I shall ring the undertaker myself. And don't forget to sign the certificate when you come down. We must have everything in order. Give me your hand . . . I hope you appreciate, George, how deeply grateful I am for your support and sympathy in this dark hour. Deeply, truly grateful. I shall never forget this.

JOHNSON (*uncomfortably*). Oh, that's all right . . . I'd better go up.

He disengages his hand from ANGELUS'S *and* EXITS. ANGELUS *picks up the telephone.*

ANGELUS. City 4514 . . . Thank you . . . Is that Lucas and Small ? Dr. Angelus, 17, Woodbank Place, speaking. We have had a sudden and melancholy event in my household . . . Yes, yes, someone's dead . . . Yes, a relative, an old lady . . . No. There isn't a nurse here. Will you send a reliable woman ?

And will you ask Mr. Small to call on me tomorrow morning. Tell him I am anxious that no expense should be spared. Within reason, of course. Within reason. Is that all clear? Very well. Good night.

> *He puts away the whisky ; locks it up ; and puts the key in his pocket. Then he sits down at the desk and takes a big envelope from a pigeon hole.*
>
> JOHNSON *comes back.* ANGELUS *swivels round to face him, and hands him the certificate book.*

ANGELUS. Fill it up, like a good chap. It had better be all in your handwriting. The name is Elizabeth Ann Wotherspoon or Taylor. Age sixty-four. Duration of illness, one year. Primary cause of death, gastric tuberculosis. Secondary cause, syncope ... Haven't you got a pen? Take mine.

JOHNSON. I was wondering whether ...

ANGELUS. You mustn't wonder. You must sign the certificate. The undertaker will be round at any moment. What's the matter with you?

JOHNSON. I don't suppose there'll be a Coroner's inquest.

ANGELUS. There are no coroners in Scotland. Why should there be an inquest? I'm satisfied. Sir Gregory Butt is satisfied. Aren't you satisfied?

JOHNSON. Yes, of course. But there seemed to be some doubt ... I mean about the exact cause of death.

ANGELUS. There was no doubt whatever. What is the matter with you?

JOHNSON. I'd rather you signed the certificate yourself. I mean, you were really in charge of the case.

ANGELUS. It is most unusual for a relative to sign a certificate. Besides, as you are aware, I was about to hand the case over to you when the—when the calamity occurred. I am really at a loss to understand why you are hesitating. It is only a matter of form. Come, sit down here.

> *He gets up and moves to the fireplace.* JOHNSON *sits down and begins to write.*

ANGELUS. By the way, I want to talk to you about a very

serious matter. You may well say, " Why, in the circumstances, can you not let it wait till the morning ?" But I am a
man who likes to be open and frank. Anything secretive is
foreign to my nature. I am a plain, blunt person. I hate
brooding over unpleasant matters.

My wife found time, in the intervals of her manifestations
of natural distress, to give me a very disquieting piece of information. As if I had not enough to upset me. I hope she
was wrong. She was in no condition to make accurate obser-
vations. But she tells me that, a very short time ago, at a
moment when a member of this household was hovering on
the brink of dissolution, she found you and a female patient
in a somewhat equivocal position. I hope she deceived herself.
I sincerely hope so . . . Have you finished the certificate ?

JOHNSON. Yes.

ANGELUS. Thank you. Give it me.

He reads the certificate.

JOHNSON. I can explain that all right.

ANGELUS. My dear boy, I shall not ask you to explain it. I
am not setting myself up as a ruler and a judge over you. It is
a matter for your own conscience. But I hope you look upon
me as a friend ; and I must warn you of the dreadful dangers
you incur by behaving in the least way incorrectly in such
matters.   Mrs.—What's her name ?—Mrs. Corcoran is a
married woman.

JOHNSON. I know that. I was just going to ask your advice
I mean, tomorrow . . .

ANGELUS. Please, please let me finish. I am advising you
now. I am advising you to keep a very strict guard on your
impulses when you are dealing with ladies like Mrs. Corcoran.
What has happened will go no further. But you ought to be
aware that it constitutes what is described as infamous conduct in a professional respect. It is treated very harshly indeed
by the General Medical Council. And rightly so. Our profession must be kept secure from the breath of scandal. I
have done. I think that all I need do is to mention the matter.
I believe you to be, on the whole, a well-principled young

man. I hope you will remain so, while you are associated with me.

JOHNSON. I'm sorry ; but you're making a mistake, sir. It must have looked very funny to Mrs. Angelus . . .

ANGELUS. Nothing looked funny to Mrs. Angelus at that melancholy time. An unfortunate choice of adjective.

JOHNSON. Well, you know what I mean. But it wasn't really like that. You see . . .

ANGELUS. My dear George, I have been labouring under considerable strain, not to say distress, not to say anguish, this evening. I hope that you will not try to prolong this discussion. I have said what I had to say. I do not blame you. I merely gave you a friendly and paternal word of warning. I am sure that you were only thoughtless. Nothing worse. Now, please go home and leave me in the shadows of this place of sorrow.

JOHNSON. Well . . . Isn't there anything I can do ?

ANGELUS. Nothing. Nothing. You have been splendidly helpful. Good night, my boy, and God bless you.

> JOHNSON *is about to speak, but gives it up. He collects his hat and overcoat.*

JOHNSON. I'll do all the visits tomorrow. I'll look in first thing in the morning. Good night, sir.

ANGELUS. Good night, my dear fellow. And again, God bless you.

> JOHNSON *goes out.* ANGELUS *waits till the front door bangs, then collects the big envelope from the desk and takes it over to the armchair. It is an Insurance Policy.*

CURTAIN

END OF ACT I

ACT II

The same as in ACT I. *A fortnight later. About 9 a.m.*
MRS. ANGELUS *scurries in nervously, wearing a flowered
wrap. Her hair is in pigtails. She has just got up out
of bed. She goes to the bookcase, selects a book on
Toxicology and turns over the pages rapidly, looking
for something. She obviously can't find it; sighs;
and tucks the book under her arm. Dust on a piece
of furniture attracts her attention. She writes her name
on the dust as* JEANIE ENTERS, *in a morning wrapper
and apron.*

MRS. ANGELUS. Jeanie !

JEANIE. You're not supposed to be up. I'll tell the Doctor.

MRS. ANGELUS. Where is he ?

JEANIE. He's out.

MRS. ANGELUS. I know. But where is he ?

JEANIE. How should I know ? He wouldna tell me, would
he ? where he was going.

MRS. ANGELUS. This room's filthy. I can write my name on
the dust, look.

JEANIE. A great thing, education.

MRS. ANGELUS. Don't be impertinent. Go at once and get
a duster.

JEANIE. Ugh, I've no time.

MRS. ANGELUS. Don't speak to me like that.

JEANIE. I'll speak the way I like.

MRS. ANGELUS. Listen, I've had about enough of your
nonsense. What will the Doctor say when he comes in and
finds his consulting room like a pigsty ?

JEANIE. He'll never notice.

MRS. ANGELUS. He'll notice when I tell him.

JEANIE. Tell him what you like.

MRS. ANGELUS. *I'll* tell him what I like. I'll tell him I don't
like your manner.

III   [27]

JEANIE. Well, I don't like yours.

MRS. ANGELUS. Do you know who you're speaking to ?

JEANIE. Oh, aye.

MRS. ANGELUS. I'm still the mistress of this house.

JEANIE. Are you ?

MRS. ANGELUS. You know very well that I am.

JEANIE. I wouldna be too sure.

MRS. ANGELUS. What do you mean by that ?

JEANIE. Never mind.

MRS. ANGELUS. But I will mind. I'm not going to have an ill-tongued slut say things like that to my face.

JEANIE. You can take that back. I'll not be called a slut by you or your likes.

MRS. ANGELUS. But you are. That's just what you are.

JEANIE. Did you hear me tell you to take that back ?

MRS. ANGELUS. I'll nothing of the sort take it back. I still have some dignity.

JEANIE. *You* have ? I've never noticed it. It's no' very dignified to hang onto a man and him no' wanting you.

MRS. ANGELUS. Don't you dare to say that.

JEANIE. You've outstayed your welcome. Everybody's making a mock of you. He canna abide the sight of you.

MRS. ANGELUS. Be quiet.

JEANIE. You can believe it or not as you like. He told me so himself.

MRS. ANGELUS. You're a liar.

JEANIE. I *am not* a liar. You'd wonder, the things he tells me.

> MRS. ANGELUS *is beside herself. She tries to speak, but can't. She throws the book at* JEANIE'S *head, missing by a yard.* ANGELUS *appears in the doorway. Neither woman notices him at first.*

JEANIE. You would murder me, would you ?

> *She is about to attack* MRS. ANGELUS *when she sees* ANGELUS.

JEANIE. Oh !

She hurries past him out of the room. ANGELUS *walks
over and picks up the book.*

ANGELUS. This is very strange conduct. The wreaths are
hardly withered on your mother's grave. And I find you
brawling with the servants.

MRS. ANGELUS. It was something she said.

ANGELUS. What did she say?

MRS. ANGELUS. Nothing, dear.   She was impertinent.
That's all. I really took no notice.

ANGELUS. You took no notice. I see. Come along, what
did she say?

MRS. ANGELUS. It was a lot of nonsense. She said you told
her things.

ANGELUS. What sort of things?

MRS. ANGELUS. Things about me.

ANGELUS. I discuss my wife with the servants, do I?

MRS. ANGELUS. No, Cyril. Of course you don't.

ANGELUS. Then why do you say so?

MRS. ANGELUS. I didn't say so . . . Oh, Cyril, send her
away. Please. Please do.

ANGELUS. Why are you not in your bed?

MRS. ANGELUS. I felt a wee bit better . . . I—I came down.

ANGELUS. Did I give you permission to get up?

MRS. ANGELUS. No.

ANGELUS. You know that you are not at all well?

MRS. ANGELUS. I felt better.

ANGELUS. You know that you are having symptoms very
like those your poor mother had?

MRS. ANGELUS. They're not the same. They're not exactly
the same. It wouldn't be that. I'm feeling better.

ANGELUS. You don't look it.

He looks at the book, opens it and turns over the leaves.

ANGELUS. What were you doing with this book?

MRS. ANGELUS. I wanted something to read.

ANGELUS. Are you particularly interested in Toxicology?

MRS. ANGELUS. I didn't know what it meant. I was just putting it back.

ANGELUS. Put it back now.

He hands her the book. She obeys him.

ANGELUS. It is a book about poisons. I suppose you didn't know that.

MRS. ANGELUS. No, Cyril.

He looks at her keenly for a moment.

ANGELUS. You are a little troublesome to me, from time to time, my darling. More than a little troublesome. Now go back to your bed. I will bring you your medicine presently.

MRS. ANGELUS. I don't want any medicine, I'm feeling better, I don't think it's the right medicine, it disagrees with me, I feel awful after it, every time. I do. Please let me up. I'll be fine. I think it's a holiday I'm needing, don't you?

ANGELUS. No.

MRS. ANGELUS. I don't think you understand my case, do you think I should go round and see Professor Butt?

ANGELUS. You don't think I understand your case.

MRS. ANGELUS. Well, could I see Dr. Johnson, or somebody, it would put my mind at rest, and yours too, if you're anxious about me, but you needn't be, I'm all right, except when I take these retching turns, honestly I'm all right.

ANGELUS. Go upstairs to bed. I will bring you your medicine.

MRS. ANGELUS. No. No, I won't. I won't take any more medicine.

ANGELUS (*mournfully*). I had thought you would be a little more grateful. I have neglected my work, my patients, my research—everything, to make you well. I have watched over you with the tenderest care. And this is my reward. This!

MRS. ANGELUS. I can't help it. I can't.

ANGELUS. Why do you treat me so cruelly?

MRS. ANGELUS. I don't mean to be cruel, Cyril; but, oh, do you think the medicine is doing any good? I've a feeling it makes me worse, not better, I don't know, of course . . .

ANGELUS. Of course you don't know, my darling.

MRS. ANGELUS. I don't mean half I say, of course . . .

ANGELUS. How could you mean what you say? You are terribly nervous and overwrought. The past six weeks would be enough to unbalance a stronger mind than yours. But you must try to control yourself. And you must be patient with your poor, plodding old husband. He does his best for you. You know that.

MRS. ANGELUS. Yes, dear, I know you do. But . . .

ANGELUS. But me no buts. Run away up to bye-byes and I'll bring you your nice medicine-pedicine. And I promise you you won't require very much more of it.

MRS. ANGELUS. I'm glad of that.

ANGELUS. Run along, then.

> *He kisses her and gives her a playful push.*

MRS. ANGELUS. I'm sorry for what I said.

ANGELUS. Forget all about it. All about it.

> EXIT MRS. ANGELUS *as* JOHNSON *comes in. She says,*
> *" Oh, hello, Doctor, good morning " as she hurries out.*

JOHNSON. Good morning, Mrs. Angelus. I hope you're better.

MRS. ANGELUS' VOICE. Much better, thank you.

ANGELUS. I wish she were.

JOHNSON. What's that?

ANGELUS. I heartily wish she were better.

JOHNSON. Oh? Isn't she? I thought when she was up and about . . .

ANGELUS. She strayed downstairs in a sort of mild delirium. I am very worried about her. I think, if you are not too busy, I should like you to examine her.

JOHNSON. I'd rather not, really. Why not get Butt?

ANGELUS. Come, come. You are too modest. You are worth twenty of that stuffed old antique image.

JOHNSON. I'll have a look at her if you like. By the way, I wanted to do a gastric analysis yesterday and I couldn't find the stuff. The tubes and the reagents and the pipettes and

115

things. I thought you had done a series of analyses on Mrs. Taylor.

ANGELUS. I had. But I do not allow anyone else—even you—to use my instruments. I hope you don't mind. I am a curious obsessional sort of fellow about such matters . . . Poor Mrs. Taylor. I hope there isn't an hereditary element in my wife's affliction.

JOHNSON. Hereditary? Gastric T.B. isn't hereditary.

ANGELUS. Let us hope not. Let us hope not . . . Thirst, enlarged pupils, epigastric pain, vomiting, fainting—I don't like it.

JOHNSON. What are you giving her?

ANGELUS. Not much. A little bismuth. A mild opiate. A dram of liquor of pepsin. Expectant treatment. Expectant treatment . . . A strange phrase that, expectant treatment. What do we expect? Too often we hardly know what to expect. We are blind leaders of the blind, and the ditch gapes for us on either side.

JOHNSON. Yes. I suppose so.

ANGELUS. I was going to ask you if you would be good enough to take my morning consulting hour.

JOHNSON. Yes, if you like.

ANGELUS. Will you let me see the appointments list?

JOHNSON *brings it over to him.*

Aha! Aha! I see the first name on the list is that of our charming and on-coming Mrs. Corcoran.

JOHNSON. Is it?

ANGELUS. The god of love that sits above and knows me, and knows me . . . I hope that you are not the sad young rascal you were a fortnight ago. Have you seen much of our obliging friend in the interval?

JOHNSON. No.

ANGELUS. Come, come. Look upon me as your father confessor. No little stolen minutes? No furtive caresses? No pink and perfumed *billets doux*? You disappoint me.

JOHNSON. Look here, sir; I hope I've as much sense of

[32]   116

humour as the next man, but I don't think that's very funny.
I've paid two visits to Mrs. Corcoran, very much against my
will. I think there's damn all the matter with her. And I wish
you would see her this morning.

ANGELUS. No. It will be a good exercise for your moral
stamina. And you are right. It is not a subject for jesting.
Not at all a subject to be considered lightly. You will forgive
me for masking my anxiety in a certain flippancy . . . And
now, you have still a few minutes. Would you very much
mind having a look at Mrs. Angelus now ?

JOHNSON. Yes, if you like.

ANGELUS. I shall not come with you. Or I shall join you
in a few minutes. I have one or two things to do.

JOHNSON. Very well.

> EXIT JOHNSON. ANGELUS *rings the bell.* JEANIE
> *comes in and stands by the door.* ANGELUS *sits by the
> fireside.*

ANGELUS. Come here.

> JEANIE *comes over to him. He seizes her by the wrist.*

ANGELUS. Well ?

JEANIE. You're hurting me.

ANGELUS. I'll hurt you a good deal more before I've
finished with you, you damned bitch. Can't you keep your
mouth shut ?

JEANIE. She angered me.

ANGELUS. She angers me too ; but I don't make a fool of
myself.

JEANIE. It was all the same. She knows fine about you and
me. Ever since that time old Mrs. Taylor found me in the
cupboard.

ANGELUS. Do you think a gentleman enjoys finding women
throwing the library about and scratching each other's eyes
out all over his establishment ?

JEANIE. Well, she angered me. So I had to anger her.

ANGELUS. We could not help old Mrs. Taylor finding you
in the cupboard. That was an act of God. But we can help

unseemly exhibitions in what is, or ought to be, a house of mourning. Do you understand that?

JEANIE. Yes, but she angered me.

ANGELUS. Don't say that again. If you can't behave yourself, I won't marry you. I am not going to anchor myself to a harridan.

JEANIE. But you will marry me. That's the first time you've said you wouldn't. You'll have to marry me, and me the way I am.

ANGELUS. Then you will have to behave yourself.

JEANIE. Is the divorce going through?

ANGELUS. Yes.

JEANIE. They were saying . . .

ANGELUS. Who were saying?

JEANIE. A lassie I was talking to. She was saying you couldna get a divorce unless the other one did something bad.

ANGELUS. Your friend knows nothing about it. And I won't have you gossiping. If I have any more scenes or any more gossiping, it will be the worse for you.

JEANIE. How will it be the worse for me? I could make it the worse for you too.

ANGELUS. Are you threatening me?

JEANIE. You were threatening me.

ANGELUS. I don't understand you. You are everything to me and I thought I was everything to you. It would be a bitter thing if you, of all people, deserted me in my dark hour. I couldn't survive it, Jeannot. But I know that your heart is not so hard as that. It is not conceivable that there should be that amount of evil in human nature. I trust human nature. I reverence it. You mustn't say harsh things to me, my beautiful. You must not shake my faith in human nature.

JEANIE. O.K. I won't if you won't.

ANGELUS. I'm sometimes hasty, I know. But it springs from genuine warmth of feeling. Never mind. We have many golden days before us, my dear. We must have patience. We must have patience with time, with events and, above all, with each other. Go now. God knows I am not a sentimenta

man ; but I am deeply moved. Leave me. I shall come down
to the kitchen in a few minutes, when I feel more composed.
Go now.

Doorbell rings.

JEANIE. There's the door. Will I answer it ?

ANGELUS. Yes, yes.

> *As* JEANIE *goes out, he goes to his desk and immediately
> becomes a wise and reliable physician.* JEANIE RE-
> ENTERS *with* MRS. CORCORAN. ANGELUS *rises to
> meet her as* JEANIE *goes out and closes the door.*

ANGELUS. My dear Mrs. Corcoran, you are a stranger. And,
alas, I'm afraid it is my fault. I hope my young colleague
has been kind to you. You know the lamentable reason for
my defection, don't you ?

MRS. CORCORAN. Yes. Is Dr. Johnson in ?

ANGELUS. Do you wish to see him ?

MRS. CORCORAN. Yes. If he's not in I can come another
time.

ANGELUS. Dear, dear. *La Donn' e mobile* indeed.

MRS. CORCORAN. I beg pardon, I didn't quite catch.

ANGELUS. I shall have to get rid of Dr. Johnson. He has
alienated the affections of all my most charming patients. I
shall be left ministering to chronic alcoholics and old ladies
with varicose veins. But he is a sterling fellow. A sterling
fellow. You must not say a word against him.

MRS. CORCORAN. I wasn't going to.

ANGELUS. Dangerous, though.   All these handsome,
sympatico young men are dangerous, if they happen to be
Doctors.

MRS. CORCORAN. Yes. Is he likely to be long ?

ANGELUS. No, no. He is upstairs talking to my wife. You
see I have the utmost confidence in him.

MRS. CORCORAN. How is your wife ?

ANGELUS. Ah, poor creature, I am very anxious about her.
She is having a hard time. Indeed, she is quite seriously ill.
But I hope that the united endeavours of Dr. Johnson and

myself will pull her into the desired haven. Dr. Johnson, for all his tender years, is a most accomplished physician. And a thoroughly good fellow. A highly principled fellow.

MRS. CORCORAN. Yes, I'm sure he is.

ANGELUS. And you have excellent opportunities of forming a judgment. I am glad that jealousy is foreign to my nature. Very glad. Ah! I hear his footstep on the stairs. I shall leave you together.

ENTER JOHNSON, *looking thoughtful.*

ANGELUS. And how did you find poor Margaret?

JOHNSON. I couldn't find anything very positive . . . Oh, hello, Mrs. Corcoran. She said she felt better, but her pulse was irregular and her tongue was pretty awful. It's a peculiar case.

ANGELUS. I shall go to her. It is almost time for her medicine.

JOHNSON. What about getting a nurse?

ANGELUS. She will have nobody but me near her. It is gratifying, in a way; but a great strain. A great strain. However, I am happy to undergo it for Margaret's sake, bless her . . . I am always telling the Doctor, Mrs. Corcoran, that nobody who has not experienced it can begin to imagine the blessings of a happy married state. I am sure that you agree with me. Good morning, good morning.

EXIT ANGELUS. JOHNSON *places a chair for Mrs. Corcoran at some distance from the desk.*

JOHNSON. Won't you sit down?

MRS. CORCORAN. Thank you, Doctor.

Both sit.

JOHNSON. Well? And how are we today?

MRS. CORCORAN (*giggles*). Sorry. I can't help it. You looked so professional.

JOHNSON (*gravely*). I hope so.

MRS. CORCORAN. All that, " How are we "; and putting the tips of your fingers together. It looked so funny—for *you*.

JOHNSON. I'm sorry.

MRS. CORCORAN. God knows, I don't feel like laughing.

JOHNSON. Why? Aren't you feeling better?

MRS. CORCORAN. Oh, I'm all right now, thanks, but I didn't come about myself. I came about you.

JOHNSON. I thought we had settled that there was to be no more of that sort of thing.

MRS. CORCORAN. Neither there is. Don't be afraid. But I had to come to see you. George, you must go away from here. You must get away from that abominable man.

JOHNSON. I think, really, you had better go. I'm rather busy this morning.

MRS. CORCORAN. You've got to listen to me. You're just starting this career you seem to think such a hell a lot of. You don't want to be dragged into the ditch at the outset. You *must* listen to me.

JOHNSON. I'm afraid I can't. I've listened to far too much gossip from you about Dr. Angelus and I've told you before and I tell you now that you know nothing whatever about him. You've got a sort of complex against him. That's all.

MRS. CORCORAN. But this is serious.

JOHNSON. I know all the old women in the medical profession call him a quack. But that's jealousy. It's partly because he took his degree in Edinburgh and partly because anyone with the least spark of originality is certain to set all the old, wheezy lapdogs barking at him. I've worked with the man now for nearly two months. He's a bit odd but he's all right. He's a great man.

MRS. CORCORAN. He may be a great man but he's a murderer.

JOHNSON. Don't speak like that.

MRS. CORCORAN. What did Mrs. Taylor die of?

JOHNSON. I'm not going to discuss that with you.

MRS. CORCORAN. Do you know she was insured for ten thousand pounds?

JOHNSON. No, and I don't care.

MRS. CORCORAN. I happen to know that she was. Jack—my husband—he's partly mixed up in the insurance business and he's actually seen the policy. It's a London firm. He wrote to me about it yesterday.

JOHNSON. Once and for all I'm not going to discuss my partner's private affairs with you.

MRS. CORCORAN. They may not be so very private in a couple of weeks. I came here to warn you to get out. Do believe that I came as a friend. I'm not a gossip-monger. And we are friends, aren't we?

JOHNSON. I suppose we are in a way though I'm not sure that we ought to be. Not after I lost my head that time the way I did.

MRS. CORCORAN. You didn't lose your head, worse luck. Perhaps I did a little but I'm not sure. I couldn't resist trying to pull you down off your high horse.

JOHNSON. Thank you very much.

MRS. CORCORAN. You're not a prig, are you, George?

JOHNSON. I don't know. I've never bothered to think.

MRS. CORCORAN. You know I respect you, don't you?

JOHNSON. Sometimes it hasn't looked very like it.

MRS. CORCORAN. I may be a bit mad but I'm really and truly fond of you. You know that, don't you?

JOHNSON. I don't know. I don't know much about women, except in hospitals and textbooks.

MRS. CORCORAN. You've been too much taken up with your career.

JOHNSON. Maybe; I never thought of it as a career.

MRS. CORCORAN. It was more a vocation.

JOHNSON. I don't know what to call it. Even when I was quite a kid it seemed to me that all the other fellows round about me had nothing to hang on to. They were only interested in themselves and games and girls and all that sort of rot. One or two of them were religious but I didn't like them much and anyhow I didn't see any sense in it, especially when I got down to studying biology and physics and that sort of thing. None of them seemed to have much sense of honour. I know it sounds a bit funny to talk about a sense of honour but it did mean something to me. My father had a sense of honour. He was only a small chemist and he had to pinch himself to help me through college. I felt I couldn't go racketing about with that hanging over me. Then, after he died, it was a comfort, in a way, to find something else to hang on to. I found that in medicine. It's difficult to explain . . . What the hell am I talking about? Have you had any more headaches?

MRS. CORCORAN. No, not for a week. But there's such a thing as being too loyal. I mean, you stick up for this man because he's your chief; but you can't see where it's leading you. He's got scoundrel written all over him. Anybody can see it except somebody like you. And he's a bit mad too. It's not easy to say these things to you because I know you'll hate me for saying them and I don't want you to hate me; but I can't bear to see you like the donkey in the story tied up to the axle of the train— especially with a mad engine driver in the cabin. I had to come round and tell you what people are saying. It's not only Jack. It's the women at the bridge club. Three of them are doctors' wives and know what they are talking about.

JOHNSON. I suppose you know that what you've been saying is damned like libel.

MRS. CORCORAN. Yes, I know, but I'm only telling you, George, and you wouldn't repeat it.

JOHNSON. No, I don't suppose I would.

MRS. CORCORAN. But you wouldn't, would you? I mean, that would be dishonourable if you like.

JOHNSON. I won't repeat it but I don't want to hear any more of it.

MRS. CORCORAN. But I haven't told you half of what I came to tell you.

JOHNSON. You've told me quite enough. And you had better warn your old tabby cat friends to keep their mouths shut. Angelus is too big a man to bother about what people say; but I doubt if even he would let that sort of thing pass.

MRS. CORCORAN. You won't tell him.

JOHNSON. No, I won't tell him, but I may as well tell you that what you've been saying is wicked nonsense. Mrs.

Taylor was seen by Sir Gregory Butt and he and Dr. Angelus
agreed in the diagnosis. I signed the death certificate myself

MRS. CORCORAN. You didn't, George !

JOHNSON. Of course I did. Now I think you had better go
on with the tonic and let me know if the headaches come back

> JOHNSON *goes to the door.* MRS. CORCORAN *does no
> get up.*

MRS. CORCORAN. I can't leave it like this. I can't have you
mixed up in this sort of thing.

JOHNSON. I think you can leave me to look after my own
affairs.

MRS. CORCORAN. No I can't. You're blind, you're blind,
George, I said I hadn't lost my head about you but that was
a lie. I'm crazy about you. I'd kill myself if anything went
wrong with you. You must leave this man at once. I don't
care if it means that I never see you again and if you've any
sense you know what that means.

JOHNSON. I think you had better go.

MRS. CORCORAN. You fool . . . His wife's ill now too,
isn't she ? What's the matter with her ?

JOHNSON. I can't stand this any longer. Please go away.

> MRS. CORCORAN *gets up*

MRS. CORCORAN. All right. But I'm not giving up.

> JOHNSON *shows* MRS. CORCORAN *out. He has jus
> returned to the room when* JEANIE *comes in, pale and
> trembling.*

JEANIE. Will you go up to Mrs. Angelus, Doctor ? The
Doctor was down in the kitchen—it was about the cockroaches
behind the grate—and Mrs. Angelus' bell began to ring and
ring. I think she's taken badly again. Oh I'm terrible
feared . . . Will you go up, Doctor ?

JOHNSON. Yes, I'll go up.

> JOHNSON *runs out,* JEANIE *staring after him.* CURTAIN
> *to denote lapse of time.*
> *When the* CURTAIN *goes up again, it is eleven o'clock a.
> night. The consulting room is fairly brightly lit by a*

*gas chandelier and brackets. The green shaded lamp is
also alight. Some rugs and a couple of pillows have
been put on the examination couch to make it into a
temporary bed.* JOHNSON *is moving about the room
restlessly. A large tray has been set beside the fireplace.*
JOHNSON *has disturbed his end of the tray without
eating anything. A cover is on the trivet in front of the
gas fire, waiting for* ANGELUS *who comes in presently.*
JOHNSON *turns to him quickly.*

ANGELUS. She's asleep. I think she is better. I trust so.
I hope so. Ah! Supper. Good.

> *He sits down and attacks his supper heartily.*

JOHNSON. I'll go up.

ANGELUS. No, no. She's all right. Sleeping like a little
child. Jeanie is sitting with her. I shall go up again when I've
had a little bite ... What time is it? Five past eleven. I shall
call you at four o'clock. That will give you a good spell of
sleep. I see the good Jeanie has arranged a bed for you. My
dear gracious goodness me, you haven't eaten anything!

JOHNSON. I didn't feel like it.

ANGELUS. Sit down at once. You can't give of your best
unless you have something inside you ... Look, take this key.
You will find a little stimulant in the lower cupboard.

JOHNSON. I don't think I want any.

ANGELUS. Tuts, man, do as I tell you. I shall be having you
on my hands next. Besides, I want some myself. I am a teetotaller, but I think I shall take a little for my stomach's sake.

> JOHNSON *fetches whisky and soda.* ANGELUS *pours out
> two stiff glasses.*

ANGELUS. I feel happier about Margaret tonight. Much
happier.

JOHNSON. She was pretty bad earlier in the evening.

ANGELUS. I know. I know. It was probably some sort of
crisis. But I feel much more confident now. She has picked
up remarkably. I'm almost persuaded that the whole thing

[41]

has a psychological basis. We shall see. I shall try a little mild hypnosis tomorrow, I think. Drink up. It will give you an appetite. And do sit down. Don't wander about. It makes me nervous.

> JOHNSON *sits down absently and drinks his whisky.* ANGELUS *only pretends to drink his.*

This is very trying for all of us. Very discomposing and upsetting. I can get nothing done. Poor Margaret occupies my entire field of consciousness. This day week I have to give a paper to the Church Literary Society and I haven't put pen to paper. You have heard that I am to be Honorary President?

JOHNSON. Yes.

ANGELUS. I try hard not to feel gratified. It is a great compliment; but I must not be smug. To be smug is almost the unpardonable sin. Do you read Francis Bacon?

JOHNSON. No.

ANGELUS. You should. You should. Bacon should be the main standby of a young man setting forth on his career; with, of course, the Holy Scriptures as his fried eggs; if you will forgive me for being playful. I find a few facetiae light this wilderness of a world like glow-worms. So long as one avoids profanity. Profanity is to be eschewed ... Bacon. You know his classification of the idols that beset men's minds?

> *He fills up* JOHNSON'S *glass.*

JOHNSON. No, I don't think so.

ANGELUS. Very ingenious. Extraordinarily true. He says that they are the Idols of the Tribe; the Idols of the Cave; the Idols of the Market Place; and the Idols of the Theatre. The Idols of the Tribe are part of our Nature; part of our identity with the great pattern of Evolution. Our Nature is at war with our understanding, George. But we must use our understanding to overthrow the animal side of our Nature. With the help of the Grace of God, of course, and of prayer and fasting. I may humbly claim that I have overthrown those idols in myself. But even I must continually watch and pray.

I may quite modestly claim that I have also overthrown the Idols of the Cave. The wise Francis points out that every individual is bounded by his own individuality—that he lives in a little Cave. I have looked out upon the great world from my Cave. I have ventured forth. So that I can now return and spit upon my Idols.

The Idol of the Market Place is set up when our intercourse with the rest of mankind predisposes us to conventional thoughts, to conventional acts, to living by what others think rather than by the inner light. You would not call me a conventional person, would you ?

JOHNSON. No. I wouldn't call you that.

ANGELUS. I am glad of that. It is of the Idols of the Theatre that I am most afraid. They are not, as you might suppose, the temptations of the Playhouse or that peculiar kind of exhibitionism associated with the Drama and its devotees. I myself was once quite a talented amateur actor and I found that it did me little harm. It strengthened my character and gave me confidence. And my religious principles were strong enough to serve me as a sure buckler against the licentiousness of the Green Room. No. To Bacon's mind, the Idols of the Theatre are those systems of philosophy that create for their devotees an unreal world, in which people act artificially, according to a predetermined book of words, as they do in Stage Plays. You must be on your guard against such idols, my dear lad. You must not be ruled by systems.

You can understand now, why it is wise to break, every now and again, even such a salutary system as Total Abstinence.

He gives JOHNSON *more whisky.*

JOHNSON. No thanks. No thanks, really.

ANGELUS. I insist . . . I proposed to examine these points in the little essay I was preparing for my Honorary Presidential Address. Even a Church Literary Society is the better of a little guidance in Clear Thinking. But you don't go to church.

JOHNSON. No. I don't.

ANGELUS (*sighing*). A pity. A pity. "A correspondence fixed with Heaven is sure a noble anchor." But there it is. It is an Age of Unbelief. You young fellows never experience the sublime satisfaction of becoming, even for an hour or two, as a little child. I find public worship a purifying experience.

JOHNSON. Doctor, what do you really think is the matter with Mrs. Angelus?

ANGELUS. I was hoping that you yourself might be able to throw some light on this perplexing case.

JOHNSON. I think we ought to take some specimens round to the pathologist at one of the Hospitals.

ANGELUS. I have examined several specimens myself.

JOHNSON. Yes, but a pathologist . . .

ANGELUS. I am myself a bit of a pathologist. I have little confidence in the fellows. I would back my own judgment against any of theirs.

JOHNSON. That's not quite the point.

ANGELUS. What is the point?

JOHNSON. Well, you see, in a case of doubt like this . . .

ANGELUS. Doubt? Where is the doubt? The case is one of chronic tubercular infiltration of the gastric mucosa, in an acute or sub-acute phase. As frequently happens in such cases, there is a strong psychological background confusing the diagnostic issue. If you are in any doubt as to the correctness of my description, will you kindly make yourself a little clearer?

JOHNSON. I don't see how it can be tubercular.

ANGELUS. I have demonstrated tubercle bacilli under the microscope.

JOHNSON. Yes. You showed me a slide. But are you quite sure it was the right slide? It looked like an old one to me.

ANGELUS. I see. You think I deliberately attempted to deceive you?

JOHNSON. Of course not, sir. I thought you might have made a mistake.

ANGELUS. You think I am callous and incompetent enough to make such mistakes in a matter of life and death?

JOHNSON. No, I don't mean that.

ANGELUS. Then what do you mean? Has Mrs. Angelus said anything to you?

JOHNSON. No. At least ... She was a bit delirious and ...

ANGELUS. And what? She probably said that I was a fiend incarnate; that I was unfaithful to her; that I let Mrs. Taylor die. That sort of thing. Did she?

JOHNSON. Something like that. I didn't pay any attention.

ANGELUS. How many cases of delirium have you seen?

JOHNSON. A few.

ANGELUS. You know that such illusions are as common and stereotyped as pink rats are in delirium tremens.

JOHNSON. Yes, I know. I thought nothing of them.

ANGELUS. Have I behaved to you like a fiend incarnate?

JOHNSON. Of course not.

ANGELUS. In the short time we have been in partnership, I thought that we had built up between us a life-long feeling of trust and mutual respect. It appears I was wrong.

JOHNSON. No, no.

ANGELUS. A passage of sick raving—which you could find described word for word in any good textbook—and you take occasion to insult me.

JOHNSON. Honestly I didn't mean to. I never thought for an instant ...

ANGELUS. Then think in future, please. I am not a very sensitive man, but some things are intolerable.

JOHNSON. I'm sorry, sir. You've taken me up wrongly.

ANGELUS. I hope so. I hope so. I'll take your word for it.

He laughs.

ANGELUS. I'm as bad as you are! It's nearly midnight. We are two overworked medical men, with our nerves on edge from anxiety and loss of sleep; and here I take your every word as if it were a considered opinion. We'll have a drink and forget all about it.

He pours another drink for JOHNSON.

JOHNSON (*with rather tipsy solemnity*). I am very sorry,

Dr. Angelus, if I have been offensive to you in any way. I've always taken my profession very seriously. All my life. But I fully realise that you have had much more experience than I have. I fully realise that. I do want you to know that I respect you both as a man and a clinician. And I can't forget the kindness and tolerance you have shown me since I joined you in practice.

ANGELUS (*much affected*). Thank you, my dear boy. That means a great deal to me. More perhaps than you know. The gratitude is not all on one side. Let us drink to a long and happy association.

JOHNSON (*drinking*). To a long and happy association. And to a speedy recovery for Mrs. Angelus.

ANGELUS. With all my heart.

JOHNSON. Now I want you to let me do one thing.

ANGELUS. What is that?

JOHNSON. I want you to let me go on duty tonight with Mrs. Angelus. I'll let you know if I want any help. I don't feel a bit tired. I never felt better in my life.

ANGELUS. No. You shall take your watch at four o'clock as we arranged.

JOHNSON. No. You look tired, Dr. Angelus. You would be much the better of a good sleep. You go to bed and have a good sleep. I'll look after Mrs. Angelus. I'm really a damned good doctor. You don't need to be anxious. She'll be quite safe with me.

ANGELUS. You haven't taken your supper.

JOHNSON. No. No, neither I have. I don't seem to want it somehow.

ANGELUS *pours him another drink.*

ANGELUS. You must fortify the inner man. And then you must sleep. I shall wake you at four.

JOHNSON *gets up and leans on the mantelpiece, looking at the big oil painting of the barrister in his robes that hangs there.*

JOHNSON. He's got a very stern sort of look on his face

tonight. I know he's Mrs. Angelus' great uncle but I've gone and forgotten his name. Stupid of me.

ANGELUS. He is Sir Roderick Taylor, at one time His Majesty's Solicitor General for Scotland.

JOHNSON. Did you know him?

ANGELUS. No, he was before my time. But they were a very good family, the Taylors. A very good Edinburgh family. Sir Roderick was the most distinguished member. They're all dead now—except Margaret.

JOHNSON. He's very like Sir Gregory Butt.

ANGELUS. Is he? No, I don't think so. Not at all. Not the slightest resemblance.

JOHNSON. Anyhow he looks pretty grim (*laughs*) . . . Like my professional conscience.

ANGELUS (*looks at his watch*). It's a quarter-past eleven. I'm taking up the time you should be spending in sleep. That is very selfish of me. You must wake up bright and alert at four o'clock in the morning. You must go to sleep now.

JOHNSON. It's funny, I do feel a little sleepy. You'll be sure to waken me, won't you?

ANGELUS. Yes, I'll wake you. Good night, my dear boy, and happy dreams, good night.

JOHNSON. Good night, Doctor, and thank you very much for all your kindness.

> EXIT ANGELUS. JOHNSON *begins to take off his collar and tie, muttering away to himself. While he is talking to himself he wanders round the room turning off the gas until only the table lamp is left. He keeps darting puzzled glances at the portrait.*

JOHNSON. Thank you very much for all your kindness. Thank you very much, Dr. Angelus, for all your kindness. They can say what they like about you, Dr. Angelus, but you've been an angel to me. That's facetious but it's true. You've been a blooming Angelus to me. Here am I a stranger in the big city and not much more than a kid after all and you take me into partnership. It's damned decent of you,

131   [47]

Dr. Angelus. I don't care what anyone says. I don't care what Dodo says. I don't care what all the flat-bottomed old barges at the bridge party said. What did they say anyway?

> *He sits down on the couch and thinks, taking off his coat and waistcoat and kicking off his shoes. Suddenly his expression changes. He looks again at the portrait then he makes a sudden dash for the telephone.*

JOHNSON. Woodside 723.

> *A pause.*

Is that Sir Gregory Butt's house? . . . Oh, he's gone to bed? Well, this is rather urgent. Dr. Johnson speaking. I'm speaking for Dr. Angelus. Could Sir Gregory come round? Will you ask him? Yes, it's very urgent.

> *Another pause.*

Oh, is that you, Sir Gregory? I'm sorry to disturb you at this time of night; but I'm very anxious—I mean Dr. Angelus and I are very anxious about Mrs. Angelus . . . Yes, it's the same kind of thing. I mean the symptoms are the same. Could you come round? . . . Oh, I'm sorry . . . Well, she's asleep just now . . . Very well, sir, tomorrow at ten o'clock . . . Very good, sir. Thank you. I'm terribly sorry to disturb you but I was very anxious . . . (*his voice trails away as* SIR GREGORY *has obviously cut him off. As he goes towards the couch*). Mistake. Shouldn't have done that. Not etiquette. Not done. Stupid lout, me. Sorry, Dr. Angelus. But you understand, don't you? I mean, Doctor . . . There's no harm in another opinion. I mean, it's . . . it's . . . not only me. It's you too. It's safeguarding both of us. In case anything happened. It's a safe . . . *guard.*

> *He turns down the lamp to a peep and goes back to the couch and lies down. The stage is very dark but the light gradually grows to illuminate the portrait.*
> *The figure of* JOHNSON *is seen standing downstage with his back to the audience. The figure on the couch is also clearly seen.*

There is no doubt about it now. It is SIR GREGORY BUTT
*in a nineteenth century barrister's wig, gown and whiskers.
He holds a brief in his hand and consults it from time
to time.*

BUTT. How long have you been qualified?

JOHNSON. Two and a half years.

BUTT. Will you give his Lordship and the Jury some account
of your qualifications?

JOHNSON. I am a Bachelor of Medicine, a Bachelor of
Surgery of Durham University; I am also a Member of the
Royal College of Surgeons and a Licentiate of the Royal
College of Physicians; I was a medallist in botany, in anatomy
and in physiology; I received a first-class certificate in the
class of Pharmacy; I studied for two years in St. Thomas's
Hospital in London and was prizeman in clinical medicine.
I was for six months Resident Assistant in the Bilberry County
Hospital.

BUTT. A very brilliant career. I congratulate you.

JOHNSON. Thank you, sir.

BUTT. At the beginning of September of this year you
answered a certain advertisement in the medical press, did you
not?

JOHNSON. Yes.

BUTT. As the result of some correspondence did you visit
Dr. Cyril Angelus of Glasgow?

JOHNSON. Yes, sir, I did.

BUTT. Do you see Dr. Angelus in Court.

*A spotlight fades in over the dressing screen at back. It
is now a dock and* ANGELUS *stands in it in a black
frockcoat, black stock and black gloves.*

JOHNSON. I do.

BUTT. As a result of this interview did you enter into partnership with Dr. Angelus?

JOHNSON. I did.

BUTT. You were to have one-third share of the gross pro-
ceeds of the practice, were you not?

133   [49]

JOHNSON. Yes sir.

BUTT. Bearing in mind the fact that you are an extremely young man, were these terms favourable or unfavourable?

JOHNSON. Very favourable.

BUTT. Had you every reason to be satisfied with your bargain?

JOHNSON. Yes, sir, every reason.

BUTT. Now I want you to cast your mind back to the evening of October 17th. At that time the mother-in-law of the accused was very ill indeed—practically in articulo mortis. Is that correct?

JOHNSON. Yes. I believe so.

BUTT. Had she been ill for some time?

JOHNSON. Yes.

BUTT. Had you given this lady any medical attention?

JOHNSON. No sir.

BUTT. Am I correct in saying that the supervision of this case was undertaken wholly by the panel himself?

JOHNSON. That is so.

BUTT. Did he discuss the case with you?

JOHNSON. Yes sir, he did.

BUTT. Were you as a prizewinner and a medallist and a student of St. Thomas's Hospital thoroughly satisfied that the diagnosis was correct and the treatment sufficient?

JOHNSON. Well sir, you see Dr. Angelus was a good deal senior to me . . .

BUTT. I'm not asking you about the panel's seniority. I'm asking you whether you were satisfied.

JOHNSON. Well, in some ways I was perhaps a bit doubtful.

BUTT. Then you were not satisfied?

JOHNSON. No, not entirely.

BUTT. You were not satisfied. Did you or did you not urge the panel to call in a consultant?

JOHNSON. Well, I suggested that he might.

BUTT. You suggested that he might. That seems to me to be putting it very mildly. Were you afraid of the panel?

JOHNSON. No sir, I wasn't.

BUTT. I put it to you that you were convinced that he was shamefully mishandling this case and yet you only suggested that he might call in a consultant.

JOHNSON. No sir, it wasn't like that at all.

BUTT. Oh, it wasn't, wasn't it? Is it a fact that the panel presented you with at least two different and contrary diagnoses?

JOHNSON. Yes, that is true. He seemed to be a little doubtful.

BUTT. He was doubtful and yet he refused you access to the case.

JOHNSON. No he didn't. In fact he specially asked me to see her.

BUTT. When? On the night she died?

JOHNSON. Yes.

BUTT. Did he ask you to see her on the following morning?

JOHNSON. Yes sir.

BUTT. But most unfortunately she died in the interval.

JOHNSON. Yes sir, that is so.

BUTT. I have here a copy of Mrs. Taylor's death certificate. Does it bear your signature?

JOHNSON. Yes sir.

BUTT. You allege on your soul and conscience that this woman died of gastric tuberculosis and syncope. Had you any reason for believing that she died from these causes?

JOHNSON. Yes sir.

BUTT. What reasons?

JOHNSON. Dr. Angelus told me.

BUTT. He told you. And you signed the certificate in blind obedience although you knew perfectly well that the diagnosis was in very grave doubt. Why did you do that?

JOHNSON. I thought, at least after Sir Gregory Butt had seen her . . .

BUTT. Did Sir Gregory Butt express any direct opinion to you on the nature of the case?

JOHNSON. No sir.

BUTT. So you accepted the diagnosis against your better

135   [51]

judgment and on pure hearsay. You are now aware that
Mrs. Taylor died of something very different are you not?

JOHNSON. Yes, sir.

BUTT. Are you aware that the body was exhumed and that
two professors from Edinburgh discovered in the stomach
and intestine enough tartrate of antimony to kill an elephant
and enough tincture of opium to destroy a rhinoceros?

JOHNSON. I have heard that.

BUTT. Were the symptoms described to you by the panel
consistent with the fact that this unfortunate woman was
being slowly and deliberately poisoned?

JOHNSON. Yes.

BUTT. Are you familiar with the symptoms of antimonial
poisoning?

JOHNSON. Yes.

BUTT. And yet no suspicion crossed your mind that she
was under the operation of this substance?

JOHNSON. Not then, sir.

BUTT. Not then? Not then? NOT THEN! Aha ha!
That implies that a suspicion arose in your mind at some
later date. When did that suspicion arise?

JOHNSON. When Mrs. Angelus took ill.

BUTT. When the *late* Mrs. Angelus took ill. How did
suspicion first arise in your mind?

ANGELUS. I can tell you that. Dodo told him.

BUTT. And who, pray, is Dodo?

ANGELUS. She is a married woman. She stands in the
relationship of patient to doctor with our dear young friend
in the witness box. In spite of this our high-minded and
particular young friend is carrying on an adulterous intrigue
with this black-hearted harlot in the absence of her husband.
He is throwing stones from a veritable crystal palace.

JOHNSON. It wasn't Dodo at all. She had nothing to do
with it. I told her to shut up. I didn't believe a word of it.
Honestly I didn't, Dr. Angelus.

BUTT. Be that as it may your suspicions were aroused. Did
you take any steps?

JOHNSON. I rang up Professor Butt. I asked him to come round. He couldn't come. He said he would come round next morning.

BUTT. And, in the interval, the patient unfortunately died. You've heard that history repeats itself, Mr. Johnson?

JOHNSON. Yes.

BUTT. You were in a position to prevent history from repeating itself and yet you took no effective action. I see. You may cower like a frightened rabbit behind the screen of medical etiquette but there are higher laws than medical etiquette, Mr. Johnson. Infinitely higher laws; could you or could you not have saved the life of this unfortunate woman?

JOHNSON. I rang up Professor Butt.

BUTT. You thought you would pass the buck to Butt.

JOHNSON. No, I didn't, I thought . . .

BUTT. You didn't think at all. You were as drunk as a judge. And you were in a blue funk. The truth is that you hadn't the guts, isn't that it?

ANGELUS. He hasn't the guts of a louse.

JOHNSON. Don't you turn against me, Dr. Angelus. I didn't know what sort of man you were. Honestly I didn't. I thought you were a great fellow. You had been very decent to me. I thought all the stories were just jealousy. I had read about people poisoning people and I believed it in a way but I thought you were my friend. I couldn't believe that anyone I knew could do a thing like that. I thought you were only eccentric.

BUTT. *Ach Himmel*, don't use that word again.

JOHNSON. But what was I to do? I didn't know what to do. I don't know what to do. I don't believe he poisoned her at all. I don't believe he poisoned Mrs. Taylor. There must be some mistake. There must be some mistake.

While he is speaking the figures in his dream fade and disappear and the stage is dark again.

CURTAIN

END OF ACT II

ACT III

The morning following ACT II. *It is ten o'clock but the curtains are still drawn. Sunlight filters round the edges.* GEORGE *is still asleep, muttering and restless. He wakes as from a nightmare, looks round the room, his gaze resting finally on the picture. He realises that it is all a dream. While this is going on the clock strikes ten with a very musical chime. He jumps up quickly and draws the curtains.*

JOHNSON. Ten o'clock. My God!

He rushes into lavatory and we hear sounds of running tap.
ENTER JEANIE, *sniffing and sobbing. She goes to window and pulls down the blind. Collects tray, leaving the whisky, then goes out.*

ENTER GEORGE *drying face. Delayed awareness that blind is down and the significance of this. After a long pause he dashes to telephone and picks up receiver.*

Christ! No! It can't be!... Oh, sorry, Miss. It was a mistake.

He hangs up the receiver. ENTER ANGELUS, *a subdued and pious figure. As* JOHNSON *stares at him, he realises that the boy has been using the telephone and drops the mask for a moment.*

ANGELUS. What the Hell do you think you're doing?
JOHNSON. What do you mean?
ANGELUS. To whom were you speaking?
JOHNSON. Nobody. I thought I heard a ring.
ANGELUS. Put on your collar and necktie. Are you aware that it is half-past ten and that there has been a death in the house?
JOHNSON. I'm sorry.

He puts on his collar as ANGELUS *recovers his suavity.*

ANGELUS. My poor, unfortunate wife passed away an hour

ago. In her sleep. Her breathing stopped suddenly and, when I got to the bedside, she had gone. In the end, thank God, she didn't suffer. Thank God for that.

He pats JOHNSON *on the shoulder.* JOHNSON *flinches.*

Don't take it too hardly, my dear boy. I know that you are practically a member of the family, but you are a medical man and you must always remember that in the midst of life we are in death. Even in the extremity of our grief, we must remember that life must go on. Death is one of the wise provisions of Nature—of kind Mother Nature. We must remember that. Poor Margaret is at peace. Her weary journey is ended. She is in Abraham's bosom. And we can only hope that she's comfortable. Her story is told. To me, at least, it will always be an inspiration. You will find your breakfast in the dining-room. But first, will you be good enough to sign the death certificate? Here it is. I have filled up the details myself.

JOHNSON. Sign it yourself.

ANGELUS. What is the matter with you? Are you drunk?

JOHNSON. No. I'm not drunk. You made me drunk, but I'm not drunk now. What did you do to Mrs. Angelus?

ANGELUS. What did I do to Mrs. Angelus?

JOHNSON. Yes. You gave her something. You've been giving her something all these weeks. What was it? What did you give to Mrs. Taylor? Out with it, damn you!

ANGELUS. I hope this is hysteria. I sincerely hope so. (*As* JOHNSON *is about to speak.*) Keep calm. Now please try to explain yourself.

JOHNSON. Do you know who I was ringing just now? The police.

ANGELUS. Now you *have* got yourself into trouble.

JOHNSON. I didn't speak to them. I wasn't sure. I didn't think you would do a thing like that. I stuck up for you. I couldn't believe it.

ANGELUS. Believe what, my poor fellow? Do you think that I have made some blunder in my treatment of these two

difficult cases ? If you think so, tell me. I am always anxious
to learn and I have tried to take you with me step by step.

JOHNSON. They—they shouldn't have died.

ANGELUS. Weren't you satisfied with the diagnosis ?

JOHNSON. No.

> ANGELUS *tears up the certificate and throws it in the
> waste paper basket.*

ANGELUS. Well, well. You are perfectly entitled to your
opinion. Perfectly. I'll give you a fresh certificate and you
can fill it up for yourself. You will understand, of course,
that it is rather painful to me to discuss fine clinical points at
this particular time. You may do exactly as you like.

> *He lays the certificate book on the desk and holds out a pen.*

Come. Sign. If your hand is steady enough.

JOHNSON. No. I won't. I'm not satisfied.

ANGELUS (*patiently*). With what are you not satisfied ?

JOHNSON. I don't know how Mrs. Taylor died or how
Mrs. Angelus died.

ANGELUS. But you signed Mrs. Taylor's certificate. You
were even more closely associated with me in the treatment
of Mrs. Angelus. If you were not satisfied, why didn't you
say so ? It is late in the day to say so now.

JOHNSON. Yes. It's late in the day.

ANGELUS. If I was going wrong you owed it not only to me,
but to my poor wife to speak out.

JOHNSON. I know that.

ANGELUS. And now, when it is too late, you deliberately
add to the torture I am suffering. Is not that a little cruel ?

JOHNSON. I know. But I can't help it. I'm—I'm not
satisfied.

ANGELUS. There are many who would call it inhuman.

JOHNSON. I can't help it, I tell you.

ANGELUS. But you must help it. I'm terribly disappointed
in you, George. I never thought you brilliant ; but I thought
you a balanced, sensible kind of fellow. It has been a great
grief to me to find . . . several things. To find you can't be

trusted with women patients. To find you liable to alcoholic outbursts without the least capacity for holding your liquor. Go and have a cold bath and come back and talk to me when your head is clearer.

JOHNSON. No. We've got to have it out now.

ANGELUS. I am in no mood for wild talk. It boils down to this, that I can't trust you. I've been almost criminally patient with you. I made allowance for the fact that you were young and inexperienced. If I did my duty, I'd report you to the General Medical Council and have you off the Register. You aren't fit to be a Doctor—to hold lives in your hand. And now you have the impudence to accuse me—ME—of incompetence. Do you ever think at all, boy? Fill up that certificate in any way you please, but let us have no more nonsense.

JOHNSON. I can't, I tell you. I can't.

ANGELUS. Why?

JOHNSON. Because I'm not satisfied.

ANGELUS. Don't go on saying that. Are you trying to accuse me of making away with my wife?

JOHNSON. Well . . . I mean, it couldn't be tuberculosis. And, I mean, the two, following one after the other . . .

ANGELUS. I see. I must repeat my question. In your ravings just now, you mentioned the police. Are you accusing me of murder?

JOHNSON. Yes. No. I don't know.

ANGELUS. If I am to believe my ears, this is a very serious matter, Johnson. You will, no doubt, be prepared to repeat your accusation in the presence of witnesses.

JOHNSON. I didn't make any accusation.

ANGELUS. But it is in your mind that these patients were improperly treated. At least, that my wife was. Now, don't deny it!

JOHNSON. I said I didn't know.

ANGELUS (writing). Look. I have put down the primary disease as gastritis. Pure and simple. There can be no doubt in the mind of the veriest tyro that Mrs. Angelus had gastritis.

141   [57]

Gastritis is simply inflammation of the stomach. Have you any doubt that she had gastritis? And that gastritis was the cause of death?

JOHNSON. I don't know what caused the gastritis.

ANGELUS. Nobody is asking you what caused the gastritis. Do have the common honesty to answer Yes or No to a plain question. Did she die of gastritis?

JOHNSON. Yes. I suppose so.

ANGELUS. Then you can have no motive, other than a malignant desire to attack and ruin me, for refusing to sign this certificate. I cannot understand how I have deserved this at your hands. I have overlooked your faults. I have treated you as a friend. I have trusted you implicitly. Is that true or not.

JOHNSON. Yes. It's true. But all the same . . .

ANGELUS. My nerves are at breaking point. I can't talk to you any more. If you sign now, at once, I shall try to forget what has passed. I shall take no further action. Sit down. Pull yourself together. You're committing yourself to nothing. Read it first. Read it. Now sign.

> JOHNSON *sits down at the desk; signs the certificate book and hands it to* ANGELUS, *who reads the certificate carefully.*

Thank you.

> EXIT ANGELUS. JOHNSON *sits with his head buried in his arms. The doorbell rings. He goes to the window.*
> ENTER JEANIE.

JEANIE. It's the Professor to see you. Come in, Professor.

> BUTT *comes in and* JEANIE *withdraws.* JOHNSON *gets up to meet him.*

BUTT. Good morning to you.

JOHNSON. Good morning, sir.

BUTT. *Ach Himmel!* What an inspissated miasma of putrescence! Is this a professional man's consulting room or a model lodging house in a Clydeside rookery?

JOHNSON. I'm sorry, sir. I slept here last night. I had to stand by. There was illness in the house.

BUTT (*sitting down*). I am not astonished that there was illness in the house.

JOHNSON. Mrs. Angelus died this morning.

BUTT. Do you tell me so? Mortality advances in this household with remarkable rapidity. Of what did the good lady perish?

JOHNSON. I don't know.

BUTT. Dear me! You show a strange lack of confidence in your own diagnostic ability. Very unusual in one so young. Do you know why I came here?

JOHNSON. Well, sir . . . Yes.

BUTT. I have great compassion on pudding-headed Youth. I've decided to overlook your recent impertinence and I've come to give you a friendly warning.

JOHNSON. That's very kind of you.

BUTT. Not at all. But I perceive that you have something on your mind.

JOHNSON. No. Yes. Look here, sir, have you any experience of antimony poisoning?

BUTT. Antimony? Yes.

JOHNSON. I was looking it up yesterday. Just out of curiosity.

BUTT. And what excited your curiosity?

JOHNSON. Nothing. It just crossed my mind to look it up. There's a hot, tight feeling in the throat, isn't there—and sweating?

BUTT. That is so.

JOHNSON. And vomiting, of course.

BUTT. Your teachers have no doubt informed you that antimony potassium tartrate is known to the vulgar as tartar emetic. And not without cause, sir. I have seen a case of chronic poisoning, sir, when the mere sight of a Bath Oliver set the unfortunate patient off like a Roman Candle.

JOHNSON. Would you very much mind looking at a microscope slide, sir? I have it here.

143   [59]

He goes to the window, pulls the blind up a little, and uncovers a microscope.

BUTT. Ah! Our friend has a microscope! Apparently he dabbles in Science in his exiguous spare time.

JOHNSON (*putting in a slide*). There were some crystals here, sir . . .

BUTT *goes over to him.*

Triangular crystals. I wondered if you could recognise them. I wasn't sure myself . . . There they are, sir.

BUTT *looks into the microscope. A silence.* BUTT *looks searchingly at* JOHNSON.

BUTT. So that's what you think, is it?

JOHNSON. I don't know what to think.

BUTT *walks heavily to a chair;* JOHNSON *watching him.*

BUTT. I had a visit from the Police this morning.

JOHNSON. Oh Lord!

BUTT. I sent the flat-footed lumps about their business. I've had no dealings with police court dirt, and, please God, I never will . . . You'd better lie down on that couch. You look like a shade on the bonnie, bonnie banks of the Styx.

JOHNSON. I'm all right . . . All the time Mrs. Taylor was ill, I felt he was hiding something. He kept putting me off. He kept sort of hinting that Mrs. Taylor was too fond of the bottle. I thought maybe he was right. I thought he didn't want me to know. I was pretty—pretty young, you know, and he hadn't known me long . . . They had had some sort of a row. He was very nice about her, but you could see, somehow, he didn't like her . . . I didn't think it was my business . . . You see, Sir Gregory, he was damned decent to me. I mean, he was always helping me out of little jams without letting me see he was doing it. He talked to me like a colleague and he treated me like one. I know he used to buck a lot and he had a highfalutin kind of way of talking; but there was always a lot of sense in it when I could follow what he meant . . . I couldn't believe there was anything wrong. I can't yet, really. You see, he was so *decent* . . . of course, he gave me one or two rather phoney diagnoses about Mrs. Taylor. I felt funny about that. But after you'd seen her, I thought he must be right and I was wrong.

BUTT. Don't drag me into this. You never asked me what I thought. You gave me a lecture on professional etiquette.

JOHNSON. Yes. I did, in a way. But after that there were one or two things.

BUTT. What things?

JOHNSON. Well, I found he was in some sort of tangle with the servant girl. It worried me. But I thought, after all, he's only human. There's often a side to the best of us we can't control. I mean, I'd a special reason for thinking that way. I'd made rather a fool of myself. I'd got a bit keen on a lady patient, without meaning to be. There was nothing wrong, really, but there might have been. I rather saw his side of it because of that.

BUTT. Then his wife took ill?

JOHNSON. Yes. It was damned awful. It was like a nightmare and trying to wake up. Everything came back. I wanted to come round and see you and then I felt like Judas Iscariot. I saw her last night and I felt certain then. I rang you up.

BUTT. Round about midnight?

JOHNSON. Yes.

BUTT. I see. Had you any other reasons for suspicion?

JOHNSON. Mrs. Angelus said something; but I thought she was delirious. I told Angelus. He said she was delirious.

BUTT. But you took his word for it?

JOHNSON. I tell you, I didn't want to believe—anything of that sort. There was something about insurance too. I didn't want to believe that. And I had nobody to talk to. I couldn't discuss my partner's affairs with strangers. I tried to find out for certain. I tried to get him to send her to hospital. I tried to get him to call you in. But he kept edging me off. And I felt a stinking cad all the time. Perhaps I am. Whenever he talks to me I sort of know in my bones that he's all right. I mean, it would be so *unlike* him to—to . . . But when I'm

145   [61]

by myself the doubts come back . . . I mean, they're more than doubts . . . Sir Gregory, are these antimony crystals ?

BUTT (*getting up*).   You will observe that I am not asking you where you found the specimen that contains these crystals. You will oblige me, in return, by asking me no more questions.   I don't know anything about you, except that you've got yourself into an ugly mess.   If you had asked me in time, I might have helped you.   But you preferred to rest on your own damned conceit.

JOHNSON. But I want help now.

BUTT. I can't help you.   If these two women have been murdered—and I'm not saying they have—you're as much responsible as anyone.   You had your suspicions and you should have had the guts to speak out.

JOHNSON. But how could I ?

BUTT. You seem to me to have considerable powers of articulation.   You're a weakling and a coward, sir ;   and I should be consulting neither my reputation nor my professional honour if I stooped to pull you out of the sheugh. Who signed the death certificates ?

JOHNSON. I did.

BUTT. Pah !   The effect you have on me, sir, is what I should expect from an overdose of your favourite tartar emetic.   You can lie seething in your own juice, sir.   I take my leave of you.   I was a stupid old man to allow myself to be cajoled to within a thousand miles of this unsavoury midden.   Where's my hat ?

JOHNSON. There's your bloody hat.   You can go to Hell, you yammering old Pharisee.

BUTT. What did you say ?

JOHNSON. I'll take whatever rap is coming to me without your help.   I said you were a Pharisee and so you are.   You can slink out of it as fast as you like.

BUTT. In all my experience I never met such a case of effrontery.

JOHNSON. No ? Because you're an old tin idol and a pompous old quack. Angelus may be a murderer and I may be a bloody

coward but you're not fit to black our boots. If you'd come a-
cross the chap in the Bible who fell among thieves, you wouldn't
have gone by on the other side. You'd have stamped over
his bloody face. I am going to the police now to give myself
up as an accessory after the fact. I'll see this through myself
without your damned help or anybody else's and you can go
to Hell.

He strides into the lavatory and slams the door.

BUTT (*shouting at the closed door*). You are a very foolish
young man, sir. It was a sorry day when I first cast eyes on
your foolish countenance. I shall blot the day out of my
calendar. Good-bye, and God forgive you !

He pulls the door open. ANGELUS *is standing in the doorway.*

ANGELUS. Ah, Sir Gregory, you find us once more at a sad
time.

He offers to shake hands. BUTT *glares at him and stamps
out.* ENTER JOHNSON *from the lavatory, wearing hat
and coat. He makes straight for the door but* ANGELUS
intercepts him.

ANGELUS. Stay here, George. I want to talk to you.

JOHNSON *turns and faces him.*

I'm going to ask you a great favour.

JOHNSON. Yes ?

ANGELUS. I would only ask it from one I have learned to
regard as a very dear friend. My actions may seem to others
to be curious, almost heartless ; but I know that you will
understand.

JOHNSON. Go on.

ANGELUS. I have arranged for my dear wife's obsequies. I
have given orders that, although the funeral will be private,
no expense is to be spared. But I shall not be there.

JOHNSON. What do you mean ?

ANGELUS. What I say, my dear boy. For one of my sensitive nature, those two overwhelming calamities, both within
the space of one short month, have been more than I can bear.

147   [63]

I fear for my reason. I must get away. Now. I must lift my eyes to the Hills. I must commune with Nature. If I am sufficiently restored in a day or two, I may return and pay the last sad tribute to what is left of the dear partner of my joys and sorrows. If not . . . My boy, I look on you as a son—a beloved son. I want you to take my place.

JOHNSON. What sort of a bloody fool do you think I am?

ANGELUS. I am at a loss to apprehend your meaning.

JOHNSON. Do you know where I'm going? I'm going to the Police Station. Do you know what I'm going to do there? I'm going to give myself up as an accessory to murder. Do you damned well apprehend my meaning now?

> *He makes for the door.* ANGELUS *hits him over the heart and follows with a right hook to the jaw.* JOHNSON *falls.*

ANGELUS (*sucking his knuckle*). I used to box a little. Just a little. It was a useful sport. A manly exercise. I have never regretted it. Get up when you can and do as I tell you.

> JOHNSON *gets up and immediately attacks him.* ANGELUS *knocks him down again.* JOHNSON *staggers across and falls over the couch.*
>
> ANGELUS *helps* JOHNSON *up and lays him on the couch. While he is talking, he examines and dresses the wound on* JOHNSON'S *forehead with iodine.*

Yes. I plan a little excursion. A little change. A little solitude. I must invite my soul . . . I hope I haven't hurt you. But I had no alternative. No alternative at all.

> ANGELUS *lights all the lights, talking as he does so. He then settles himself comfortably for a long cosy chat.*

" More light," said jesting Pilate, and did not wait for a reply. You are walking in darkness, my dear George. We must enlighten you . . . I have noticed in the last few weeks that you have harboured a paranoidal system of suspicion against me. This has grieved me. This has grieved me very much.

At the same time I must warn you not to act on these morbid impulses. You will only get yourself into serious trouble. I should be driven to protect my good name by suing you for slander and, incidentally, your rather shameful association with a married patient would be discussed in open court. I should also warn you not to hope for any help from Sir Gregory Butt. He would not have attained his present position if he had not been a thoroughly selfish and self-centred person. No, my boy, you have no prospect but ruin if you pursue your fantasy into fact.

Morbid and idle as your speculations are, last night I allowed them to occupy my mind. In the long watches of the night, as I sat by poor Margaret's bedside, weary but vigilant, I tried to enter into your thoughts. I asked myself what if I had justified your suspicion and made away with those who were nearest and dearest to me in such a lamentable fashion ? Would it have been possible to justify these acts to my conscience so that, on the great day of Judgment, I could face my Maker unafraid ?

Suppose I had destroyed my mother-in-law and my wife, what could possibly have impelled me to do so ? Mind you, this is all hypothetical. Strictly hypothetical.

I have all my life been a man of action. I may without vanity describe myself as a religious man, a philosopher and a man of science. This is a rare combination, but I consider it necessary if a man is to fulfil the full purpose of his being. At the same time I regard religion, philosophy and science not as ends in themselves but as means to an end.

This realisation of oneself is the aim and object of existence. My religion, my philosophy, my science have taught me that and I owe whatever little success I have gained in life to my knowledge of this truth.

Can we now imagine a man who holds this firm conviction being placed in a situation in which what is called murder would be a perfectly logical and reasonable solution of his difficulties ? At a critical period of his life, suppose him to be frustrated, hog-tied, hemmed in on every side in such a manner as to prevent the fulfilment of his destiny.

Let us take a fantastic and laughable instance. Let us suppose that he is a doctor devoted to the study of his art and determined to take his rightful position as a benefactor to all mankind. He must have free play to the wings of his imagination. He cannot be cramped by the petty embargoes of a general practitioner's environment. Even the sanctions of his own earthly, animal nature tend to hold him fast to the ground and they cannot be allowed to do so. Suppose this man to have made an unfortunate marriage. Suppose him to be subjected to the incessant attempts of two ignorant and narrow-minded women to mould him to their miserable conception of what a right-thinking domestic animal ought to be. At every turn they trip him with their beastly apron strings. They are forever trying to lower him into that barber's chair where Samson, Judge of Israel, was shorn of his strength. Suppose this man to have passionate physical longings. Unless they are satisfied he cannot plan, he cannot think, he cannot invite his soul, he cannot rise above the earth. Above all he cannot make his wretched female gaolers understand his necessities. What is he to do ?

You may answer to this that the world is wide. He can leave those creatures and seek other fields. But that is not the solution of a man of courage, to run like the wandering Jew from city to city seeking rest and finding none. He must stand and fight. He must not run away from circumstances. He must make circumstances, like Napoleon. He must break the bonds of oppression. He must be ruthless. He must hew Agag in pieces before the Lord. It is the only thing he can do consistent with his self respect.

He applies smelling salts to JOHNSON'S *nose.* JOHNSON *recovers slightly.*

Always remember that, my dear boy, when self respect is gone there is nothing left. Self respect should always, of course, be tempered with a proper humility and I have always striven so to temper it. But humility does not mean selling oneself body and soul to live in accordance with the ideas of

persons who are incapable of thought. No, no. The free
spirit must rise and crush his would-be masters with as little
compunction as if he were stepping on a disgusting beetle.

He gets up.

Well, my dear lad, I have enjoyed our little chat. It has been
an oasis on the desert of tragedy. It has no bearing on the
present circumstances. I am an idealist—sometimes a ruthless
idealist—but I am still warmly alive to the sanctity of
domestic affection. I have lost all that is dearest to me in life.
It will take me many months to gird up my loins and once
again march breast forward. The married state is a blessed
one, George. It will be the happiest day of my life when I see
you standing at God's altar taking those solemn vows which
can only be dissolved by death. Alas, death has dissolved
my vows and there remains an emptiness that can never be
filled. A great void, George.

> ANGELUS *goes towards the door but turns again to*
> GEORGE.

And God bless you, my boy. God bless you.

> *The doorbell rings loudly and continuously. The following
> scene is played at a great pace, the speeches overlapping.
> The door swings open and* JEANIE *stands in the doorway
> speechless with indignation.* ANGELUS—*looks at her
> for a moment and then runs to the window and looks
> out round the corner of the blind. He gives a scream of
> terror.*

Don't let them in! Don't let them in!

JEANIE. You were going away without me. That's a fine
thing. You had your bag packed and you never told me. You
were going away without me.

ANGELUS. Don't let them in!

> *The bell goes on ringing and heavy knocking is heard.*
> JEANIE *has taken two or three steps into the room.*
> JOHNSON *dashes from the couch suddenly and goes out
> behind her.*

JEANIE. Why would you do the like of that? Why would you leave me the way I am? I canna believe anybody would do the like of that.

ANGELUS. Don't let them in! Don't let them in!

> *The hall door is heard opening and voices are heard in the lobby.* ANGELUS *runs through the doorway and rushes upstairs.*

MACIVOR (*outside*). Get after him, sergeant, like the hammers of hell! You too, Dougal!

> *He appears in the doorway holding* JOHNSON *by the arm and heavy feet are heard running up the stairs.*

MACIVOR. And see you search him properly. We canna let him do himself a mischief.

> *He leads* JOHNSON *into the room and sets him down in the armchair.* JEANIE *has thrown herself face downwards on the couch and is sobbing wildly.* MACIVOR *leans against the mantelpiece and consults a notebook.*

You'll be Dr. Johnson, I'm thinking? Dear me, you're a very peely-wally looking Dr. Johnson. That's a sore dunt you've got on your head. It seems to be a dangerous life, a doctor's, and me thinking the constabulary had a hard enough time.

JOHNSON. Are you a policeman?

MACIVOR. Well, I'm a police inspector.

JOHNSON. I want to give myself up.

MACIVOR. Dear me, it would be wise to think a little before you speak. What would you be giving yourself up for, now?

JOHNSON. Dr. Angelus murdered his mother-in-law and his wife. I knew he was doing it and I did nothing about it. That makes me an accessory, doesn't it?

MACIVOR. His wife, too? Well, well, isn't he the villain?

JOHNSON. I want to make a statement.

MACIVOR. Take your time, take your time. It's a very impulsive character you are.

> JEANIE *sobs more loudly.*

Dear me, are we to have no peace and quiet? Hold your wheesht like a good lass.

> JEANIE *howls loudly.* MACIVOR *walks over to her and gives her two sharp punches in the kidneys.* JEANIE *stops instantly and sits up.*

MACIVOR. Janet McAdam, it'll be?

JEANIE. Yes, sir.

MACIVOR. Well, well, you can sit there if you behave yourself, but I don't want another cheep out of your head until I ask you.

> *He goes to the door and shouts upstairs.*

Have you got him, sergeant?

SERGEANT'S VOICE (*above*). Yes, Mr. MacIvor.

MACIVOR. Take him into the dining-room and leave him there with Dougal, and go you over the house with MacIntyre. I'll call for him when I want him.

> *He shuts the door and comes back into the room to his stance against the mantelpiece.*

MACIVOR. Well, now, we were talking about something but I can't remember for the life of me what it was. Is your head clear enough for a wee talk?

JOHNSON. Yes.

MACIVOR. Fine, man, fine. You'll be acquainted with a lady called Mrs. Corcoran?

JOHNSON. Yes.

MACIVOR. Her and me had a very interesting talk not so very long ago. A nice lady. You yourself seem to be a lot in her mind. You'll be well acquaint with her, maybe?

JOHNSON. I know her. She's a patient.

MACIVOR. Yes, yes, poor thing.

JOHNSON. Look here, inspector . . .

MACIVOR. Now don't you be trying to talk. It's bad for your head. There's one or two things I have to ask you but you've just got to say yes or no. Take it easy.

JOHNSON. You'd better warn me first.

MACIVOR. Oh, there's no occasion. No occasion at all. It

was just a wee thing or two I was going to ask you. You can
trust me all right.

JOHNSON. I'm never going to trust a living soul as long as
I live.

MACIVOR. Well, you may be right and you may be wrong. I
would not say. You've a long time to live and I wouldn't be
making rash promises if I were you.

He holds out the certificate

Have you seen this before? It's poor Mrs. Taylor's death
certificate.

JOHNSON. Yes.

MACIVOR. That'll be your signature?

JOHNSON. Yes.

MACIVOR. The Doctor got you to sign it? He didn't forge
your signature?

JOHNSON. No.

MACIVOR. It's as well to make sure. It says here that Mrs.
Taylor died of gastric tuberculosis and syncope. Now, do
you feel quite sure in your mind that that was the cause of the
decease?

JOHNSON. No. Not now. You see I . . .

MACIVOR. Nay, but at the time. You would be saying,
" I'm a young man and the Doctor's an old one. He'll likely
know better than me."

JOHNSON. I'm responsible for my own opinion.

MACIVOR. Just that. And that was your opinion at the time.
Well, we'll see at the post mortem whether you were right.

JOHNSON. I signed Mrs. Angelus's certificate too.

MACIVOR. Yes, yes. So you would. And she's passed
away, the poor lady. It's a great pity we were too late to save
her. A great pity. But you'll understand, there are certain
formalities, Doctor. Certain formalities. A sad affair.

JOHNSON. I knew damned well he had poisoned her and I
hadn't the guts to say so.

JEANIE. Don't you listen to him. He had always a spite
against the Doctor. He's telling lies.

[70]

MACIVOR (*roaring like a bull*). Hold your tongue !
    He looks fiercely from one to the other and then suddenly resumes his bland manner.

MACIVOR. What was this spite he had against the Doctor ?

JEANIE. He was carrying on with a lady patient. Dr. Angelus told him off. He had a spite against him after that. Dr. Angelus told me himself.

MACIVOR. When you were having a wee bit chat with him, like ; about this and that ?

JEANIE. Yes.

MACIVOR. You'd often have a bit chat with the Doctor.

JEANIE. Yes.

MACIVOR. When he was helping you to wash the dishes and the like. He'd be a nice, open-hearted frank kind of man, Dr. Angelus—very kind and condescending to the domestic staff.

JEANIE. Yes. He was.

MACIVOR. Patriarchal kind of gentleman. Like Abraham or Solomon or the like.

JEANIE. I don't know what you're speaking about. All I know is he told me about the young Doctor having a spite against him.

MACIVOR. He would be sorry about that.

JEANIE. Yes. He was.

MACIVOR. It's a hard thing to a sympathetic nature when somebody has a spite against him. You'll understand that fine. You've a sympathetic nature yourself, Miss McAdam, I'm sure. He would often come to you with his troubles.

JEANIE. Now and again he did.

MACIVOR. He'd be grateful for a kindly lassie to talk to. He'd maybe show his gratitude by giving you a wee cuddle now and again.

JEANIE. He nothing of the sort did. I'm a respectable girl. I don't care who said it, it's a pack of lies.

MACIVOR. Oh, dear me, I wouldn't blame him. I would be very pleased myself. And he was for leaving you without so much as saying good-bye.

JEANIE. Oh!

She begins to cry.

MACIVOR. That'll do. Go like a good girl into the dining-room and tell the police officer to send the Doctor in here.

EXIT JEANIE, *snivelling.*

MACIVOR. A sonsy bit, yon. I'm not a Doctor. I'm only a married man. But would you say she was three months or four months gone, Doctor? Just as a matter of opinion.

JOHNSON. I don't know. I never noticed.

MACIVOR. Well, well. I'm thinking it's no wonder we didn't take your diagnosis on the certificate for gospel. It's experience you're needing. Just experience.

ENTER ANGELUS. *Sergeant closes the door behind him.*

MACIVOR. Ah, good morning to you, sir. It'll be Dr. Angelus, I make no doubt.

ANGELUS. Good morning. What is the meaning of this?

MACIVOR. Oh, it's just that I have a warrant in my pocket for your arrest.

ANGELUS. On what charge?

MACIVOR. Murder, Doctor, murder. But before I put it into effect, I'd like to have a wee talk with you. Just as you like, but it would be an obligement. And anything you say can be taken down and used against you as evidence at your trial.

ANGELUS. Do you want this young man to be in the room?

MACIVOR. Ah, well now, the young Doctor isn't like you and me. He's not too old to learn. He'll sit and listen to our brotherly conversation and maybe learn a little about human nature.

ANGELUS. He's as ignorant as a beast.

MACIVOR. You mean he knows nothing of your carryings on?

ANGELUS. I mean what I say.

MACIVOR. 'Deed, he doesn't seem to know very much . . . By the way, you'll excuse me for having you searched. We had to make sure that you were not taking precautions.

ANGELUS. I never take precautions.

[72]   156

MACIVOR. Well now, that's very foolish of you. Maybe if you'd taken precautions I wouldn't be here leaning against your mantelpiece and you wouldn't be looking like poor Mary's ghost.

ANGELUS. What has he said to you? What possessed me to take that malignant idiot into my employment? What possessed me? What possessed me?

MACIVOR. Sit down.

ANGELUS. Why should I take your orders? You will be sorry for this. I solemnly assure you you will be sorry for this.

MACIVOR. Ah, well, I'll try to bear up.

ANGELUS. Do you think I will let myself be pawed all over by your disgusting myrmidons without protest? I shall speak to the Chief Constable.

MACIVOR. That's fine, and I've no doubt he'll enjoy it. But I explained why it was necessary to search you.

ANGELUS. You thought I was going to poison myself. You must be a goddam fool. Do you think I value my life as little as that, I who have been given this heart and these lungs and this brain to act according to the dictates of my intelligence? Do you think I would destroy this mighty instrument my body? You come here, you clumsy idiot, with your bullying and your threats. What sort of man do you think I am? I've crushed better men than you and flicked them out of my way. My object was to go on living and living more abundantly. You think I would take my own life now?

MACIVOR. There's no telling. I see in my wee book that you're an expert on insurance, Doctor. I don't think an insurance company would rate your life very high at this moment.

ANGELUS. What do you mean?

MACIVOR. You know very well what I mean. There's a wee room in His Majesty's prison in Duke Street where better men than you have shaken hands with their lives for the last time.

ANGELUS (*staring*). You are talking about . . . me?

MACIVOR. Just that.

ANGELUS falls into the chair.

ANGELUS. I didn't think of that. You may not believe me, but I didn't think of that.

MACIVOR. That would be one of the precautions you did not take——thinking of that?

ANGELUS. Even when I saw you at the door I didn't realise . . .

He rapidly grows hysterical.

George, it never entered my mind. You believe that, don't you? You know me, George? I only saw one way ahead of me. There were no crossroads like this. I did what I had to do and got on with the journey. I never thought of this. I can't bear it . . . I didn't do it, George. You know I didn't do it. Tell them I didn't do it.

MACIVOR *produces handcuffs.*

Don't let them touch me. Margaret would tell you. She knows I was always good to her. Her blessed spirit is looking down from Heaven. Margaret! Look what they're doing to me, Margaret! Tell them I wouldn't hurt you.

MACIVOR *slips the handcuffs on his praying hands.*

They're trying to kill me, Margaret. You wouldn't let them kill me, would you? Help me! Help me! Come down from Heaven, Margaret! Bring some angels with you! They're killing me, I tell you. They're going to choke me with a rope. They're going to murder an innocent man.

MACIVOR. Get up, you whining brock! Stand on your feet.

He jerks ANGELUS to his feet.

I arrest you, Cyril Angelus, for the murder of Elizabeth Taylor.

ANGELUS. No, no! Don't you understand? You *must* understand. I swear before Almighty God . . . Margaret, speak up for me! You and your mother. Go to God and speak for me . . . Oh, Jesus tender Shepherd, hear me! This cross is too heavy for me to bear. Margaret! Margaret!

MACIVOR *thrusts him through the doorway.*

MACIVOR. Sergeant, take him to the dining-room. I'll be with you in a wee minute.

The SERGEANT *is glimpsed in the passage as he takes charge of* ANGELUS, *who is now howling like a dog.* MACIVOR *shuts the door and turns back into the room. He lights a cigarette.*

There goes one who'll be none the worse of a hanging.

A dirty type, yon. Wait you an hour or two and he'll be enjoying himself fine. He'll have the prison chaplain bubbling and greeting and him as pleased as Punch and quite certain he's put everything right with his Maker. It'll be a cleaner world when the hangman pulls the snib on him.

JOHNSON. I'm as bad as he is.

MACIVOR. Eh? Man, I think you flatter yourself.

JOHNSON. I'm an accessory after the fact.

MACIVOR. Tuts! You're havering. There's no such and a thing in Scotland. Art and part we call it in Scotland. It's easier understood and it's poetry forbye. But you're neither art nor part.

JOHNSON. I could have saved that woman's life.

MACIVOR. Not you. It's only a good stout bit of hemp round his neck will stop that one from murdering.

JOHNSON. I knew what he was after and I didn't speak out. I'm as bad as he is.

MACIVOR. Not you. I was saying before that you had a lot to learn, and it's a fact sure enough. You young ones don't know the difference between good and evil. You should have a talk with the police now and again. Och, I know what you're thinking. But if the Procurator Fiscal and the Criminal Investigation Department couldna get off the mark quick enough to save Mrs. Angelus there's nobody going to blame you, and you little better than a bairn. We'd all have been the fine, clever and courageous ones if we had seen every situation from its beginning to its end. You've taken a kind of tumble to your self respect, but that's no harm, no harm at all. You

did your best and it wasna very good and that's a fair epitaph
for most of us.   Away you now with Dougal to the police
station.   You'll have a statement to make.   See that it's a
sensible statement.

> *While he is speaking he is moving* JOHNSON *towards the
> door.   He pushes him through with a friendly push
> and stands looking after him.*

MACIVOR. Dougal !

CURTAIN

END OF THE PLAY

IT DEPENDS WHAT YOU MEAN

An Improvisation for the Glockenspiel

A PLAY IN THREE ACTS

PERSONS IN THE PLAY

ANGELA PROUT, B.A.

THE REV. WILLIAM PARIS, C.F.

GEORGE PROUT, R.O.I.

JAMES MUTCH, D.LITT.

PTE. JESSIE KILLIGREW, A.T.S.

VISCOUNTESS DODD, D.B.E.

JOE BYRES, M.P.

HECTOR MACADAM, M.D., F.R.C.S.ED.

PTE. WALTER GEIKIE, R.A.S.C.

TIME : 1942.

PLACE : North Britain.

SCENES : A Studio and an Army Recreation Hut.

NOTE :—*The Characters in this Play are not intended to represent any existing individuals*.

IT DEPENDS WHAT YOU MEAN

ACT I

SCENE :—*A small bare, but untidy, Studio in a small country town. The Stage is empty. A car is heard braking fiercely just outside, and immediately after a knocker is heard banging at the door.*

ANGELA PROUT ENTERS *through a curtained doorway, crosses the stage and opens the door. She is a slatternly but not unattractive woman of about thirty-five with an extremely intelligent face. She admits a* CLERGYMAN *in Battle Dress.*

ANGELA.   Oh, do come in ; I am sorry to have kept you waiting, but this is an artist's house, and you know what that means.

PADRE.   Oh yes, thank you.   It's quite all right.

ANGELA.   Won't you sit down ?

PADRE.   Thank you, yes, rather.

HE sits.

A very jolly place you have here, Mrs. Prout.

ANGELA.   Oh, do you think so ?   It seems to me a dreary little hovel.   Thank God my husband's an artist and I'm not supposed to keep it clean, though mind you, I've searched three counties for a charwoman.   I think the race must be extinct. Such a pity. I didn't exactly love them in the old days, but absence does make the heart grow fonder, doesn't it, Mr.——I mean Captain, of course.

PADRE.   Oh, Mr.'s quite all right.   I'm a padre, as a matter of fact.   Paris is the name.

ANGELA.   Oh, I'm so sorry, but one never knows these days, does one ?   I got quite a shock when our doctor in Chelsea suddenly turned up looking the perfect man of blood.   Such a kind little chap he was too.   An osteopath really, though he was a proper doctor as well. He's a major now—eating raw beefsteaks and using terrible language. Now I'll get you some tea. George and Jimmy Mutch are arguing about spring onions and neither of them knows a thing about spring onions. I'll shout for them. (*Goes to the window.*)

PADRE. Oh no, really, please, you mustn't bother.

ANGELA. Don't you want tea?

PADRE. Well, persons of my cloth have the name of being addicts, haven't they?

ANGELA. That's all right then. That's settled. Besides, we were having it anyhow. (*Shouting through the window.*) Georgie! Come in; we've got a visitor.

GEORGE (*without*). Oh hell!

ANGELA. And it's tea-time.

GEORGE (*without*). Blast!

ANGELA. I'm so sorry there's no whisky. Do you find that tea is very bad for your patients' tempers?

PADRE. Patients?

ANGELA. Oh, I forgot, you're not a doctor, but George is much easier to live with when there is plenty of whisky in the house, and tea seems to have just the opposite effect. I say, what about your driver?

PADRE. Well, if you would be so extraordinarily kind I'll take out a cup.

ANGELA. Is it a he, or a she?

PADRE. It's a she.

ANGELA. Is she good looking?

PADRE. Well—yes, I suppose so, rather.

ANGELA. Bring her in then. George is terribly fond of pretty girls.

PADRE. Really? Do you mind? She's rather good fun. Rather a character in her way.

ANGELA. Right-ho then. Bring her in. I'll go and fetch the tea.

EXIT ANGELA. PADRE *opens the door and calls.*

PADRE. Jessie! Will you come in, please? Mrs. Prout is going to give us a cup of tea.

JESSIE (*without*). Oh, hoorray!

ENTER PROUT *and* MUTCH. THEY *almost bump into the* PADRE.

PROUT. Hello!

PADRE. Hello!

PROUT. I say, look here, I'm terribly sorry. We can't billet anybody here. The place isn't fit to keep a pig in. Professor Mutch here has much or less to sleep in the scullery.

PADRE. That's all right. I'm not the Billeting Officer. I'm not an officer at all actually. I'm only a padre.

PROUT. Only a padre? What an appalling thing to say. A direct representative of the Almighty isn't *only* anything. Is he, Jimmy?

MUTCH. Well, I mean to say, after all. . . . Humility, I mean. Isn't it one of the apostolic virtues?

PADRE (*laughing*). Ha, ha! Well, I suppose it ought to be, oughtn't it? Oh, there you are, Jessie.

ENTER *a very smart member of the* A.T.S. SHE *is at her ease, but a little on guard.*

This is my driver, Private Killigrew. Mrs. Prout very kindly said she might come in for a cup of tea.

PROUT. Naturally, yes, of course. Very pleased. How do you do?

JESSIE. How do you do?

PADRE. You're the celebrated Professor Mutch, aren't you?

MUTCH. Well, as a matter of fact, yes.

PADRE. I thought I recognised you from your photographs. Private Killigrew, this is Professor Mutch.

JESSIE. How do you do?

MUTCH. How do you do?

PADRE. And you're Mr. Prout, aren't you?

PROUT. Yes.

PADRE. I'm Paris.

PROUT. Good. Now we know each other. And now I hope that draggle-tailed harridan, the wife of my bosom, is hurrying up with the tea.

PADRE. I do wish she wouldn't bother. As a matter of fact I only called in for a minute. I wanted to ask you to do us a great favour.

PROUT. Who's us? Sit down, Miss What's-your-name.

MUTCH *gets a chair for* JESSIE. *All sit.*
Who's us?

PADRE. Well, the troops, you see.

PROUT. Have you a cigarette, Padre?

PADRE. I only learned last night that we had three such celebrated people in the neighbourhood and the O.C. and I decided to cash in on it.

PROUT. Got a match?

PADRE. I'm sorry, I don't smoke. Where was I? The Welfare Officer's in hospital you see, and I'm sort of stooging for him. I wonder if you'd care to take part in the Brains Trust we're holding in the Canteen next week?

PROUT. Brains Trust? But I've got no brains and Jimmy here is practically an imbecile. He's no worse than his stupider sort of neighbour in ordinary conversation, but wait till you see him before an audience.

PADRE. Oh come, come, come, come, come, come, come. (*To* MUTCH.) I'm afraid our friend is a bit of a legpuller, isn't he?

PROUT. I'm nothing of the sort.

MUTCH. You are in a way, old boy. You've a sadistic streak in you.

PROUT. But I've never pulled anyone's leg in my life. Why should I? Where is that infernal woman? I want my tea. At least I don't want it, but I need it. Angela!

ANGELA (*without*). Coming, coming.

ENTER ANGELA *carrying a tray with tea things. With the rather fussy assistance of the* PADRE *she puts it down on a low table and the tea-party starts.*

MUTCH. I have noticed that sculptors, and people generally who make things with their hands, are very often deficient in self-criticism.

ANGELA. Can you take goat's milk, Padre?

PADRE. Yes, thanks. Thanks very much.

MUTCH. I don't mean they don't criticise themselves. They do.

ANGELA. We've no sugar, I'm sorry, but we are rather proud of our goat's milk.

MUTCH. But it is usually a very inexpert sort of criticism.

PADRE. Do you mind if I use my saccharine? Would anyone else like some?

ANGELA. I'm sure they would.

PROUT. Thanks very much.

JESSIE. Yes, thank you.

MUTCH. Over their work I mean.

PADRE. There you are. Help yourselves.

PROUT. Thank you very much.

MUTCH. I don't mean after it's completed and, so to speak, away from them. A picture or a piece of sculpture is budded off from the artist.

ANGELA. Did you know we had a nanny goat?

PADRE. No, really?

MUTCH. It's like that sea water creature—I forget it's name.

ANGELA. She's called Lady Cabstanleigh, after Beachcomber. She's got the same kind of expression in her eyes.

MUTCH. It grows its young like little buds from the stalk——

PADRE. Now you come and sit here, Mrs. Prout.

ANGELA. Bring that chair down.

MUTCH. They grow their young on a kind of stalk, but the stalk breaks off and the infants float away and become separate entities. It's only when the artist's work has budded off and floated away and grown up a bit that the artist is really fit to give any opinion about it at all. It's then an entity like himself and not part of himself, if you see what I mean.

ANGELA. Yes, dear Jimmy, we see what you mean. (*To* JESSIE.) I suppose the boys at the camp get plenty of sugar?

JESSIE. Yes.

PADRE. I tell the boys they don't know they're born, they get lashings of sugar.

ANGELA. The lucky fellows!

PROUT. What do you mean by "lucky"? I had a year of the army before they chucked me out and I never went through such indiluted hell since I was at school.

ANGELA. I often think——

PROUT. Nonsense.

ANGELA. My dear George, I am accustomed to the peculiar Chesterfieldian grace of your interjections, but I wonder what Mr. Paris will think of us.

PROUT. Who's Mr. Paris?

ANGELA. This is Mr. Paris.

PROUT. Oh, I know what he thinks of us. He thinks we're a ready-made Brains Trust.

ANGELA. Brains Trust?

PADRE. Yes. In point of fact, I called to see whether you and Mr. Prout and the Professor would help us. I hate the name Brains Trust, but the troops always call it that and they love it. Will you help us?

ANGELA. Yes, of course we will. What fun! Is Professor Joad coming?

MUTCH. My God!

PADRE. No. We're relying on what I may call local talent. I'd better tell you who the other members are. There's the local doctor, he's a very clever man. He won all sorts of medals at Edinburgh. Then, of course, there's Lady Dodd.

PROUT. Why "of course"?

PADRE. Well, she's a very busy woman, and it was very nice of her to jump at the suggestion—and she's very popular with the troops. And then there's Mr. Byres.

PROUT. Who's he?

PADRE. He's the Member of Parliament for the county. Of course he's a Labour Member, but I don't think we should

[6].

168

allow that to weigh with us in war-time, do you ? I've told him he mustn't talk politics.

PROUT. Why shouldn't he ? If he's a Labour Member politics are the only things under heaven that he knows anything about. Are you going to forbid me to talk about painting ? Aren't you going to allow Angela to talk about poetry ? Aren't you going to talk about religion ?

PADRE. Well, I'm not as a matter of fact. You and Mrs. Prout can talk about what you like. But one has to be so careful, hasn't one ? We don't want to hurt anyone's feelings.

PROUT. That's why nobody goes to church nowadays. You don't want to hurt anyone's feelings. You can't say, " It's a fine day " without hurting somebody's feelings ; so you've got to talk meaningless gibberish.

ANGELA. Darling, the Padre is not talking meaningless gibberish.

PROUT. I know. But the result is that he's hurt my feelings very severely.

PADRE. Oh, have I ? I hope not.

PROUT (*walking up and down*). I'm a workman—a plain man of my hands. But I'm the best workman in my own line of business in the British Islands ; and I'm to be made a cock-shy with a row of other Aunt Sallies, including my Lady Dodd, God bless her, to keep the British soldier out of the public-house where he'd be much better employed. Do you realise, sir, that I take the profession of Michael Angelo and Velasquez with some seriousness ?

PADRE. Of course I realise that. I take my own humble profession with some seriousness also. But that has nothing to do with the point. Even Michael Angelo could bring himself now and again to answer a polite question or two. And that's all I'm asking you to do. You'll persuade him, won't you, Mrs. Prout ?

ANGELA. I can't persuade him to do anything—even to change his underclothing.

MUTCH. I'll persuade him.

PADRE. Will you ?

69   [7]

MUTCH. Well, I don't know whether you would exactly call it persuasion. But if I hear him standing on his dignity as an artist something will impel me to lick the living soul-case out of him.

PADRE. Dear me!

ANGELA. He could, you know. He used to box for his university. And George is a terrible physical coward. He won't even milk Lady Cabstanleigh because he's afraid she might butt him.

PROUT. Of course if you wish to lay bare the most secret corners of our private life to every Tom, Dick and Harry who happens to drop in. . . .

ANGELA. Nonsense, George. Mr. Paris and Miss What's-her-name aren't Tom, Dick and Harry. Besides you said yourself that it would be a better world if we all told the truth about ourselves.

PROUT. There you go again. I told you that in confidence.

ANGELA. That's another thing about him, Mr. Paris. He talks platitudes in confidence.

PROUT. All right, let's take all our clothes off. Show him your appendix scar, Angela, won't you? And I've got a most entertaining birth mark. I don't think there's anything particularly interesting about Jimmy—except that he looks damned funny in the buff.

MUTCH. Really, George. But come along, let's get cracking. We're wasting time. The Padre wants to know all about us.

ANGELA (to JESSIE). What a lovely ring you're wearing.

JESSIE. We're not supposed to wear them when we're in uniform, but the Padre lets me wear it when I'm driving him.

ANGELA. It's a beauty.

JESSIE. Yes, isn't it? I wouldn't have got a ring like this only Walter—that's my boy-friend—saved an old pawn-broker from getting beaten up in the black-out. I don't know how he did it. He's like your old man, he's not much of a scrapper; but he says he remembered one or two dirty tricks from the unarmed combat course. He wouldn't tell me what they were. Said they weren't fit for a lady to hear.

ANGELA. Still, you must be very proud of him.

JESSIE. Oh, I don't know.

ANGELA. You don't know! He comes back to you like a privateering captain and throws the spoils of the Indies into your lap and you say you don't know!

JESSIE. Well, I don't, and that's the truth. You see, he hasn't got much of an education.

MUTCH. He seems to have picked up one or two quite valuable pieces of information in his physical training class. After all, that's what education does, doesn't it? Or ought to do. It fits one to meet emergencies.

JESSIE. Oh *that* kind of education! He's got plenty of that, and he's a good mechanic too. But that's not what I call education.

MUTCH. What do you call education?

JESSIE. How should I know? I never had any.

ANGELA. Then what do you mean?

JESSIE. Oh, I don't know. Being able to talk about things like you three here and the Padre and that. The way I look at it, Walter can only talk about what I look like, and his blooming engines and that. That's all right in its way, but it's going to spread out a bit thin over thirty or forty years. And education makes you understand people. Walter doesn't understand me a bit. He says so himself.

ANGELA. But surely if you're both at the same level of education. . . .

JESSIE. Well, it seems to me that if you are neither of you is any better off. I think people should marry to better themselves, don't you? Or anyway at least one of them ought to be better off.

ANGELA. Dear me! That is very materialistic of you. Almost commercial. What about falling in love?

JESSIE. I don't know so much about that. I mean falling in love's very nice and all that, but where's your guarantee that both of them are going to be in love till death doth them part? It's taking a big risk.

ANGELA. But if a thing's worth doing it is worth taking a big risk for it.

JESSIE. That's what my father used to say, and mother and me had to whip round the neighbours to pay for his funeral. You see where I come from in Civvy Street we only talk about things. We don't talk about what they're all about. They go on happening and they don't seem to mean anything, somehow. That's why I sometimes think I'd like to marry a man with brains and spend the rest of my life trying to find out what it all means.

ANGELA. I wouldn't do that if I were you.

JESSIE. But I want to know, you see.

PADRE. Well, well, well, we can thrash that out on Friday.

ANGELA. On Friday, is it ?

PADRE. Yes, next Friday. I'm sorry it's such short notice, but may I take it that you will come ?

ANGELA. But of course we'll come. We are boring each other stiff here, and it will be a great treat to bore somebody else for a change.

MUTCH. I don't know whether I shall be here next Friday. I only came down for a week-end and I've been here for ten days.

ANGELA. You can go away on Saturday, so it's all arranged.

PADRE. Splendid, splendid. We'll send a car for you at half past seven and that will give you time to have a glass of South African sherry in the Mess before we go round to the Recreation Hut. I'm certain that you will enjoy it and I know that the troops will be immensely honoured.

HE *gets up*.

Now I must get back. Oh, my goodness, my saccharine ! (*Picks up box.*) Thank you so much for the tea, Mrs. Prout. We shall all look forward to a most interesting evening.

ANGELA. I suppose we'll have to answer a lot of terrifying questions ?

JESSIE. I shall ask one.

MUTCH. Oh, will you ? What will you ask ?

PADRE. That's not fair. You mustn't know the questions beforehand.

ANGELA (*to* JESSIE). You must come round and have tea again. You can bring any of the girls who would like to come, and Walter too if you like.

JESSIE. If you don't mind I would rather come myself.

PADRE. Now we must get cracking. *Au revoir.*

OMNES. Goody-bye. Good-afternoon.

ANGELA (*going out*). I'm afraid we've not been very hospitable to the camp people, but then we're not very hospitable people.

PADRE (*going out*). Oh, indeed you are.

EXEUNT ANGELA, JESSIE *and* PADRE.

PROUT. I say, Jimmy.

MUTCH. Yes, George?

PROUT. That was an odd thing you said.

MUTCH. What?

PROUT. You said you'd give me a hammering if I didn't go. Do you know that I suddenly believed you?

MUTCH. Oh, well, I mean to say, good gracious me!

PROUT. Do you remember my first day at school?

MUTCH. Well, no, not exactly.

PROUT. My old man put me in your charge, and you took over quite solemnly, and he gave you half-a-sovereign. Then you took me into your stinking little cubby-hole and do you remember what you said?

MUTCH. No. No, I don't.

PROUT. You said to me—" You were always a conceited little bastard, and I don't like the way you walk on your heels, or, indeed, anything about you. But I promised your guv'nor I'd do my best for you, and I will . . . I'm going to knock some of the bloody side out of you to save the beaks and the other fellows the trouble." Then you gave me the hammering of my life. You sadistic little swine that you were. . . . I had exactly the same feeling a moment ago. It was astonishing and most unpleasant.

73

[11]

MUTCH. Well, I hope it did you no harm. I remember now you *were* a cocky little brute. I probably did you a damned good turn.

PROUT. I spent the next fortnight thinking out ways of killing you. But it never came to anything.

MUTCH. Not yet, eh?

PROUT. Not yet, but I don't suppose I ever will kill you; you amuse me and Angela likes you—I can't think why.

MUTCH. Probably because I'm not rude to her in public.

PROUT. Rude to her? In public? Me? Good Gubbins. Pull yourself together, Jimmy. Angela and I are terrific pals.

MUTCH. I know that.

PROUT. I think in the whole circle of my acquaintance we're the only happy couple who are legally married. We're terrific pals. I don't know what I should do without her, blast her! Where is she, by the way?

MUTCH. She must have gone down to the gate with the Padre.

PROUT. Trying to fascinate him, I suppose. Poor old devil, that's not her line of country. I think that's probably why I like her so much—she's so completely unfascinating. I'd hate to be married to one of these disturbing women. They're as selfish as hell, and full of unscrupulous tricks. But Angy's not like that. She's no Helen of Troy, and I know it, and she knows it, and she knows I know it. And so we get on like a house on fire.

MUTCH. Oh, you do, do you? I mean, do you?

PROUT. Well, don't we? You know as well as anybody that we do—damn it.

MUTCH. Yes, I suppose you do. Yes, oh yes, rather, of course, yes. Now, about onions. I mean you can say what you like, but I'm perfectly certain that you should have earthed them over. I mean to say in a climate like this with late frosts and God knows what . . . I mean my point is this, that it stands to reason. . . .

PROUT. Reason's got nothing to do with it. It's a matter

of experience. You only plant the roots. You leave the rest of the onion above ground.

MUTCH. Well, I'm perfectly certain that's wrong.

PROUT. My dear fellow, it's no use evolving methods of growing onions out of your inner consciousness. You can only grow imaginary onions that way. And what's the good of an imaginary onion? It won't cheat you of a sigh or charm you to a tear.

MUTCH. But if a thing is logically and demonstrably wrong, surely to goodness. . . .

PROUT. You don't know what you're talking about.

MUTCH. Neither do you.

PROUT. That's perfectly true, but a jobbing gardener told me——

MUTCH. But nobody would be a jobbing gardener if he had any intellectual capacity whatever. I mean to say, it's notorious. . . .

PROUT. You'd better ask your wonderful Brains Trust if you want to know how to grow onions.

MUTCH. But we are the Brains Trust.

PROUT. Speak for yourself, I'm not going.

MUTCH. You damned well are.

PROUT. My dear Puggy. . . .

MUTCH. Now what in the world made you call me that? Wasn't it funny? I haven't been called Puggy for twenty-five years.

PROUT. I don't know. Funny that.

MUTCH. Anyhow you must admit there's something *wrong* with the onions.

PROUT. I know that; but it's nothing to do with the way they were planted. You don't suppose I would plant onions without getting some sort of expert advice? Good heavens! I know my own limitations.

RE-ENTER ANGELA.

MUTCH. Then what are you talking about?

PROUT. Hullo.

ANGELA. Are you two quarrelling again?

PROUT. More or less, but you needn't look so pleased about it. We're not quarrelling about you.

ANGELA. Oh.

ANGELA starts to clear the tea-things on to the tray.

ANGELA. That was quite interesting.

PROUT. What was?

ANGELA. That girl.

PROUT. What was interesting about her? A very ordinary type I thought.

ANGELA. It was her little romance that was interesting.

MUTCH. What? With the mechanic?

ANGELA. No. She's madly in love with the Padre.

PROUT. Don't be so damned silly. He's not that sort.

ANGELA. I didn't say he was in love with her, but she was watching him all the time out of the corners of her eyes. She was frightened to look at him for fear of giving herself away, except when our backs were turned. And she keyed herself up whenever he opened his mouth. Besides, what do you think she was talking about?

MUTCH. She was talking about education. She seemed to have some sort of mystical regard for it.

ANGELA. Mystical all right!

She picks up the tray.

Mind you I don't think he has the least idea that she's crazy about him.

PROUT. You think everybody's crazy about somebody else. You should write musical comedies.

MUTCH. Let me help you with that tray.

ANGELA. Oh, don't bother, Jimmy.

MUTCH. I insist.

ANGELA. You're a perfect gentleman.

Gives him the tray.

PROUT. Not like me I suppose.

ANGELA. Not a bit like you.

MUTCH goes out with the tray.

PROUT. I suppose that unfortunate love-lorn stiff will wash ¦e dishes.

ANGELA. Don't be so vulgar.

PROUT. I thought we were supposed to be.

ANGELA. What do you mean by that?

PROUT. Well, you've just been poking your nose into the ¦mours of a little A.T. driver who's got nothing to do with ¦ou.

ANGELA. Everybody has to do with everybody else. We ¦n't all lead utterly selfish lives like you.

PROUT. I'm selfish, am I?

ANGELA. Yes, very.

RE-ENTER MUTCH.

PROUT. Aren't you going to wash up?

MUTCH. Oh, do you want me to?

PROUT. Of course. It isn't my turn.

ANGELA. Let them alone. I'll give them a wallop round ¦hen we're getting the supper ready. Sit down, you must be ¦red.

MUTCH *throws himself down on the settee.*

MUTCH. Do you know, I think you're right.

ANGELA. Right about what, Jimmy?

MUTCH. About the A.T. She had that sort of faithful dog ¦ok.

PROUT. You don't call female dogs, dogs.

ANGELA. He can if he likes—go on, Jimmy. Besides, she ¦n't.

MUTCH. Of course not. She looks a very decent little girl ¦ me. What does she see in him, do you think? And she's ¦gaged to another fellow.

ANGELA. I expect she thinks he's a perfect gent. She's quite ¦ght, so he is.

MUTCH. She raised two very interesting points.

ANGELA. Yes, she did. What were they by the way—I ¦rget.

MUTCH. Well, there was a point about whether one shoul
marry into a higher intellectual level than one's own with th
idea of making some sort of positive profit. There ought t
be some sort of biological gain in that, if you see what I mear
I mean if they have offspring.

ANGELA. Yes, but it cuts both ways, doesn't it ? If on
marries up the other marries down.

MUTCH. Yes, on the intellectual plane. But we've got t
consider the physical plane too. What you lose on the shi
you make up on the round-abouts.

ANGELA. I see. What was the other point ?

MUTCH. Oh, whether an intellectual background fits on
specially to solve the problems of life.

ANGELA. I should have thought there was no doubt abou
that.

MUTCH. I wonder.

PROUT. An intellectual background wasn't much help t
you in attacking the problem of spring onions. I'm going o
to have a look at them. I'll try instinct and experience.

MUTCH. Instinct's got nothing to do with it, and you've ha
no experience.

PROUT. No, but the gardener has.

EXIT PROUT. *Short silenc*

ANGELA. No, but honestly. . . .

MUTCH. Honestly what ?

ANGELA. It is rather touching, isn't it ?

MUTCH. You mean the little atsie ?

ANGELA. Yes.

MUTCH. An infant crying in the night, an infant crying fo
the light, and with no language save a cry.

ANGELA. Yes. I wish we could help her. We ought to b
able to help her.

MUTCH. What exactly do you mean by " help her " ?

ANGELA. You of all people ought to know.

MUTCH. Well, I don't quite know what line you think w
ought to take. Should we do a bit of fifth column work o

the Padre, I mean to say? And then help her to break down his defences? I mean to say she'd probably be much better off with Walter.

ANGELA. No, no, no, no, no. I don't mean that at all. No. I mean, these people haven't been taught to think clearly and straightly and *starkly*. When they get into an emotional tangle they don't know what to do. I found that out when Polly Wotherspoon used to take me down to her Girls' Club. I mean they simply didn't know what I was talking about; and I'm a simple enough soul.

MUTCH. Yes, you are.

ANGELA. But what about this girl?

MUTCH. What about her?

ANGELA. Well, you know as well as I do that these unsolved problems grow into complexes and complexes grow into neuroses. Now I should think this girl has a very good brain. Not a first-class brain, and undeveloped, of course. But I think one could make something of her.

MUTCH. The difficulty is to make some sort of contact. I mean to say, after all, in the name of goodness, she doesn't speak our language.

ANGELA. Yes. Yes. There's that.

MUTCH. And should anyone, I mean, interfere in anyone else's life? I mean to say it never comes off.

ANGELA. But, Jimmy. It isn't interfering if somebody who can't swim falls into the water and you've had swimming lessons and dive in after them.

MUTCH. Yes. There's that. But I've a feeling it's a false analogy.

ANGELA. Not at all. She's floundering and splashing and puffing and blowing. She doesn't know what to do. It's a perfect analogy.

MUTCH. Well, you may be right.

ANGELA. And she wants our help. She promised to come to tea.

MUTCH. She said she'd ask the Brains Trust too.

ANGELA. Yes, she did. But I don't see much good in that. You can't answer questions like that in a Brains Trust.

MUTCH. Why not? I mean to say, what's the use of sitting there and answering questions that don't matter?

ANGELA. I wonder what her question's going to be. I wonder whether we can answer it.

MUTCH. Oh well, after all, I mean to say, one has a good deal of experience in answering much more complicated questions than this girl is likely to excogitate.

ANGELA. Yes—you are clever, Jimmy.

MUTCH. Oh, good heavens. I mean to say, it's my job, that kind of cleverness.

ANGELA. All the same, if you don't mind my saying so, do you know I sometimes think you—intellectualise—*things*—a little too much?

MUTCH. Well, now, perhaps it is quite true that I have a sort of a tendency to sublimate emotions and impulses into some sort of rationalised and connected intellectual system. But why not? I mean to say, we have developed ratiocinating faculties no doubt for some sort of coherent purpose—or at least as part of a more or less intelligible process. And after all there's a certain satisfaction in the exercise of one's more highly developed faculties.

ANGELA. Yes . . . I suppose so . . . yes. I suppose there *is* a certain satisfaction.

MUTCH. Well, I mean, isn't there? I mean, take you and me. I mean, there you are.

ANGELA. Yes.

> *They look at one another. It almost seems as if they were about to exercise their less highly developed faculties when* PROUT *shouts.*

PROUT (*calling without*). Jimmy!
MUTCH. Yes, George?

HE *gets up*

What is it?

[18]

18c

PROUT. Come here a minute—I want you.

MUTCH. Right-ho.

                                    EXIT MUTCH.

    ANGELA *blows her nose rather loudly and* EXITS *by the curtained doorway.*

CURTAIN

END OF ACT I

ACT II

The scene is the stage of a Recreation Hut in som
military centre or other in Scotland. It is set for th
first scene of an old-fashioned pantomime. The villa
inn is on one side and the squire's manor is on th
other. The scenery is extremely shabby. A long de
table is set downstage with seven Windsor chair
behind it. The lighting is very brilliant.

The PADRE *in battle dress and clerical collar bustles i*
He notices that the curtain is up and turns
the audience after laying a sheaf of papers on th
table.

PADRE. I say, excuse me, won't you? We've got the cur
tain up rather prematurely. Oh dear, what a frightful glar
of lights; I must do something about it. Jessie! I won't be
minute. . . . Electrics! Jessie!

ENTER JESSIE *in khaki dungaree.*

Look here, Jessie, we can't sit here below all these light
We'd be blinded. Look, could you take down those thingum
bobs a bit and put on the amber floats? You see what
mean? We don't want to be blinded.

JESSIE. Rightio.

EXIT JESSIE *to Prompt sid*

The lights begin to go through a series of vagarie.

Green ligh

PADRE. Oh, no, not green, Jessie, anything but green.

Amber foots alon

PADRE. Yes, that's all right, but look, Jessie, it's here w
want the light, here on the table.

Foots off—white glare at the back. Doesn't see them fo
a moment then looks.

PADRE. No, no, Jessie, we're sitting down there.

Lights change to moderate lighting.

PADRE. Look now, Jessie, can you hear me? I only wanted the slightest modification.

Black out.

Discovers audience.

PADRE. Jessie, now please keep your head, and bring up your ambers; Jessie, you must have ambers.

Ambers up and foots.

PADRE. Now we're getting somewhere, Jessie—now just a little bit more on the table.

Foots out.

Jessie, I said leave it at that.

Lights properly.

The stage is gradually lit by an unconventional but rather agreeable glow.

PADRE. I'm terribly sorry, ladies and gentlemen. Walter, the electrician has had a motor bicycle accident and I'm afraid Jessie isn't quite up to it yet. He recommended her, but, you see, she's his fiancée and perhaps his judgment was a little bit biased. I don't know whether she's responsible for the rather *exotic* setting. Most of you saw the A.T.S. pantomime last night. I confess I feel a bit like a demon king.

Black out. Red light.

EXIT PADRE.

Ad lib JESSIE ENTERS, *sits down in front of Proscenium and begins to eat an apple.* RE-ENTER PADRE *ushering in the* BRAINS TRUST :—LADY DODD, ANGELA, MUTCH, JOE BYRES, DR. MACADAM *and* GEORGE PROUT. *They sit down at the table in the following order :—* BYRES, PROUT, LADY DODD, PADRE, MRS. PROUT, MUTCH, MACADAM. *The* PADRE *at once rises.*

PADRE. Ladies and gentlemen, it is my pleasant duty as Question Master to introduce to you tonight's Brains Trust.

On my extreme right, without further ado, is Mr. George
Prout. He is a very celebrated painter of—er—oil paintings
He is a—a—Member of the Royal Institute of—of—Oi
Painters. A very distinguished body of men who—whe
paint oil paintings. If there are any questions about art,
feel perfectly certain he will be able to deal with them—
especially if they have anything to do with—ah—oil paintings
Next to him, I am very happy to be able to tell you, is Pro
fessor James Alexander Mutch, of the University of Skerry
vore, and, at one time, of Balliol College, Oxford. He is
great expert on Metaphysics—and has written several books o
the subject—besides being a well known anthropologist an
one of our best known collectors of postage stamps. So i
there are any questions about metaphysics or postage stamp:
I am sure that they will be very ably dealt with——Jessi¢
must you sit there? Can't you get a seat?

JESSIE. I'm sorry, sir, I can't hear from the switchboar¢
I won't get in your way.

PADRE. But are you comfortable?

JESSIE. Oh, quite, thank you.

PADRE. I need not introduce Lady Dodd. Many of u
have been, I hope, welcome visitors to her house and groun¢
and to her kennels and we are under a very deep debt ¢
gratitude to her. Lady Dodd is, as you know, the Presider
of the County Branch of the Friends of the Fourfootec
Feathered and Furry. This by no means exhausts her act
vities, but perhaps I can spare her blushes and pass on t
Mrs. Prout—I hardly know whether to call her Mrs. Prout ¢
Angela Kilpatrick. She is the author of several delightf
books—often of poetry—and has edited a children's mag
zine. She also is very interested in puppets and will, perhap
some day, give us a little show. Will you? Thank you :
much. Then we have our old friend Dr. Macadam—
distinguished graduate in medicine of, I believe, Edinbur;
University. Then we are very happy to have with us Mr. J¢
Byres, who is a Member of Parliament for the Borough ¢
Baikie. We have no politics here and we are very happy

have him with us. And now we shall get down to the business of the evening. The questions are on anything that comes up your backs. The Brains Trust hasn't seen any of them. I've picked them more or less as they come. Naturally I have barred questions on politics and religion and questions showing ill-timed facetiousness. We really can't discuss politics or religion in a mixed gathering like this and, of course the C.O. won't have smut. What's left makes a pretty good lot.

The first is from Leading Aircraftswoman Dixon. She asks, " What makes cows in a field run after railway trains ? " Perhaps we might ask Lady Dodd to kick off. Now, Lady Dodd, " What makes cows in a field run after railway trains ? " (*Sits.*)

LADY DODD. Well, now. That *is* a question ! I've often wondered myself. My aunt was a great friend of Sir James Barrie and he told her that they were running to catch any babies that might fall out of the windows. I hardly think it can be that, though, mind you, cows are frightfully intelligent. They have such speaking eyes. I often wonder what they are speaking about. If we only knew !

PADRE. Thank you, Lady Dodd. Professor ?

MUTCH. Well, I mean to say, are we entitled to suppose that they have any, at least, I mean, reason in point of fact for running after the train at all, if you follow me ?

LADY DODD. Oh, they must have, they must have !

MUTCH. Well, I don't know. When one talks about *reason,* I mean to say one is going head over heels into the psychological aspect, and, I mean, after all, *have* cows a psychological aspect ? I mean to say, we don't know enough about it. It may be a simple problem in bio-physics. But we simply don't know. Do we ? I mean, you see my point ?

PADRE. Yes, of course. Thank you. Mr. Byres ?

BYRES. They get excited by the noise and the clatter. You'll no' see cows running in a field where a lot of trains pass. They get used to it.

PADRE. Thank you. Mrs. Prout ?

ANGELA. I agree with Mr. Byres. I think any kind of vague tumult is exciting and makes us want to jump or run or something. I think they run after the train instead of away from it because they like it. They like the monotony to be broken. Cows have very monotonous lives, you must remember.

PROUT. I don't agree. Most human beings live far more monotonous lives than cows. And if there's one thing they hate it's to have the monotony broken. Besides, cows don't run after trains.

ANGELA. Yes, they do, George.

PROUT. No, they don't. Anyhow, cows are females. What's the good of worrying about why they do anything on the living earth?

PADRE. Order, order! Dr. Macadam. Perhaps you will sum up.

MACADAM. What? What was the question?

PADRE. Why do cows run after railway trains?

MACADAM. I haven't the slightest idea.

PADRE. Well, I think we've had very varied and satisfactory answers to that most interesting question. I think the Trust has decided that it would be unwise to go too far into the cow's motives. . . . The next question is a very interesting one. It is from 857643 Lance Corporal Jenks W., of the Corps of Military Police. Corporal Jenks asks: "What are the guiding principles that lead a community to accept a canon of aesthetic values?" Yes. . . .

LADY DODD. What on earth does that mean?

PADRE. Now you're asking me! I think it means, if you look at a picture, say, or a lot of chaps look at a picture and say, "By Jove, that's jolly good," what makes them think so? I think this is Mr. Prout's cup of tea. Come along now, Mr. Prout, you're an artist. (*Sits.*)

PROUT. The only man who knows how to look at pictures is the man who paints them.

PADRE. Oh, come, come, come, !

ANGELA. What nonsense, George!

LADY DODD. I don't think myself. . . .

PROUT. There are plenty of idiots who chatter about pictures, but for all they see they might have one glass eye and the other stuffed with treacle. It makes me sick.

BYRES. You might as well say the only one who appreciates you is your mother.

PROUT. That's quite true. She *is* the only one. Was, rather, she's dead.

LADY DODD. I'm so sorry.

PROUT. Not at all.

PADRE. Perhaps we should pass on to the next question. Gunner McGuire wants to know if civilisation is, in the opinion of the Brains Trust, a failure; and what is civilisation anyway? We ought to have some good answers to that. Mrs. Prout?

ANGELA. We had better answer the second part first, hadn't we?

PADRE. As you wish. " What is civilisation, anyway? "

ANGELA. Civilisation, surely, is the application of knowledge and experience to the good of the greatest number of people.

PROUT. Oh, is it? You count a certain number of fat heads, and then try how far whatever you've got'll go round? That's not civilisation. You can have a civilisation if you've got half a dozen sensible men and a thousand million mugs. But the mugs have no part in it.

BYRES. They haven't, haven't they? Then it's high time they had.

PADRE. Oh—ah—well, I'm afraid we're getting perilously near politics. Perhaps Lady Dodd can give us an idea of what she understands by " civilisation " and whether she thinks it's a failure.

LADY DODD. Oh, I don't think it's a failure at all. There are lots of things one would like to see altered—but I think that on the whole we can say that we are making for righteousness. And nobody could say during this war, at any rate, that we are not a united nation moving forward in a commo.
cause.

PADRE. I think we are all very much indebted to Lady Dodd
for her very frank and penetrating answer.

MUTCH (*Hand up*).

PADRE. Oh, you wish to say something, Professor?

MUTCH. Well, I suppose I ought to say something, as it's
a matter I've thought about a good deal. I mean to say, we
must start, I mean, *this is important*. . . . We must start by
having absolutely clear ideas about what we mean by what we
are talking about. . . . I mean to say, it isn't as if there had
only been one civilisation. There have been dozens and
dozens and dozens. It's hopeless. . . . I mean, you've got to get
down to brass tacks. I could go on all night about that, but
perhaps I'd better not.

PADRE. Perhaps not. Thank you very much. Mr. Byres?
(*Shaking his finger playfully.*) But no politics mind. What do
you think of civilisation?

BYRES. I don't think much of it.

PADRE. Well, that's very much to the point. Well, I think
I may say that the Brains Trust thinks that there is a great deal
to be said for civilisation as we know it, and that there is life
in the old dog yet.

BYRES. At the same time I must say that a civilisation built
from top to bottom out of humbug, class-privilege and the
profit motive is about as fancy a bit of jerry-building as ever
I heard of. You'll see the whole jinghang come down with
a fine-like clatter.

PADRE. Quite, Mr. Byres. Now we'll get along to the next
question.

PROUT. But I agree with every word you say. Every beautiful device that we human beings have invented to keep the
gorillas and yahoos in order will be destroyed.

BYRES. What do you mean by gorillas and yah-hoos?

PROUT. I mean your sacred proletariat.

BYRES. Well, I'm blessed! Who do you think you are,
anyhow? The Chairman here says you make your living
by painting pictures. I haven't seen any of your pictures, but
what are pictures anyway? A bit of bourgeois decoration.

[26]

My wee girl of twelve paints pictures. But if I catch her putting on airs because she can put down on paper a thing that looks like a horse or a chrysanthemum, she'd get the skelping of her life.

PADRE.   Order, order! We must get on to the next question

PROUT.   Tickle my catastrophe! You can't argue with anybody. You can only bluster and rant. I never met a Labour politician who could do anything but bluster and rant.

BYRES.   Oh, is that so? Well, if you're asking for home truths you'll get them; and if you're asking for a punch on the nose, you'll get it.

PADRE.   Order! Order! Really, Mr. Byres. Really, Mr. Prout. I think you're both out of order, if you don't mind my saying so.

BYRES.   Well, I demand an apology.

PROUT.   Well then, I apologise.

BYRES.   I accept your apology.

PADRE.   Well, that's very nice. Very nice, indeed. And now we'll get along to the next question. It is a most interesting question sent in from Bombardier Benskin. Bombardier Benskin wants to know whether there is any evidence for the belief that living creatures exist on the moon's surface?

MUTCH.   On the what?

PADRE.   On the surface of the moon. Well, Professor? Perhaps we'll ask you to answer this question. Is there any evidence of life on the surface of the moon?

MUTCH.   No.

PADRE.   I beg your pardon?

MUTCH.   No.

PADRE.   Oh . . . We . . . You mean there's no evidence whatever?

MUTCH.   No.

LADY DODD.   None at all?

MUTCH.   No.

LADY DODD.   That seems very peculiar to me.

PADRE. Well, I think we must take it, Bombardier Benskin, there's no evidence of life on the moon. We come now to the next question. The next question is from Quartermaster Sergeant Murdo MacPherson. It reads as follows : " What is planning ? Who does it ? And who is going to carry out the plans ? " I think we ought to ask the Professor what he understands by planning ?

MUTCH. Well, it depends what you mean by planning.

PROUT. We're asking what *you* mean by planning ?

MUTCH. Well, I mean, to say, isn't planning a sort of synthesis of correlated probabilities interdigitated into a sort of a—kind of a—well, *pattern*—with the ultimate idea of translating the resulting probabilities into some—some sort of concrete matrix ? I should think that's perfectly clear.

PADRE. Well. . . .

ANGELA. But who is to *do* this planning ? Experts ? Or just anybody ?

MUTCH. Oh, experts, of course.

PROUT. Experts at what ?

MUTCH. Experts on planning.

LADY DODD. But who are these experts ? I wouldn't go so far as to say the Labour Party is unfit to govern—I knew Ramsay MacDonald very well—a charming man ; and my husband was at school with Mr. Attlee. But, there it is. Organising a whole huge Empire isn't a very easy matter. I think the people who run the show ought to have some experience and *background*. Or don't you think so, Professor ?

MUTCH. Oh yes, certainly. I think that's an absolute necessity. I mean to say, but of course, it depends on what background exactly. That is most important. I mean to say, it's quite hopeless if you don't . . . well, take, for example——

PROUT. What it boils down to is, who is going to be boss ? And you and I will have damned little to say to that.

LADY DODD. You're what used to be called a mugwump, aren't you, Mr. Prout ?

PROUT. I am, and proud of it.

ANGELA. Well, you shouldn't be. I think this Brains Trust could run the Empire very well.

JESSIE. I don't.

PADRE. I beg your pardon?

JESSIE. Nothing. Sorry.

ANGELA. Wait a minute. Why don't you think so?

JESSIE. If you're going to order a lot of human beings about you've got to be human, see? This Brains Trust isn't human.

PADRE. Allowing for the fact that the interruption is entirely out of order, Jessie, and if I may be permitted to make a mild observation, I should say that if this Brains Trust has a fault it is that it has been a little too human so far.

JESSIE. It can't be too human, but you're all ladyships and M.P.s and artists and things. Look at the professor. He's not human.

MUTCH. You're a damned liar.

PADRE. Oh, I say, come, come, order, order.

JESSIE. Well show it then. You've been asked all sorts of questions what human beings are ever so interested in and all you do is show off, and not very well either at that.

PADRE. Really, Jessie, I can't allow this sort of thing.

ANGELA. But I want to know what this girl's driving at. If my husband and I aren't human I don't know who is.

JESSIE. Perhaps you are in your way. Okey-doke, carry on.

PADRE. With the young lady's kind permission we will carry on. The next question is from—let me see—Private— oh, dear me—something—it looks like Hezekiah. No. It's . . . Private J. B. I can't make this out.

JESSIE. Killigrew.

PADRE. Eh? What?

JESSIE. Killigrew, Jessie Killigrew.

PADRE. Oh, it's you, Jessie?

JESSIE. Yes, it's me.

PADRE. That's very interesting. Jessie wants to know whether . . . I can't make it out. It looks like marshmallow.

191   [29]

JESSIE. Is marriage a good idea ?

PADRE. I beg your pardon ? I wish you wouldn't speak with your mouth full.

JESSIE. That's the question. Is marriage a good idea ? And if it is what's the best way to choose a partner ?

PADRE. I thought it was marshmallow. Very stupid of me. Well then, Private Jessie Killigrew would like to know whether, in the opinion of the Brains Trust, marriage is a good idea. Lady Dodd ?

LADY DODD. I think it's an excellent idea. I think that, perhaps, with the exception of kindness to animals, it is one of the best ideas in the world ; except Christianity, of course. But Christianity takes it all in, doesn't it ? I mean they wouldn't let us get married in churches unless it were a frightfully good plan, would they ? Anyhow, I'm married, and very glad I am, although poor Lord Dodd is a martyr to osteo-arthritis as many of you know.

PADRE. Thank you, Lady Dodd. Dr. Macadam, you have been very silent. What do you think about it ?

MACADAM. I am sorry. I didn't catch the question.

PADRE. Is marriage a good idea ?

MACADAM. I don't know whether it's a good idea or a bad idea, but it's an inevitable idea. Mind you, it's a contract very few sane people would enter into ; but, in point of fact, hardly any sane people do enter into it.

LADY DODD. Oh, Doctor, what a dreadful thing to say !

MACADAM. What was that ?

LADY DODD. I said that was an awful thing to say.

MACADAM. Well, it's quite true. If falling in love isn't going mad, I've never seen a lunatic. It's a state of sub-acute mania with alternations of exaltation and depression and persistent hallucinations. Nobody's fit to make a contract in such a state.

LADY DODD. Then how—oh, I beg your pardon (*to Padre*)— do you account for the fact that there are thousands and thousands of happy marriages ? People do live happy ever after.

MACADAM. Happy ever after? Of course they are, some of them. Anyone can get on with anybody else if he tries hard enough. If I went blindfolded to any cinema queue and picked out a female, she and I could live happily enough ever after if we had to. And that's how it's done, I solemnly assure you.

BYRES. If it's as easy as all that, why didn't you get married?

MACADAM. Because I never went mad. We'd have no marriages unless we went mad, and we'd be in a fine mess without it.

PADRE. Oh, thank you, Doctor. Well, now, Mrs. Prout?

ANGELA (*gently*). I must have been mad when I got married.

PROUT. That's a nice thing to say in public.

JESSIE. Never mind about the public. Get on with it.

PADRE. Really, Jessie! This is getting to be a bit too much of a good thing.

JESSIE. But I want to know. Me and my boy-friend has had words about it, and the pictures are all hooey, and the books are just daft. If you ladies and gents, with all this background that we hear so much about, can't settle a thing like that I don't think much of you. Only you've got to be human—honest you have.

> PADRE *attempts to interrupt.*

ANGELA. It's all right. I'll do my best. I remember when I first met George. The only thing I thought about him was that I didn't think his finger nails were very clean, and he hadn't shaved properly. There was a horrid little bit of stubble at the angle of his jaw.

JESSIE. That's a bit more like it.

PROUT. To be perfectly candid I didn't think you were much to look at either. You had a way of flinching whenever you said anything; it irritated me abominably.

ANGELA. I remember noticing a rather peculiar and distinctly unpleasant smell. It is rather difficult to describe.

PADRE. I don't think you need attempt to describe it here, Mrs. Prout.

ANGELA. Well, it wasn't a religious smell and it wasn't a political smell. There was some turpentine and some rather stale tobacco. (PROUT *turns away*.) Perhaps that's why I flinched. I was out for a walk with my puppy I remember, and he suddenly began to bite Mr. Prout's shoes. That's how we got to know each other.

LADY DODD. The darling ! What kind of puppy was he ?

ANGELA. He was an Aberdeen terrier.

LADY DODD. There's no love like a dog's love, is there ?

PROUT. He was a filthy little brute called Sambo. He bit through my last shoe-lace. I didn't like him any better at first sight than I liked his mistress. She looked like a bit of damp sea-weed ; she had a cold in the head.

ANGELA. It wasn't a very bad cold. It was just starting.

PROUT. It was quite bad enough.

ANGELA. Perhaps it's true to say that I wasn't looking my best.

PROUT. But your best isn't much either. . . . What the devil did we talk about ? I forget.

ANGELA. Wait a bit. I was just coming out of our house on the main street. My father was a country solicitor, you know. We had an old house right on the High Street with a most beautiful walled garden at the back with a little green gate and steps running down to the river.

Goes up steps. JESSIE *rises.*

Do you remember, George ?

PROUT. Yes, I remember.

ANGELA *wanders about up-stage in a vague manner.*

ANGELA. On the day we are speaking about I was going out to buy butter, and I thought I'd just take Sambo for very nearly his first walk. George was just coming out of the pub.

JESSIE. Like that pub over there ?

ANGELA. Yes. It was called the " Fox and Grapes." It was very like that pub.

PROUT (*jumping up*). Yes, by Jove. I remember thinking it

it was like a scene in a pantomime. The village street, I mean.
The village green was up there, nearly as green as that. The
main street ran down right where you chaps are sitting.   The
pub and the lawyer's house were just at the top of it. I was
living in the pub.

JESSIE (*excitedly*). Go into it. It's only a canvas pub. But
go into it now. We'll reconstruct the crime like they do in the
" Who Done Its."

PROUT. Shall we ? All right.

JESSIE. Hurry up, get cracking. Double march.

> PROUT *responds to the command and trots into the pub.*

ANGELA. Shall I go into the Manor ?

JESSIE. Yes, yes. Go on.

ANGELA. I had a cold. I always had a cold in the early
spring.

> SHE *disappears through the doorway of the Manor.*

JESSIE (*shouting*). A February morning, Mrs. Prout ?

ANGELA (*off*). Yes. 18th of February.

JESSIE. Right-ho. I'll fix it.

PADRE. Dear me, isn't this a little unusual ? I don't know
whether——Jessie !

BYRES. Let's have the next question.

PADRE. Do you think so ? Well, now, let me see——

> *Black out. Then raw lighting with plenty of blue in it.*

Good gracious me, what's happening to the lights ?
Jessie must be doing something to them.

> RE-ENTER JESSIE, *buttoning on her A.T.S. uniform
> jacket. She is wearing a hat.*

What on earth have you done to the lights ?

JESSIE. Sorry, sir—trying to make a February morning.

PADRE. Why on earth do you want to make a February
morning ?

JESSIE. Mrs. Prout wanted one.

PADRE. Well, really, this is supposed to be a Brains Trust.

How can the Trust use its brains if this sort of thing keeps on happening?

JESSIE. I'll give you a hand if you like, sir.

PADRE. What do you mean you'll give us a hand?

JESSIE. They teach us in the A.T.S. to use our brains in time of emergency. May I sit down, sir?

PADRE. Well, you seem to be running the whole show anyhow. I don't see why you shouldn't.

JESSIE. Thank you, sir.

BYRES. Come and sit beside me, Jessie.

> JESSIE *sits in* PROUT'S *seat.*

PADRE. Now may we go on?

JESSIE. Sorry! Certainly.

PADRE. And now, perhaps, we can consider——Good heavens, what's the matter, Mrs. Prout?

> ENTER ANGELA *from the Manor House.* She goes
> *through the motions of leading an imaginary dog.*

JESSIE. Sh . . . . please, sir.

ANGELA. Now Sambo, be a good doggie and go right inside. Cook's got a nice bone for you if you behave like a good, decent little doggie. You can't come for a walk with Angy. Do you hear me? You can't. Come here at once you bad dog.

> PROUT ENTERS *from the inn carrying an imaginary easel
> and painting materials.* He stumbles over the imaginary dog.

PROUT. Ough! Get out of the way, you little brute. You nearly had me down.

ANGELA. I'm so sorry. He's only a baby.

PROUT. Oh, that's all right.

ANGELA. Come here at once, you bad dog. You are very naughty and disobedient.

PROUT. Run along—do what you're told. You mustn't eat my feet. They're not nourishing.

ANGELA. Sambo!

> SHE *runs forward and gathers the imaginary dog into her arms.*

No licks now, you bad, bad dog. Angy's not friends with you any more. What a whipping you're going to get.

PROUT. I shouldn't beat him if I were you. You'll spoil his temper.

ANGELA. Hush! I've no intention of giving him a B-E-A-T-I-N-G; but he understands every word we say.

PROUT. Oh, come, come.

ANGELA. Yes, he does. These little Scotties are terribly intelligent.

PROUT. They've their own kind of intelligence, of course, but how can they understand spoken language?

ANGELA. I don't know. . . . I don't see how anybody can know. . . . Oh, look, he's bitten through your shoe-lace.

PROUT. So he has, damn him.

ANGELA. Do just wait a minute, I'll get another for you. There are some lying on the hall table. I bought them from a hawker this morning.

PROUT. Oh, not at all. Please don't trouble. I can tie the ends together.

ANGELA. No, no, it's no trouble at all.

> SHE *runs into the house.* PROUT *sits down on the step and begins to work with his shoelace.* ANGELA *appears almost immediately with a new lace.*

ANGELA. Take your shoe off and I'll lace it up for you. There's nobody about; or would you—would you care to come in?

PROUT. Oh, no thanks, it's quite all right, but do let me do it myself.

ANGELA. Not at all. It was my dog that did the damage.

> SHE *laces the shoe.*

You should have come in; but to tell you the truth, I was ashamed to ask you in. Father's gone away for a

week's fishing and Cook and I are doing the spring cleaning.
And we're rather picnicking.

PROUT. You've no mother?

ANGELA. No, she died last year. Are you staying at the Inn?

PROUT. Yes, I've been staying there for a week. I'm going
tomorrow.

ANGELA. It isn't very comfortable at the Inn.

PROUT. No.

ANGELA. Do they give you enough to eat?

PROUT. Quite enough. More than enough. The trouble is
that it's uneatable.

ANGELA. Oh, I am sorry. I say, do come in for five minutes.
At least we've got a good fire and I'll get Cook to make you
a cup of tea.

PROUT. That is very tempting.   (ANGELA *hands back shoe.*)
Oh, thank you. (*Takes shoe.*)

ANGELA. But I forgot. You want to go and paint.

PROUT. There's a flurry of sleet coming on. I don't think
I'll paint today.

HE *puts on his boot.*

ANGELA. And one of your feet must be frozen. Yes, it is!
What a pig I am. Do come in and get warm. I'll keep the
puppy dog locked up.

PROUT. Well, it's most awfully kind of you. Thanks, I will.

ANGELA *and* PROUT *go into the Manor.*

JESSIE (*getting up*). Excuse me a minute.

PADRE. What's the matter now?

JESSIE. I nearly forgot something.

PADRE. Forgot what?

JESSIE. The moon.

PADRE. She did say the moon? . . . .

EXIT JESSIE.

Do you know I think that girl Jessie ought to see a
psychiatrist; I'll certainly see about that tomorrow. She
must see a psychiatrist.

Sudden dim to night and moon.

Oh, my goodness. This is really too much. What's happening now?

> *The moon rises. Lights appear in the windows of the Manor and the pub. A fiddle is heard playing a rustic air.* ENTER ANGELA *and* PROUT *from the Manor House* RE-ENTER JESSIE. *She sits down again.*

JESSIE. Sorrow.

PROUT. How sweet the moonlight sleeps upon this bank.

ANGELA. The bank was at the other end of the street. It never seemed to be open.

PROUT. Strange things, banks. I want to take my boots off when I go into them, as if they were mosques.

ANGELA. Oh, I'm quite happy in banks. Father always banked at the next town. They talk so much in little villages. He never would have a telephone either. Father liked. . . . I mean he likes having secrets. I like them too. That's why I'll never be a real artist, like you.

PROUT. I'm a rotten artist.

ANGELA. Are you? That's funny, I don't seem to care. And you have never asked me to read you one of my poems.

PROUT. I dare not.

ANGELA. You're afraid they wouldn't be good?

PROUT. They might not be, and I might have to lie to you— or to myself. You are not the kind of person I want to tell lies to.

ANGELA. I feel exactly that about you too. It's very queer.

PROUT. You have one of those voices I find awfully attractive. Like a nightingale.

ANGELA. It's only a bad cold coming on. It isn't my usual voice.

PROUT. I say! Ought you to be out?

ANGELA. No, I don't think so. I ought to go in now.

PROUT. Have you any toddy in the house?

ANGELA. No. Father's a very strict teetotaller.

PROUT. I'll fetch you a gill of whisky from the pub.

ANGELA. No, no. It's most frightfully kind of you, but you mustn't. I'll be all right.

PROUT. Are you sure?

ANGELA. Yes. It's nothing really. I throw them off very quickly. I'm never really ill.

PROUT. I can fetch it in a minute.

ANGELA. No, Mr. Prout. Positively no.

PROUT. Yes.

ANGELA. No, George, you mustn't. I'll say goodnight now.

PROUT. Tomorrow?

ANGELA. Yes.

PROUT. When?

ANGELA. Oh, any time. About ten.

PROUT. Nasty things, these colds. Hadn't you better stay in bed?

ANGELA. Oh, no. I'm not encouraged to go to bed when I have a cold. I've never learned the habit.

PROUT. Then I think it's a damned shame. You spend all your life thinking for others and working for others and you'll never get any thanks for it.

ANGELA. But I'm not that sort of person at all, Mr. Prout.

PROUT. I don't think you know what sort of person you are. Perhaps it's as well.

ANGELA. Why?

PROUT. Because that curious shy grace you've got might be lost. You're like a wild creature conscious of every leaf that stirs, but unconscious of yourself. I think it's the most important part of your charm. You see, you're not classically beautiful, though you've got interesting features and rather beautiful eyes. (*Takes her hand.*) And your hands are lovely. And there's a burnt amber note in your hair that reminds me of Manet. You don't walk very well, though you have a fascinating slouch—like a thoroughbred foal. I don't know what shape you are because of your hideous clothes ; but the little sage-brush shadows round your mouth and at the angle of your jaw are a knock-out.

[38]   200

ANGELA. But you can't see me. It's too dark.

PROUT. I see you all the time. I can't get you out of my head. I never in my life met a human being who interested me so much. And yet I'm afraid of you.

ANGELA. Afraid of me ? Why ?

PROUT. I wish I knew. When a woman attracts me, I'm not usually afraid.

ANGELA. You are often attracted by women ?

PROUT. My God, yes ! But you're a different kettle of fish. I told you why.

ANGELA. Sh . . . . listen !

A clock chimes twelve.

But that's dreadful. It's midnight. May I say something to you ?

PROUT. Yes.

ANGELA. It's heavenly to have found a real friend at last. Goodnight.

PROUT. Goodnight, Angela.

ANGELA. Goodnight, George.

> *They embrace suddenly.* ANGELA *breaks away and runs into the house.* PROUT *stands gazing at the windows.* JESSIE *slips out and at once a light appears in a series of windows. After several trials she decides on one of them.*

PADRE. Well, now, thank you very much, Mr. Prout. Do sit down.

> *Stage is completely lit.* PROUT, *in some embarrassment, regains his seat.*

Well—er—yes. Er—I think we are all very much indebted to Mr. and Mrs. Prout for their demonstration and, no doubt, we all feel ourselves very much enlightened. But at the same time. . . .

> RE-ENTER JESSIE *with camp-stool. She sits at the* R. *end of the table.*

JESSIE. I think myself that's a silly scene.

PROUT. I know. So it is. That's the whole point of it.

RE-ENTER ANGELA.

PADRE. Oh, there you are, Mrs. Prout. Thank you very much. Well, now, ladies and gentlemen——

ANGELA. Not at all.

She sits down. JESSIE *is wandering about upstage.*

PADRE. Well . . . we've been getting, perhaps, a little astray. . . .

PROUT. Not at all. My wife and I behaved in that idiotic way because . . . because we were each carrying about with us a microscopic bit of matter that could neither read nor write, nor see, nor hear, nor speak, nor think. It had nothing but a will. But, somehow or other, that will could call to its neighbour and say, " Hullo. Let's get together and grow into a thing which is a perfectly arranged mixture of Angela and George—with her eyes and his nose— with her tendency to be chesty and his tendency to lose his temper." " Right," says the other gene, "The first thing to do is to make them both mad. He's a scruffy looking devil and with a face like a gargoyle. She's a long, lanky creature with knock-knees and a snivelling cold in the head. Let's make him think she's Venus and make her think he's Phoebus Apollo ; otherwise they'll never be such damned fools as to chain themselves together for the rest of their lives." The Doctor's quite right.

MACADAM. Eh ?

PROUT. I said you were quite right.

MACADAM. Right about what ? I didn't quite catch what you said. Would you mind repeating it ?

PROUT. What I said was . . . .

PADRE. Please, not again, Mr. Prout.

The BRAINS TRUST *protests vigorously.*

JESSIE. But . . . oh, well.

PADRE. Jessie !

ANGELA. All the same, I don't think I was so frightful as all that.

PROUT. Yes, you were.

MUTCH. Nonsense.

PROUT. What's that?

MUTCH. Well, I mean to say, of course . . . .

JESSIE. Is that only what you think of her now, or did you think that then?

PADRE. I really, really must put a stop to this.

LADY DODD. Oh, but why? I think it's fascinating.

JESSIE. Don't you want us to learn something? I thought that's what Brains Trusts were for—to teach you something—and we've only just begun. We've seen that two people can get hooked up for life without knowing in the least what they're after.

LADY DODD. Oh, but it doesn't always happen that way. I think my husband knew what he was after when he married me.

PADRE *sits with head in hands*.

JESSIE. But anyhow that's how it happened once. I want to know what comes next. Do they live happy ever after?

PROUT. Nobody lives happy ever after, but they get on all right.

ANGELA (*doubtfully*). Well. . . .

PROUT. What do you mean by " Well "? Oh, I know we have our ups and downs, and life would be pretty dull without an occasional row; but personally I think we've made a darned good arrangement. We've had to give and take a bit, but that's a law of the Universe. I'm sometimes a bit unreasonable and Angela's never anything else, but it doesn't take long to find a *modus vivendi*.

JESSIE. A what?

PROUT. A way of living.

JESSIE. But is it the best way of living?

MUTCH (*thumping the table*). No, by God, it isn't.

A startled silence as they all look at MUTCH.

MACADAM. What did you say?   I didn't quite catch. . . .

MUTCH. I said it isn't. It's all right for George. He's got somebody to look after his laundry and cook his meals and fight with the tradesmen and listen to his ravings and tell him he's wonderful. But where in the name of all the suffering saints does Angela come in?   She's got a far better brain than he has. She's got all the qualities to make her name in the world, and she's got what he hasn't got—decent manners and the capacity for hard work. And she's got to stand like a conjuror's assistant flourishing a handkerchief and shouting "Voila" whenever he takes a mangy rabbit out of the hat. It makes me sick.

JESSIE. Yes, but how did it work out that way?

MUTCH. I'll tell you. I'll tell you all right. It's just pure damned undiluted——

> MUTCH *rises in great excitement.*

PADRE. No. Stop. Sit down, please, Professor.

> MUTCH *sits down.* PADRE *looks at his wrist-watch.*

PADRE. Ladies and gentlemen, according to the programme we should have a little interval here, and I must say I think it is high time. Coffee and soft drinks will be served at the Canteen Bar for exactly ten minutes. After that I hope you will take your seats promptly for the second part of this Brains Trust session. May I say that I hope by that time certain of the distinguished members of the Trust will have composed themselves a little as we have several very interesting questions to discuss. Thank you very much. Ten minutes only.

> PADRE *bows to the* BRAINS TRUST, *who rise and file out, except* JESSIE, *who comes down into the audience.*

> *The* CURTAIN *remains up.*

END OF ACT II

ACT III

Scene I

The BRAINS TRUST *files in.*

The members of the TRUST *let go a " feu de joie " of variegated coughs.* JESSIE *is not among them, but her camp-stool remains at the end of the table. The* PADRE *rises.*

PADRE. Well, now. We now begin the second part of this Brains Trust session, and you'll notice I've contrived somewhat less exotic surroundings. The first part was—I will not say marred—but a little disorganised by certain—shall I call them, eccentricities. But I think you'll find a cup of tea has put that all right, and I notice that Jessie has deserted us, so I think you will find that we are a little more—ah—usual in this part of the programme without, I hope, being in any way conventional. Now the first question is from Private Slater of the Royal Army Medical Corps. He wants to know what is meant by a sense of humour and how an effective sense of humour may be cultivated. Lady Dodd ?

LADY DODD. Well, now, a sense of humour is a wonderful gift. I can't imagine what it must be like not to have one. I have a very keen sense of humour myself, and I have always been thankful for it. Deeply and truly thankful. As to cultivating a sense of humour, I think that can be done by subscribing to some such periodical as *Punch* and looking at the most amusing pictures. Then there are always books like Mark Twain's *Innocents Abroad*. My father used to read it aloud to us and we always laughed when he did, even if we didn't see the joke straight away.

PADRE. Thank you Lady Dodd. Dr. Macadam, I wonder if you heard the question.

MACADAM. Yes, yes, I'm not deaf.

PADRE. Have you any remarks to make then ?

MACADAM. I haven't got a sense of humour myself. I'm too busy, but I notice some people are always giggling at something or other. People like that are usually a bit soft in the head. It's all damn nonsense.

BYRES. I don't know ; I think a good joke now and again keeps things going, so long as it's clean. Some things I hear on the B.B.C. I can hardly believe my ears ; but I'm partial to a good hearty laugh.

He relapses into a gloomy silence. JESSIE ENTERS *from audience unobtrusively and takes her seat on the camp stool.*

PADRE. I'm sure you are, Mr. Byres (*Sees* JESSIE). Oh, you're back again.

JESSIE. Yes. Sorrow. I popped over to the hospital to see Walter.

PADRE. Oh, how is he ?

JESSIE. He's all right so far. I'm sorry I'm late. Go on.

PADRE. Well, I'm sure the Brains Trust is very grateful to you for your kind permission. We have just been discussing a sense of humour.

JESSIE. Oh, I'm sorry I missed that.

PADRE. Would you like to say anything about it ?

JESSIE. No. I want to hear more about Mr. and Mrs. Prout.

PADRE (*drops mallet*). My dear girl, you must try to control your curiosity. Mr. and Mrs. Prout are entitled to some measure of private life.

JESSIE. But I want to know about marriage.

PADRE. That was the last question but one.

JESSIE. But they haven't answered it yet.

PADRE. Oh, for heaven's sake. Well, Private Slater, the Brains Trust thinks that a sense of humour is difficult to define, but that it is a very valuable thing to have. We think you can cultivate one by reading suitable books and magazines, and refraining from listening to the B.B.C. We shall pass on to the next question. It is anonymous. The questioner wants to know how a bluebottle walking on the ceiling takes off when it wants to fly. A most interesting question. How does a bluebottle take off from the ceiling?

JESSIE. Who cares?

PADRE. Obviously the person who asked the question. Now Lady Dodd—you're a great animal lover. Do you know the explanation? How does a bluebottle take off from the ceiling?

LADY DODD. A bluebottle is not an animal.

JESSIE. That's right—it's an insect.

PADRE. Ah. Then perhaps Miss Killigrew, who seems to be so well informed in natural history, will enlighten us as to how a bluebottle takes off from the ceiling?

JESSIE. What a soppy question! It doesn't need to take off, at all. It just drops.

PADRE. That is your opinion?

JESSIE. That's right.

PADRE. Well, Doctor? How does a bluebottle take off from the ceiling?

MACADAM. Talking of a sense of humour. It's quite true that you do come across some laughable things in general practice. I remember an old fellow with a swelling on his backside the size of your head. . . .

PADRE. Yes, yes, Doctor, but. . . .

MACADAM. I had a surgeon in to see him, and we both agreed that we ought to take a wallop at it.

PADRE. Yes, but Doctor. . . .

MACADAM. So we just did the operation on the kitchen table with me giving the chloroform. I must say the young fellow made a good job of it.

PADRE. We're straying a little from the point.

MACADAM. As neat a bit of work as ever I saw. It left a beautiful scar. A credit to the surgeon.

PADRE. It's about bluebottles.

MACADAM. A pity the old fellow couldna show it—owing to its situation if you understand. But as I was saying.

PADRE. Yes, Doctor, but I'm afraid we're straying a little from the question. It's about bluebottles.

MACADAM. So we helped him into his concealed bed, and as soon as he came out of the chloroform he said. . . .

PADRE.   IT'S ABOUT BLUEBOTTLES ! BLUE-BOTTLES !

MACADAM. He didnae need a bottle, just a whiff. So this old fellow he felt under his pillow and took out a handful of dirty greasy notes and asked the doctor what his fee was. " Oh," says he, " ten guineas." So the old fellow went—one, two, three, four, five, six, seven, eight— and then says he, " You can take it or leave it. Eight pounds. And if you dinnae like it you can put the swallin' back."

PADRE. Yes, ha, ha. Quaint old characters you meet some-times. Well, the opinion of the Brains Trust about bluebottles is——

MACADAM. I mind another time when I was walking the hospital. . . .

PADRE. Yes, yes, quite, another time.

MACADAM. Aye, another time, I was just a laddie though, mind you, you'd have thought I was Joseph Lister and Syden-ham rolled into one.

PADRE. Will you tell us about it later, we have to get on ?

MACADAM. Surely, surely. It's all the same to me.

ANGELA. Do you know, I wish someone would explain to me how bluebottles manage to walk on the ceiling at all.

PROUT. Don't be so damned stupid.

MUTCH. That'll do.

PROUT. What's that ?

MUTCH. I said that'll do.

PROUT. Well, upon my word, Mr. Mutch, I don't see why the devil I can't make a remark to my wife without you brawling and blustering in.

ANGELA. He wasn't brawling, George.

PROUT. Yes, he was.

PADRE. Mr. Prout, please, please, please. And Professor, please to you too.

JESSIE. What's the matter ?

PADRE. What's the matter with what ?

JESSIE. What's the matter between these three?

PADRE. There's nothing the matter you silly girl. Sit down and keep quiet.

JESSIE. There is, there is. And I want my question decently answered. It's a matter of life and death to me, Padre. I've got to tell Walter tonight.

PADRE (*holds* JESSIE). Jessie, Jessie, Jessie. Control yourself. You're getting quite hysterical.

JESSIE. No, I'm not. We never had hysterics in my family. We had to work too blooming hard. But I want to know.

PADRE. You want to know what?

JESSIE. I want to know what happened. Everybody here wants to know. Come on, Mrs. Prout, get on with it.

PADRE. I can't allow this. I simply can't allow this. . . . Jessie, go away, go away at once.

JESSIE. No, no, please, sir, no. Please, Mrs. Prout—it means a lot to me. It means a lot to Walter too. Please, Mrs. Prout.

ANGELA. I—I—I don't know. I don't think I. . . .

> ANGELA *burst into tears*. MUTCH *leaves his seat and goes to her.*

MUTCH. It's all right. Don't worry, don't cry, I'll take you away.

PROUT. Take your hands off her, will you? (*To the* PADRE.) Get out of the way.

PADRE (*vaults table*). Now, now, Mr. Prout. Behave yourself.

> He *twists* PROUT's *arm round behind his back and gently levers him into his seat.*

I ought to tell you that I've done a bit of scrapping in my time. I was amateur middle-weight champion of. . . .

PROUT. I know, I know. Like that damned swine Puggy there. Your sort of repartee is knocking people about like a couple of navvies. You'd dare to put your filthy paws on a

209   [47]

man like me, you infernal bullies! Damned bullies, that's just what you are.

HE throws his head on his arms and begins to cry.

PADRE. Oh, dear me, what a state of affairs? What on earth am I to do? Jessie, let down the curtain.

JESSIE. No.

LADY DODD (*rising*). I think perhaps I'd better go.

PADRE. Jessie—let down that curtain. That's an order.

JESSIE. It's not working, sir.

PADRE. This is terrible. Mr. Prout. Pull yourself together, be a man and not a cry-baby. Lady Dodd, I'm most frightfully sorry—I don't know what to say.

LADY DODD. Oh, it isn't your fault. It's that girl's fault.

JESSIE. I didn't tell them to get married.

LADY DODD. I know that, but you bullied them into talking about it, with all these people looking on too. You ought to be ashamed of yourself.

JESSIE. Please, Lady Dodd, sit down for a minute please. Please, Professor, you too. Padre, please! Now I'll try to explain.

For want of anything better to do, they obey her.

JESSIE. Listen. In our street in Civvy Street they never tell you about anything. They talk about things that have happened, but they never tell you how they happened, and it's all a mess. If you ask them they tell you nothing but lies. Them that have been through it, I mean. The young ones like ourselves, they'll talk about it, but what do they know? They don't know anything. And the pictures and the books are all lies too. I never see anyone that's got an education from one year's end to another, and now I've got you here you're going to stay here until you tell me whether it's worth while getting married or not. You said you were here to answer questions, so get on with them. Did you choose right or didn't you? And if you didn't, what was wrong?

[48]   210

Answer that one and you can bubble and scream as much as you like. I don't mind. We're used to it in our street.

Short silence.

ANGELA (*drying her tears*). She's quite right, you know. We ought to answer her question.

PADRE. No, please ; I really must put my foot down. After all, I'm supposed to be the Question Master. Does the Brains Trust wish me to continue in that office, or would you rather I handed over to Private Killigrew ?

LADY DODD. No, no, please go on. You're doing splendidly.

BYRES. You're quite good enough.

PADRE. Well, if I am to be Question Master, I must insist on being Master ; I suppose, Mr. Byres would say that no man is good enough to be another man's master, but at the same time. . . . Jessie, do you want to be Question Mistress ?

JESSIE. No, I don't.

PROUT (*uncovering his face*). No woman is good enough to be another man's mistress.

PADRE. Order ! Order ! Now what do you want me to do ? Do you want me to go on to the next question or what ?

ANGELA. I still think we should answer Miss Killigrew's question.

PADRE. Lady Dodd.

LADY DODD. Oh, yes. But we needn't have any more of these horrid charades, need we ?

PADRE. I hope not. Mr. Byres ?

BYRES. Let the lassie have her way. We havnae answered her question yet.

PADRE. Professor ?

MUTCH. Oh, all right, all right.

PADRE. Mr. Prout ? Are you feeling better ? Would you care to continue this discussion ?

PROUT. *I* don't give a damn.

PADRE. Doctor ?

MACADAM. I didn't quite catch the question.

PADRE. Do you think we should go on discussing matrimony?

MACADAM. We've been discussing matrimony since the Garden of Eden. I don't see why we should stop now.

PADRE (*sighing*). Very well, then. Mrs. Prout, I think you had something to add.

ANGELA. Well, what exactly does Miss Killigrew want to know?

JESSIE. Oh, I know the facts of life, if that's what you mean. But I want to know how it works out.

ANGELA. I don't really know. You go mad more or less all of a sudden, but you recover quite slowly and by degrees. I suppose a family makes all the difference. We've had two— a boy and a girl. It was very exciting and very unpleasant. But perhaps Dr. Macadam could tell you more about that. He was our doctor both times, and the referee sees more of the game than the players.

PADRE. I hardly think we can ask Dr. Macadam to go into these—ah—obstetrical details.

JESSIE. Why did you stop having children?

ANGELA. It didn't seem a very good idea somehow. I mean they're all right in their way. They're charming kids.

JESSIE. What happened then?

PROUT. They grew up into a couple of devils incarnate. They made it impossible to work or think or do any mortal thing that wasn't centred on their caprices and inordinate desires.

ANGELA. They *were* hard to manage. We sent them away to school four years ago. The boy was eight and the girl was seven. Then we had time to notice each other again.

JESSIE. And what did you think of each other?

ANGELA. It's difficult to say. All these things happened so gradually. I think we felt very jolly and hearty and friendly and helpful, like people who have just been through a blitz. I mean to say, children get on your nerves deliberately, and most grown-ups try not to.

PROUT. They're not always very successful.

ANGELA. No, they're not always very successful. I began noticing things about George that I didn't like very much, and I suppose that hurt his vanity, because he began to lose his temper very often.

JESSIE. You stopped loving each other?

PROUT. What?

ANGELA. No, no, no. Of course not.

PROUT. Good heavens, no.

ANGELA. I wonder where you got that idea. It wasn't the same, of course, as it was at first; but you aren't the same as you were when you were three years old. George and I are devoted to each other.

PROUT. Absolutely.

JESSIE. But you didn't see any of his faults at first?

ANGELA. But I've told you that I did. All of them. Only they didn't seem to matter. It was as if they belonged to some other person.

JESSIE. Because you were a bit cracked?

ANGELA. That's what Doctor Macadam seems to think.

LADY DODD. I think it's all summed up by Lord Tennyson when he says that a friend should bear a friend's infirmities. And if you've got to bear a friend's infirmities, how much more ought you to bear a husband's? It's all a matter of give and take.

PADRE. Very true, and excellently put. And now perhaps we may sum up the discussion by saying that marriage is a very good idea indeed if we are prepared to give and take as Lady Dodd says.

MUTCH. But not if it's all on one side.

PADRE. Of course it mustn't be all on one side. I think Lady Dodd made that quite clear.

MUTCH. But it *is* all on one side. I mean to say, what the devil?

He stands up and begins to thump the table with his fist to emphasise the points he imagines he is making.

I mean to say you don't know these people as I do. I mea
I've known Angela for fifteen years and George for near
forty, and I mean to say he's a decent enough fellow and a
that sort of thing, but he's bone lazy and bone selfish, an
as conceited as a peacock with three tails ; though what he
got to be conceited about I don't know, though it's partly he
fault of course. I mean, after all, she's got a personality of he
own, and what the hell . . . I mean to say, the point is th
. . . of course I can't say anything, for some reason or othe
nobody's supposed to say anything about things like tha
until the damage is done. But it *is* done. And there's some
body had her whole life spoilt by the bone-headed concei
and stupidity of a little twirp like that ; but it's high tim
someone told him, and I don't care if he knows it.

He sits down abruptly

PADRE. The Professor is of the opinion that both partner
must be prepared to make some sacrifice, that there mus
be some give and take, so we'll pass on to the next question

PROUT. I beg your pardon, we'll do nothing of the kind
This man has had the impudence to come in and out of my
house like a tame lap-dog and pretend to be my friend, and
now he stands up at a public meeting and insults me in
intolerable terms. I want to know what he means by it, if he's
capable of stringing a couple of intelligible sentences together

PADRE. I think you can settle that on a more suitable
occasion.

PROUT. No, I insist. He's either said too much or too little
He's got to stand up there and tell us what the devil he means.

MUTCH. I should think I've made my meaning clear enough.
I've called you a selfish, conceited, bone-headed twirp, and I
mean it. You are one.

PROUT. And what am I supposed to do now ? Fight you ?
You know damn well I can't fight you. You'll hear from my
solicitor.

MUTCH. He's my solicitor too. He'll tell you not to be a
damn fool. Upon my Sam, I don't know how she sticks him.

PROUT. You keep my wife out of this.

ANGELA. But it's true, George. You are very difficult.

PROUT. That's right. You turn on me now. A minute ago ou were rolling your eyes up to heaven and telling the British Navy, Army and Air Force how much you loved me, ut it's just like you. I'm not surprised. You insist on being reated like a rational being and at the same time claim the ight to behave like a spoilt child. I forgot your birthday hree weeks ago and you sulked for ten days. How can I nake a comrade and friend and partner out of a creature like hat?

MUTCH. I should begin by trying to behave like a gentle-nan.

PROUT. I suppose you call your behaviour gentlemanly.

MUTCH. I only discuss terms with people who know what hey mean.

ANGELA. Oh, stop. I can't bear this.

LADY DODD. Well, to tell you the truth, it's getting a little oo much for me.

PADRE. I'm not in the least surprised. Gentlemen, you must ither behave yourselves in a civilised fashion, or leave this olatform.

MUTCH. Certainly I'll leave this platform, and I'll take Mrs. Prout with me.

PROUT. You'll do nothing of the sort.

MUTCH. Who's going to stop me?

PROUT. I am. (To ANGELA.) Are you going to sit there and hear me insulted? I can't imagine a woman with a spark of spirit sitting still and hearing her husband insulted.

LADY DODD. Oh, can't you, Mr. Prout? It's one of the few pleasures we poor women have.

ANGELA. If we're talking about insults, I've been steadily insulted ever since this thing began, and by you, George. And I may tell you I've had about enough of it. You can go on washing our dirty linen in public as long as the Padre will et you. I'm going with Jimmy.

PROUT. I forbid you to do anything of the sort. Why should you? Is he your lover, or what?

ANGELA. Yes, he is. I mean he is—in a way. I mean he is

A short silence

PROUT. Do you mean to say this has been going on under my very nose?

MUTCH. Nothing's been going on under your very nose. Don't be silly.

PROUT. I beg your pardon, Professor Mutch. My wife has just stated in the clearest possible terms that she has been deceiving me with you. You set great store by your gentility. Do you accuse my wife of telling lies?

ANGELA. But it isn't what you think it means, George. It isn't at all, honestly.

PROUT. What *do* you mean then? At least I am entitled to an explanation.

ANGELA. Of course, Jimmy and I are very fond of one another—but not in that way.

PROUT. May I ask what you mean by " that way "?

PADRE. No, sir. You certainly may not.

> *The whole battery of stage-effects is suddenly turned on. Thunder, rain, lightning. In the pandemonium, the startled* BRAINS TRUST *sits down and looks at itself, in a dazed sort of way.*

> *The tumult dies, except for the sound of galloping horses' hooves dying in the distance.*

JESSIE. When did you begin to feel that way about the Professor, Mrs. Prout?

PADRE. Stop a bit. I don't understand. Who's monkeying about with the light and effects?

JESSIE. Never mind, sir, please sir. Please sit still. I'll tell you later.

PADRE (*severely*). Do you know I have a strong suspicion, Private Killigrew. . . .

PROUT (*rising*). I said that when I married I would marry the perfect woman or die a bachelor. I was ugly. I was poor, but an artist can marry anybody he likes. A wise man told

e that and I believed him. I was determined to marry a
oman who was graceful and beautiful, without blemish,
ut curiously touched by humanity that she might escape the
orror of perfection. I could hear only her voice. It would
und, I thought, like bees on the clover, like quick accidental
aterfalls, like the lower notes of the skylark, like the song of
ie thrush. A voice full of sympathy, but not impertinent
ympathy. And talking good sense. And talking good
nglish. And not trying to be clever. The woman would
ave a personality strong and individual but ready to blend
ith other personalities, to warm and illuminate them. I
new her. I could hear her. But I could not see her. All I
new was that she would be a surprise. Dark? Fair? It
as nothing to me. Height? As high as my heart. But
eautiful she must be, and honest and gentle and strong.
.nd look what I married! That!

> *He walks out abruptly. The* BRAINS TRUST *sit looking
> at each other in a stunned silence which is broken by*
> JESSIE.

JESSIE. He didn't want much, did he?

ANGELA. I must go to him. He's so impulsive. The Lord
nows what he'll do. He might do anything.

> *She gets up hurriedly.*

PADRE. I'll meet you outside in two minutes.

LADY DODD. I'll drive you back. We'll catch up with him
n the road.

ANGELA. Thank you, Lady Dodd—could we go now?

LADY DODD. Yes, yes. I'm perfectly certain it will be all
ight.

> EXIT ANGELA *and* LADY DODD *followed vaguely by*
> MUTCH.

PADRE. Ladies and gentlemen, I think I'm safe in saying
hat the Brains Trust is of the opinion that Holy Matrimony
s not . . . is hardly a topic for discussion before a mixed

audience, so we had better draw these proceedings to close.

JESSIE. Let down the tabs, Walter.

PADRE. What's this? Walter? What Walter? Where's Walter?

JESSIE. I wangled him out of the hospital. He wanted t hear the Brains Trust. O.K., Walter.

> *Curtains draw together and* PADRE *gets entangled wi*
> *them and eventually appears in front.*

PADRE. Ah! There you are, ladies and gentlemen. Jus before I rush off to see what I can do about this most un unfortunate *contretemps*, I have to tell you that tomorrov night ENSA is presenting on this stage, Mr. Pete Schach and his Jiving Strawberries.

> EXIT PADRE. *The house lights remain out and th*
> *orchestra, if any, plays to denote the passage of ha.*
> *an hour.*

END OF SCENE I, ACT III.

ACT III

SCENE II

As soon as it is humanly possible, the Curtain goes up on the Prouts' Studio. It is completely dark and there is silence for a moment till the purr of a very good motor car is heard, and shortly after somebody turns the key in the door, and ANGELA, LADY DODD, MUTCH *and the* PADRE ENTER, *guided by the Padre's electric torch.*

MUTCH. Half a jiffy; I'll put on the light. Where the devil is it?

ANGELA *switches on the light.*

Oh good, I never could find switches.

PADRE. I'm certain it's going to be quite all right.

LADY DODD. So am I. I'm never wrong about these things.

ANGELA *has been busy about the fireplace. She stands up suddenly.*

ANGELA. Do you think he could have got here before us?

PADRE. He could quite easily if he caught the last bus. That puncture held us up twenty minutes, and we didn't pass it on the road.

ANGELA. Jimmy, the rat poison!

SHE *runs out, followed by* MUTCH.

PADRE. Oh dear, perhaps I'd better go too. Excuse me a minute, Lady Dodd.

EXIT PADRE.

LADY DODD *dusts a seat carefully and sits down, looking round her with some distaste and some curiosity.* RE-ENTER ANGELA *quickly, followed by the two men. She carries a tin of rat poison.*

ANGELA. Well, that's all right, thank God! The tin hasn't been opened.

LADY DODD. Well, that's a blessing anyway. I don't approve of rat poison. I'm told the poor little things suffer terribly.

ANGELA. Perhaps he's in his room.

Noise.

I'll go to him.

PADRE. No; perhaps it would be better if Mr. Mutch and I went. Or perhaps it would be better if Professor Mutch didn't go. One never knows exactly how people feel about these things.

MUTCH. I could show you where his room is.

PADRE. Splendid, splendid. Well, come along; and be quite calm, Mrs. Prout. I'm perfectly certain it's going to turn out all right.

EXEUNT PADRE *and* MUTCH.

ANGELA. I hope it's all right. He's so very impulsive.

LADY DODD. I think we can leave him to Mr. Paris. Mr. Paris is wonderful. I did admire the way he took complete control of the situation. He even wanted to bring the Medical Officer. It's a pity the poor fellow was so tipsy, and I must say I hadn't much confidence in that old Dr. Macadam. He's quite out of date. I only have him for the servants.

ANGELA. Do you think we'll need a doctor?

LADY DODD. No, of course we won't. People don't need doctors if they lead ordinary, simple, clean, healthy lives.

ANGELA. But George doesn't lead an ordinary simple, clean, healthy life. And anyhow that's not the point. He may have done something awful.

LADY DODD. Nonsense! He seemed to me a very sensible cultivated kind of man—in a way. A nice, quiet, well-bred type.

PROUT (*without*). Will you get to hell out of here and mind your own business?

PADRE (*without*). But I say, look here, Mr. Prout. Do be sensible.

ENTER PROUT *in a rage followed by the* PADRE *and* MUTCH.

PADRE. But look here, Mr. Prout—really !

PROUT. I'm not going to have any bloody old woman interfering in my private affairs. Oh, hullo, Lady Dodd, I didn't notice you.

LADY DODD. Good evening, Mr. Prout. You're here, after all. We were very anxious about you ; and you mustn't call me an old woman. It isn't civil, and it isn't true.

PROUT. It wasn't calling you an old woman—I didn't know you were here. I was calling this dog-collared nosey parker an old woman.

MUTCH. Shut up, George, will you ? You're making a damned fool of yourself.

PROUT. And no doubt you're a damned good judge.

ANGELA. George, are you all right ?

PROUT. Of course I'm all right. Who wouldn't be all right after having his private life dragged through the gutter in front of a lot of gaping baboons ? A most stimulating and delightful experience.

ANGELA. Well, it was all your fault. You began it.

PROUT. *My* fault ? *I* began it. Who was it started these damned private theatricals ?

ANGELA. You did.

PROUT. I did ? You did. Split my windpipe, I have my faults but I'm not a damned exhibitionist like you. And as for Jimmy. . . .

MUTCH. I chipped in when I thought you were going too far.

PROUT. You mean you lost your temper—in front of all those people.

MUTCH. I didn't ; anyhow how could anyone keep his temper ?

ANGELA. It all seemed to come over me somehow.

PROUT. It's always coming over you.

MUTCH. Shut up, you.

PROUT. Why should I?

PADRE. Now, now, now, now. This isn't very helpful.

PROUT (*turning on him*). And now thank you for your visit, your reverence, and will you be good enough to take yourself out of here and leave me to the peace of my family circle?

PADRE. I shall do nothing of the sort. Jessie's bringing round a jeep for me presently; but until she comes I'm going to do my best to get you into a better frame of mind.

PROUT. Even at the risk of being kicked out.

PADRE. I'm afraid you can't do that very well. You see I happen to be. . . .

PROUT. I know, I know. The ex-middle-weight champion of the Monastery, but look out.

LADY DODD. This is quite, quite ridiculous. When any of my friends had trouble with their wives, they often wanted to horsewhip the other fellow or shoot him or something. They never thought of kicking the vicar.

PROUT. No doubt you're right, but if he doesn't clear out I'll send for the police. Or I'll set Jimmy on him. He likes brawling and mauling and punching people on the nose.

ANGELA. Jimmy won't do anything of the sort.

PADRE. There isn't going to be any punching on the nose. Do let's sit down and behave like civilised beings.

PROUT. You're not going to clear out?

PADRE. No.

PROUT. Then I will.

MUTCH. Chuck it, George, for God's sake. We've got to get this straight.

PROUT. I know we have, but what's he got to do with it?

MUTCH. I don't know; but he seems to be able to keep his head, and—well—I mean to say, the rest of us are hardly a picture of sound commonsense.

LADY DODD. The professor is perfectly right. Let's all have a cosy chat. I've always found it doesn't lead anywhere,

[60]

but it lets off steam, and you sometimes hear the most fright-fully interesting things. Come along, Mrs. Prout, make your husband behave himself.

ANGELA. I don't seem to have any influence over him at all.

LADY DODD. Well, in that case, you'd better do as I tell you, Mr. Prout. Sit beside me.

> ALL *sit*. PROUT *beside* LADY DODD, MUTCH *beside* ANGELA, *and the* PADRE *a little apart*.

LADY DODD. Well, now. The three of you have got your-selves into a mess, and you have been silly enough not to keep quiet about it. In fact, I never saw any three people quite so silly about an ordinary little domestic upset. If people started pulling the roof down every time somebody took a fancy to another man's wife there wouldn't be a single good family left in Britain. Now, Mr. Paris, tell them what you think, and don't be afraid.

PADRE. It all seems perfectly simple to me.

PROUT. As the bomb said when it landed on the Art Gallery.

LADY DODD. Please don't interrupt, Mr. Prout.

PADRE. We all have absurd inclinations and we don't always behave very wisely, but there's one thing we owe to our self-respect and that is to play the game.

MUTCH. What game?

PADRE. You're a public schoolboy. You should know what playing the game means. We must have some kind of standards, and I don't know of any better than the good old sporting standards of the New Testament.

MUTCH. Well—I mean to say—good gracious—for heaven's sake. . . !

PADRE. If only you fellows would read your Bibles you would understand exactly what I mean by "playing the game." Professor Mutch, I must be absolutely frank with you. You are not playing the game.

PROUT. Hear, hear.

223   [61]

PADRE. You seem to me to have deliberately set yourself to break up the family life of two of your friends. That is what I mean by not playing the game.

MUTCH. Do you know anything about their family life?

PADRE. Not a great deal. But family life is family life all the world over.

MUTCH. If that means that family life is the same all the world over, I mean to say, for heaven's sake! It isn't the same in two semi-detached villas. It certainly isn't the same in Aberdeen and Timbuctoo.

PADRE. It is essentially the same in Aberdeen and Timbuctoo. It is based on a solemn contract between a man and a woman. If you break the contract the whole system falls down.

MUTCH. Yes, but I mean to say, what's the basis of the contract? I mean to say, the point is, it's out of date. It was framed to meet the needs of a primitive society nearly two thousand years ago.

PADRE. It's a good deal older than that and we're still a primitive society.

ANGELA. Oh, but Padre—we are *not* a primitive society. At least not *our* kind of people. We know more about ourselves. I don't mind telling you I've been psycho-analysed three times. I mean really *deep* psycho-analysis, and I ought to know what I'm talking about.

LADY DODD. Well, I don't know. You remember that little girl who was eating apples and fiddling with the light? She put a question to the Brains Trust and you tried to help her out of her difficulty, and all you did was to get yourselves into the most outrageous mess.

PADRE. That's very interesting. But perhaps I'd better say this—Professor Mutch has behaved very badly, and Mrs. Prout has exercised very little self-control. I am quite clear in my mind about that. If Mr. and Mrs. Prout have stuck it for fifteen years they can stick it for another twenty-five, and they've just jolly well got to. The Professor ought to go and

[62]

get married and settle down. It would do him a world of good.

LADY DODD. I quite agree.

MUTCH. It's not so easy as all that.

ANGELA. It isn't by any means.

MUTCH. I'm sorry for George. He can't help it. I mean to say, he's quite a decent fellow, but he and Angela aren't suited to one another. You saw for yourselves that it was a pure accident that they got married at all. I mean to say, there was no reason—no foresight in it. The result has been fifteen years of pure undiluted hell, I mean to say, not for Angela alone, but for George too. I mean to say, I've known them nearly all my life, and I've been very worried about it. And it was really worrying about that that gave me this sort of what-you-may-call-it—*fixation* I've got for Angela. God knows I don't want to bust up George's arrangements, to say nothing of my own, but I really think the best way would be for me to take over the responsibility for Angela and leave George to find someone more suitable. What do you think? Eh?

PADRE. Mrs. Prout, would you say that your married life for fifteen years had been pure, undiluted hell?

ANGELA. Yes, on the whole I would.

PADRE. What?

ANGELA. And it won't be any better after this. George was difficult enough to get on with as he was without being all torn up with jealousy and suspicion.

PADRE. But surely Mr. Prout would be reasonable.

ANGELA. He might be, but I've never known him try to be. Just look at him sitting there—sulking. Does he look like a reasonable man?

> PROUT *does not look like a reasonable man. He is sitting*
> *with his arms folded in a state of obstinate gloom,*
> *staring straight in front of him.*

PADRE. Mr. Prout, if your wife promises never to see

Professor Mutch again, will you forgive and forget and let bygones be bygones?

ANGELA. But I'm not going to promise any such thing. Jimmy's the only thing that's made life bearable for me. If I stay on with George and darn his socks and cook his meals he's just got to lump it.

PADRE. But that would never do.

LADY DODD. Of course not.

ANGELA. Then we've just got to go away together. George can divorce me if he likes.

MUTCH. Hold on a minute. I hardly think, if you follow me, we ought to make up our minds quite so precipitately. I mean to say, my housekeeper has got a terrible antipathy to children. She had one illegitimate child that grew up and stole all her savings.

LADY DODD. But couldn't you get rid of her?

MUTCH. I've tried to get rid of her for over twenty years. She wouldn't mind Angela—at least I don't think so—but she couldn't stand the children.

ANGELA. You might have had the decency to tell me that before.

MUTCH. I did tell you.

ANGELA. No, you didn't. Not in so many words. Of course if you prefer your housekeeper to me. . . .

MUTCH. But I don't, my darling. Only I can't afford to pension her and she's too old to get another job.

ANGELA. I think if I'm prepared to break up my domestic arrangements you might go a little way in breaking up yours.

MUTCH. But I've explained, darling. I mean to say, after all, whatever way you look at it, the point is. . . .

ANGELA. Don't you love me?

MUTCH. I love you with my whole soul.

ANGELA. And I love you too. Don't you see we've got to do something about it?

MUTCH. Yes. But why rush things? After all, we're proposing to take a terrific step. We've got to examine it from every angle.

[64]

ANGELA (*in tears*) I'm sick of examining angles.

PADRE. Look here, Mrs. Prout; pull yourself together. You've got to make a clean break. You've simply got to. There's nothing else for it. I'll talk to Mr. Prout tomorrow when he's in a better state of mind.

PROUT. You will not.

PADRE. Now, now, come, come.

PROUT. I'm damned if I'll come, come.   Mind your own business.

PADRE. But this is my business.

LADY DODD. Of course it is, Mr. Prout. Mr. Paris's business is to make people good, and you have all been very naughty indeed.

PROUT. I've been nothing of the sort.

MUTCH. Yes, you have, George. It would never have happened if it hadn't been for you.

PROUT. The cat wouldn't have stolen the milk if it hadn't been for the milkman or the dairymaid and the cow—and the parish bull, if it comes to that. I prefer to blame the cat.

MUTCH. If you had treated Angela properly. . . .

ANGELA. Oh, it wasn't that, it wasn't that at all.

PROUT. Thank you for those few nuts.

MUTCH. Well, why then. . . .? I mean to say, I always thought—— For goodness' sake! I mean to say, what did start it?

ANGELA. It wasn't George anyway. I never thought very much of him, but I was terribly fond of him and I knew he couldn't help being a bully and a brute sometimes. All artists are neurotics. They wouldn't be artists if they weren't. They'd settle down and do some honest work. I knew what I was doing when I married George, and I knew how to put up with him. I could even manage him a bit. It wasn't that at all.

MUTCH. What was it then?

ANGELA. I don't know. People who are in love get to be in love with love. And in the long, long times when George was somewhere else, or with his head all muffled in the clouds, absorbed in his painting, I felt restless and silly and hungry. I thought it was sympathy I wanted, but it was love I wanted. People don't think of that when they blame people.

LADY DODD. That's very true.

PADRE. Well, it is a sort of an excuse ; but I must say I can't find any excuse for Professor Mutch's conduct. I can only call it by a very disagreeable name indeed : philandering.

LADY DODD. Have you got an excuse, Mr. Mutch ?

MUTCH. Well, is it a matter for excuses ? I mean to say, it seems to me on the face of it that situations like this arise in a sort of a way from a variety of causes and that only a very small percentage of these causes are in any way under our control, if I may put it that way. What I mean to say is this. . . .

PROUT. Shut up !

MUTCH. Eh ?

PROUT. Shut up ! You never could explain anything. I'll explain it for you if you like.

MUTCH. But you're biassed.

PROUT (*He turns to* LADY DODD, *markedly ignoring the* PADRE). Lady Dodd, there's a certain type of man who is doomed to be a stray dog, and you'll agree, I think, that stray dogs are very pathetic.

LADY DODD. Of course they are. They're the saddest things in the whole world.

PROUT. Very well, then. Jimmy's a stray dog. If anybody's kind to him and gives him a bone and a cookhouse fire to sit at, he goes all maudlin. He goes off his head. He can bark and snarl all the way down the street. He can bite the children who try to tie tin cans to his tail . . . did you ever hear him lecturing to his students ? You'd be amazed.

LADY DODD. No.

PROUT. A famished wolf at bay has nothing on Jimmy lecturing to his students. . . . Very well then. We gave him a fireside, and some carbolic soap to get rid of his fleas, and got all his crazy devotion in return. The trouble is that no woman can be trusted with a dog.

LADY DODD. Oh, what nonsense!

PROUT. No, but it's true. They're not content with taking the brute for a run and feeding it and throwing sticks for it, and teaching it a few self-respecting tricks. They set to work and steadily undermine its morale until it's a cringing nervous little horror. It's not the dog's fault. They talk baby talk to it. They let it slobber all over their faces. They take it to bed with them at night.

A loud knock on the door is heard.

ANGELA. Answer that, Jimmy, will you.   (*To* PROUT.) You're a low despicable cad.

PADRE. Yes.

LADY DODD. I almost agree with you.

MUTCH (*at the door*). Oh, here's Jessie. Shall I bring her in?

PROUT. Bring in the Navy, the Army, the Royal Air Force and the Home Guard. What the hell does it matter?

ENTER JESSIE.

(*To* JESSIE.) Come along in.

JESSIE. I've brought the car round, sir.

PADRE. Thank you, Jessie.

JESSIE. I hope you don't mind, sir—I've brought Walter too.

PROUT. Bring him in. No doubt he's passionately interested in our private affairs.

JESSIE (*to* PADRE). Is that all right, sir?

PADRE. Is what all right?

JESSIE. Can I bring Walter in?

MUTCH. I say, this is a bit thick.

PROUT. You shut up. I may be a blooming cuckold but I'm still master of this house. Bring him in.

JESSIE. Okey-doke.

EXIT JESSIE.

PROUT. We're supposed to be helping this young couple to solve their problems. We've made a fine mess of it. I

want them to see where people land themselves by being too
damned clever.

> ENTER JESSIE *and* WALTER. *He is a self-possessed
> rather loutish young man in soiled hospital blues. H*
> *holds a spanner in his hand, but stands smartly t*
> *attention.*

JESSIE. This is Walter. He can stand easy, can't he ?
PADRE. Yes, yes.

> WALTER *stands very easy indeed*

ANGELA. Won't you sit down ?

> MUTCH *brings a chair for* WALTER, *who sits down*

WALTER. Ta.

JESSIE. I hope it's all right me bringing Walter. He told
the Provo' Sergeant he had to bring back three lantern slides

PADRE. What lantern slides ?

JESSIE. Well, there aren't any ; but the Provo' Sergean
couldn't be expected to know that. (*Then brightly.*) Well
Have they settled everything all right ?

PADRE. Half of these problems arise just because peopl
think too much about them. If more people took a cold bat
and a sharp walk before breakfast, there would be less of th
sort of thing. Now look here, all of you. The only way ou
of this is for you three to make some sort of sacrifice.

MUTCH. Why ?

PADRE. It's the only way to get back your self-respect.

MUTCH. But we've never lost it. I've got a great respec
for myself.

PADRE. I'm sorry to hear it.

MUTCH. You want me to give up. . . . By the way yo
are rather a clever fellow George — I never argue by analogy
but you hit the nail on the head — I am a bit of a lost dog. . .
You want me to give up the only patch of happiness I'v
ever found in my poor drab scholar's life. You want Angel
to give up the only thing that makes the life of a woma

[68]   23

and a poet, worth living. You want George to give up his life's work. I mean to say, why not ask us to turn on the gas and be done with it. I mean to say, do try to be a little reasonable.

PADRE. But it can't go on, on this footing.

PROUT. It certainly damn well can't.

LADY DODD. I think we should all go home to bed.

PADRE. No, I'm sorry. We can't leave it this way.

PROUT. You can all go home as far as I'm concerned—and that applies to Jimmy too. He's certainly not going to stay here. And he can take Angela with him if he likes.

MUTCH. Where the devil can I take Angela at this time of night? I've nowhere to go myself if it comes to that.

PROUT. Fat lot I care.

ANGELA. George, you must be sensible.

PROUT. Sensible!

JESSIE. Please, may I say something?

PROUT. Go on, go on.

JESSIE. I think we should ask Walter what he thinks.

PADRE. Really, Jessie, behave yourself.

WALTER. Gercher!

JESSIE. No, honestly. Walter looks a bit soft, but he's all there, all right. What do you think they ought to do, Walter?

WALTER. Well, I don't know all the facts, but when you've got a lot of blokes and judies with too much time on their hands, well, it stands to reason you get a bit of square-pushing. Well, most times it don't do no harm. It all depends how bad you've got it. Well, say a gent gets sweet on another gent's judy, the gent what owns the judy he's got two or three things he can do. He can go about yapping and bellyaching; he can clock the other guy one and give his judy something to remember. But that don't do much good in my experience. If he licks the other guy, it's the other guy the judy's sorry for. If the other guy licks him the judy thinks he's a poor enough piece of cheese. The best way in my experience is to sit down over a pint of wallop and say—" Here, chum, what about it? There's plenty of other judies in the world, yapping about and leaving their hair combing's all over the place. What do you want to come messing around my judy for ? She takes a bit of getting used to—I warn you, and I got used to her. Anyhow," you says, " love and that's all very well, but you've got your life to live. If you look at it reasonable, judies is things that most blokes can do with in moderation. There's things you've got to do. You've got to eat and you've got to sleep, but you ain't got to go running after other blokes' judies. I've seen the time I'd have give the most wonderful judy in the world for a plate of bully and a slice of bread and marge. So have a bit of sense, chum. And what about one for the road ? " That's what I'd say if I was in his place. Anyways, I think I would. You never know. . . .

JESSIE. That's right. Walter's right. You haven't got it as bad as all that, Mrs. Prout, and the Professor certainly hasn't. You'll get over it all right, if you mark time for a bit, and Mr. Prout doesn't go on whacking it up like a scene in the pictures.

ANGELA. I like that. I like that very much. You've settled it all, haven't you ? But what about you and Walter ?

JESSIE. Oh, that's all right.

ANGELA. Is it ? Aren't you in love with the Padre ?

WALTER. What ?

JESSIE. Amn't I what ?

ANGELA. That was your whole difficulty, wasn't it ?

PADRE. Good gracious me, what a terrible thing to say ! Really, Mrs. Prout, you ought to know better.

JESSIE. The Padre's a very nice gentleman, but nobody's going to fall in love with him ; not without their feeling specially holy or something.

WALTER. Ah !

JESSIE. Besides you've done me a bit of good on the Brains Trust tonight. I'm going to marry someone practical. Are you ready to go, sir ?

PADRE. Well, after Mrs. Prout's extraordinary remark, I don't think there's anything else to do. I hope, Lady Dodd, you didn't think for a moment . . . .

> PADRE *picks up his hat with braces.* LADY DODD *turns to speak to him with her hand out.* PADRE *tries to give braces to* WALTER, *who half backs away.* PADRE *looks to see if his own braces have come off. Drops them as if they were a snake.*

PADRE (*under his breath*). For God's sake let me get out of here.

EXIT.

PROUT. In love with the padre?

ANGELA. Shut up.

PROUT (*to* MUTCH). In love with the padre!

> EXEUNT JESSIE, WALTER *and the* PADRE *all murmuring* "Goodnight."

LADY DODD *makes ready to depart.*

LADY DODD. And now, Professor, if you've got a toothbrush and a suit of pyjamas I think you had better come along to the Hall for tonight, and I don't mind telling you that we have one or two quite nice firesides to sit at, and perhaps even a bone or two. And I'm very fond of stray dogs.

MUTCH. Well, I mean to say, it's most terribly good of you.

PROUT. No, no, he'd better stay here.

ANGELA. No, Jimmy. You'd better go. Go now. Your bag's packed already and I'll push in your pyjamas. You left them in the bathroom.

MUTCH *opens the door for her.*

MUTCH. I don't know. I feel a bit guilty.

ANGELA. You needn't. Only you'd better get into the car now and not keep Lady Dodd waiting.

MUTCH. But what are you going to do?

ANGELA. I'm going to town next week to have my hair done in rows of tight little lumps like iron filings. I'll feel all right then.

EXIT ANGELA.

LADY DODD *prepares to depart.*

LADY DODD. Well, now, Mr. Prout, perhaps your charming wife will forgive us if we take her at her word. You'll say goodbye to her for me, won't you ? Come along, Professor.

PROUT. Oh, yes ; all right. Thank you. Good-bye.

EXIT LADY DODD.

PROUT. Oh, by the way, Jimmy.

MUTCH. Eh ?

PROUT. Your train doesn't go till 2.45. I wish you'd look in some time in the course of the morning. I want to ask your advice about those spring onions.

MUTCH. Why . . . yes, of course ; certainly. Yes, naturally. But I mean to say, I've been thinking it over and you were absolutely right, old boy. I mean to say, they wouldn't leave them above ground unless they had some reason for it and probably a very good reason too.

PROUT. No, that's very true.

RE-ENTER ANGELA *with bag.*

ANGELA. Are you still here ? Take this and clear out.

MUTCH. Oh, yes, righto. Thank you, Well, good-bye, then.

ANGELA. Get out.

EXIT MUTCH.

PROUT. I don't think you ought to have talked to Jimmy like that.

ANGELA. I nearly threw the bag at him.

PROUT. No doubt. But he's a sensitive sort of fellow and you were damned rude.

ANGELA. My God ! . . . Oh, what's the use ? George, why must you leave braces lying about all over the place ? You know you never wear them.

PROUT. I hardly think this is a time to be talking about braces.

ANGELA. No, perhaps not.

SHE *lifts some stockings off the easel. Then sits on divan beside* PROUT *and begins to darn a sock.*

PROUT. Oh, Lord, this place is a positive dog's breakfast.

ANGELA. I thought you liked it that way.

PROUT. Yes, I do. And somehow we always seem to be able to find things. There's one thing I want, though.

ANGELA. There isn't a drop in the house.

PROUT. What about a cup of tea?

ANGELA. I'll put the kettle on.

PROUT. No; I'll put the kettle on.

> HE EXITS. *As this is the first time for years that he has ever done a spontaneously civil action* ANGELA *registers first astonishment, then delight, and darns the socks with fresh gusto.*

CURTAIN

END OF THE PLAY

THE FORRIGAN REEL

A BALLAD OPERA

" Then cried Mahound for a heiland padgean ;
Syne ran a fiend to fetch MacFadyen,
Far Northward in a nook ;
When the coronach had done shout
The Gaels so gaddened him about,
In Hell great room they took.

Thir Termagents with tag and tatter,
Full loud in Erse begood to clatter,
And roup like raven and rook.
The De'il so deaved was with their yell,
That in the deepest pot of Hell,
He smoorit them in smoke."

DUNBAR.

This version of the play was performed at Sadler's Wells on 24th October, 1945, with the following cast:

OLD MACALPIN	.	.	.	Alastair Sim.
DONALD MACALPIN	.	.	.	Duncan Macrae
MAIRI	.	.	.	Sheila McIntosh.
MRS. GRANT	.	.	.	Molly Urquhart.
GRANT OF FORRIGAN	.	.	.	Ian Wallace.
MURDO	.	.	.	Ronald Perry.
MR. MACK	.	.	.	J. Hubert Leslie.
SIR BRIAN COOKE	.	.	.	Eric Fort.
MRS. MEARES	.	.	.	Winifred Davis.
CLARINDA COOKE	.	.	.	Joan Sterndale Bennet.
WALTER PHILLIPS	.	.	.	Geoffrey Dunn.

The Music was by Cedric Thorpe Davie, and conducted by Walford Hayden.

The Play was produced by Alastair Sim

The Scenery was by Frederick Crooke.

An earlier version was performed at the Citizens' Theatre, Glasgow, at Christmas, 1944, with the following cast:—

OLD MACALPIN, James Gibson; DONALD, Duncan Maerae; MAIRI, Lucille Steven; MRS. GRANT, Molly Urquhart; FORRIGAN, Jameson Clark; MURDO, Kenneth Miles; MACK, James Cairncross; SIR BRIAN, Denis Carey; MRS MEARES, Dorita Curtis-Hayward; CLARINDA, Helen Lacy; PHILLIPS, Gordon Davies.

The play was produced by Eric Capon and designed by Frederick Crooke.

PERSONS IN THE PLAY

OLD MACALPIN	A fiddler.
DONALD	His son. A herdsman.
MAIRI	A serving wench.
MRS. GRANT	
GRANT OF FORRIGAN . .	A tacksman.
MURDO	A servant.
MR. MACK	A lawyer.
SIR BRIAN COOKE . .	A timber merchant.
MRS. MEARES . . .	His cousin.
CLARINDA	His daughter.
WALTER PHILLIPS . .	His nephew.
SERVANTS AT FORRIGAN	

TIME : 1740.

PLACES : England and Speyside.

The Author's Agents are Christopher Mann Ltd., 140 *Park Lane,
London, W.*1

The Musical Score is the property of CEDRIC THORPE DAVIE,
Master of Music, St. Andrew's University.

PROLOGUE

When the Curtain rises SIR BRIAN COOKE *and* PHILLIPS
*are discovered walking across the stage in front of a
backcloth representing a very tidy and formal Italian
garden with a prospect of forests and cultivated fields
beyond it.*

*They are deep in thought, they take eight paces to the right
and eight paces to the left accompanied somewhat
derisively by the orchestra in march time. When they
have crossed the stage four times the music stops
suddenly and* COOKE *speaks.*

COOKE. No, egad, I can see no other way out of it; was
ever an unfortunate county gentleman and timber merchant
so bamboozled and bitten by a gallimaufry of such untoward
circumstances.

PHILLIPS. It is indeed, uncle, a wellnigh insoluble dilemma.

They resume their walk and cross the stage twice.

COOKE. I *must* see these Highland forests for myself; I shall,
never again while I live trust a living soul. Those men, Walter,
in whom I had placed the most absolute trust, had no sooner
beheld the Grampian Mountains than the wine of the country
so wrought them that they saw trees as men walking and
relapsed into the condition of blindness. It is impossible
to do business by such methods and yet the Admiralty must
have their ships. I *must* go myself.

PHILLIPS. But it is impossible to transport Clarinda to such
barbarous regions in the present state of her constitution.

COOKE. Stop, you may have stumbled on a solution. It has
been the guiding principle of my life that, when I hear the
word " impossible " applied to any project, I determine that
that project must and shall be achieved. I cannot, Walter,
at the age of nigh on sixty, abandon the guiding principles of

my life. Clarinda will come with us to the Scottish Highlands.

PHILLIPS. Nay, but how ?

They sit down on a stone bench.

COOKE. I could have wished that my architect had provided a seat more commodious to my rump. But circumstances, Walter, are often plaguily difficult to circumvent and we must e'en put up with them.

PHILLIPS. A profound reflection, uncle, and one highly applicable to our present situation. But my mind is sadly troubled at the effect upon my fair cousin of the circumstances you have proposed. I have been informed that the roads in Scotland are precipitous and pocked with crevices ; that the stages are ramshackle and the inns uninhabitable. My informant found it impossible to describe the climate.

COOKE. Again the word " impossible." I have visited the country and have found it quite possible to describe the climate.

PHILLIPS. I beg of you, sir, not to harden your resolution before you have consulted Mrs. Meares, whose assiduity in implementing her responsibilities towards my fair cousin have long been an example and an inspiration to us all. Fortunately she approaches. I beseech you to ask her opinion.

ENTER MRS. MEARES.

COOKE. Ah, good morning cousin.

MRS. MEARES. Good morning cousin.

COOKE. How does your charge find herself today ?

MRS. MEARES. She slept well but, alas, the influence of the balmy comforter has not extended itself into the dawn of another day. I should say she is worse.

COOKE. Worse than what ?

MRS. MEARES. Worse than yesterday.

A gloomy silence.

I suggested that she should remain in bed but she has expressed a wish to walk for a little on the terrace and, indeed, the morning air is agreeable and may revive her somewhat.

PHILLIPS *has offered her his seat on the bench and she sits beside* SIR BRIAN.

COOKE. I am glad that she has slept—I slept very little myself. What with thinking of Clarinda and calling down anathemas upon the drunken scoundrels who have put their bellies before my interests, I hardly shut an eye ... Cousin, do you think it possible that the physicians have been wrong? May it not be that all this bleeding and blistering and poulticing and cupping has been misguided? May it not be that my daughter's distemper has its seat in the mind rather than in the body? What do you think, eh?

MRS. MEARES. I am only a poor lonely widow. It would be unbefitting for one of my sex to set her opinion against that of the faculty.

COOKE. Rat me, Madam, I have heard your opinion of the faculty before now. I doubt if you would be a widow *or* lonely if you had held by it.

MRS. MEARES. You are unkind to reproach me with my misfortune.

COOKE. Damn it, cousin, I reproach nobody. But you told me yourself that Dr. Quince was a ruffian and a scoundrel and you told him to his face that he was a murderer to boot. I don't see why you should be so particular in bowing and scraping to his profession.

MRS. MEARES. I bow and scrape to nobody. Thank God my dependent position has not ingrained in me the habit of servility.

COOKE. I meant no offence.

MRS. MEARES. None has been taken. My duty is not to bandy words with you but to give what satisfaction I can in my humble capacity.

COOKE. You give every satisfaction.

MRS. MEARES. It gives me pleasure to hear you say so.

COOKE. I give honour where honour is due. Nobody can say that I am wanting in generosity. I am a simple sort of fellow and my trust can be readily abused. Rat me, when I

think of those hellhounds I trusted to do my business i
Scotland . . . What the devil are we talking about ?

PHILLIPS. It was your intention, sir, to consult my aunt a
to a course of action which, I am bound to say, failed to com
mend itself to me.

COOKE. I don't commend any of my actions to you—
especially when they are none of your business.

PHILLIPS. It is the business of a gentleman to protect th
weaker sex at all times and on every occasion.

COOKE. Curry my wig, am I to delegate the protection o
my own child to anybody who calls himself a gentleman ?

PHILLIPS. No, sir, but I would remind you that I am you
daughter's accepted suitor.

COOKE. I have not noticed that she accepts your addresse
with any great enthusiasm.

PHILLIPS. That is an unworthy remark, sir.

MRS. MEARES. I cannot refrain from intervening. Sir Briar
you know very well that Clarinda holds Mr. Phillips in th
tenderest regard and affection. But her disorder so occupie
her mind that it is hard for her thoughts to take an amorou
cast.

COOKE. That's it. That's it. Her mind. It's all in her mind

PHILLIPS. Sir, I hope that you do not, in my presence, accus
my cousin of simulating her complaint. To the most un
tutored eye she is very ill indeed. She is pale and wan. He
hitherto hearty appetite appears to have taken wing. Sh
seems unable for exercise of any kind. How can you say th:
these are phantasmagoria of the imagination ?

MRS. MEARES. It may seem strange to you, but such :
thing is possible. When I was sixteen, an ardent passion fo
the incumbent of the parish produced in myself almost ident
cal symptoms.

COOKE. But Clarinda is not religiously inclined.

MRS. MEARES. That is true.

PHILLIPS. How were you cured ?

MRS. MEARES. Our family physician prescribed a change o
scene. The change proved efficacious. The scene w:

[4]

Brighton. It was there I met Mr. Meares. He was already, at that time, an elderly man but, except my father, I have never known a more perfect gentleman.

COOKE. So the change of scene cured you?

MRS. MEARES. It was to that we attributed the subsequent steady improvement in my condition.

COOKE. Good, we shall have a change of scene.

MRS. MEARES. To Brighton?

COOKE. To Scotland.

MRS. MEARES. To Scotland, sir?

COOKE. Have you any objection?

MRS. MEARES. None at all. Though, for all its unhappy memories, I should prefer Brighton.

COOKE. You can be ready by Friday?

MRS. MEARES. I am an Englishwoman. If the Dread Reaper with his scythe were to appear on this terrace with the obvious intention of mowing its inhabitants down, I should be ready for him.

COOKE. You think she will benefit?

MRS. MEARES. I have some hope of Scotland. I once knew of a Scotchman in Moorfields who had four fingers and two thumbs on each hand. He had second sight and could charm away chilblains. It is said that the ancient Picts were possessed of certain secrets and simples unknown to medical science. The atmosphere, at least, is salubrious and the sights are strange and various. I beheld a Caledonian one day in White-hall who made an imposing spectacle in his Highland dress. He looked the picture of health. And the cattle, I am told, are magnificent objects.

COOKE (to Phillips). You see?

PHILLIPS. I cannot think that Mrs. Meares has considered the question in all its bearings.

COOKE. I have done the considering. Where is Clarinda?

PHILLIPS. She approaches.

ENTER CLARINDA.

COOKE. Here you are my love, come, sit here beside your old father.

47   [5]

CLARINDA sits between COOKE and MRS. MEARES.
PHILLIPS stands gloomily apart.

Do you feel better my love?

CLARINDA nods.

We have been talking about you and we are all decided to give you a pleasant surprise. You know and believe that your old father is animated by one consideration only—his regard for your welfare.

CLARINDA nods.

We have determined that what you most require to restore you to your pristine health and happiness is a change of surroundings, a change of scene, a change of air, a change of occupation, a change of . . . in point of fact, a change.

CLARINDA looks from COOKE to MRS. MEARES in a
lack-lustre fashion.

We are all agreed on that point.

PHILLIPS. But not upon the nature of the change.

CLARINDA looks at PHILLIPS.

COOKE. Rat me! You will agree too or I will know the reason why.

PHILLIPS. I have been attempting to explain the reason why.

COOKE. Are you coming with us?

PHILLIPS. If you persist in your determination; yes.

COOKE. That's my bully boy. That's my heart of British oak. Blood will tell. I don't know what it will tell but it'll tell something anyway and now there is no time to be lost. Despatch. Despatch.

All rise.

(TRIO) COOKE, PHILLIPS *and* MRS. MEARES.

    COOKE. Pack and go! Let the coach horn sound!
          Let the horses trot and the wheels go round.
    MRS. MEARES. Perchance some Northern Providence
          May blow these gloomy vapours hence.
    COOKE. So may we slay a brace of birds
          Projecting but a single stone.
          Enough delay; enough of words!
          To coach, to coach and let's begone.

PHILLIPS. Alas ! I hope it may not prove
          Your metaphor all too exact ;
          And that the bird we fondly love
          Perish not in our hasty act.
MRS. MEARES. Unusual sounds ; unusual sights ;
          Pyebrocks remote on moon-lit nights ;
          This canker that our rosebud blights
          May cure—revivify—restore
          The state that she enjoyed before.
PHILLIPS. Or bandits, tempests, rain and fleas
          Intensify her sad disease.
COOKE. Pack and go ! Let the coach horn sound
          The horses trot and the wheels go round.
MRS. MEARES. The noble seeming denizens
          In rough but picturesque attire
          Sporting upon their purpled bens
          May haste the end we most desire.
PHILLIPS. Hairy barbarians ; marsh and bog ;
          And broken axles in the fog !
COOKE (*impatient*). Pack and go ! Let the coach horn sound,
          The horses trot and the wheels go round.
MRS. MEARES. Perchance that Northern Providence
          May charm these gloomy vapours hence.
PHILLIPS. Or bandits, tempests, rain and fleas
          Intensify her sad disease.
COOKE. Nay, let's begone.
PHILLIPS. If it must be.
MRS. MEARES. Count upon me.
OMNES. So let's begone.
          Pack and go, let the coach horn sound,
          Let the horses trot and the wheels go round.
          Enough of words . . . enough of words . . .
          Let us begone !

They are gone.

*The stage behind the backcloth lights up showing through
the transparency, Scene I of the play.*

ACT I

Scene I

DONALD *asleep at back but camouflaged with scenery.*

(1. OVERTURE) *A bit of high ground in front of a Highland bothy.*
It is a summer evening in the early eighteenth century.
The bothy is a thatched, tumbledown affair in the middle
of a patch cleared from the heather or drained from the
moorland bog. A narrow track leads to its door.

A very aged little ragged man with a curious resemblance
to the Pantaloon in a Harlequinade is sitting on a cutty-
stool beside the door. From different quarters of the
stage come the calls of a curlew, a plover, a skylark and
a cuckoo. He turns towards each sound as he hears it in
a bleary sort of way and at last is inspired to take up
his fiddle. After a few bars, he breaks into song to his
own accompaniment :

(2. VIOLIN MUSIC)

(3. SONG) OLD MACALPIN.

Ochan, my sorrow ! Ochanie, my trouble !
I wish I was a brown trout, floating in a pool,
With naught to concern me but to wave my tail and bubble.
Am I not the silly one ? Am I not the fool ?

Ochan, to be sitting, brooding on my sorrow.
Gin I was young, now, the way I was before
With a world full of siller to beg or to borrow
And to lie among the bracken for aye and evermore.

MACALPIN. Oh, me ! The same sorrow is on me that is on
they cloudy bens. They cannae to ought but stand there
glooming from generation to generation and I cannae play
my chanter with my mouth full of tobacco and my neb full of
Taddy's snuff. Predestination, that is what it is. Predestination. It's the sad sad world, you have been born into

[8]

Dugald MacAlpin. Well, Well. God save us from lawyers and doctors and make me a good boy. Amen.

(4. MUSIC)

> *As he broods on predestination a sturdy girl of about twenty* ENTERS *singing.*

(4a. SONG) MAIRI.

MAIRI (*off*). Go from my window, you rascal, you amadan !
Go from my window, my darling, my dear.
There is grieving and pain in the wind and the rain
But you canna get lodging here,
My love.
You canna get lodging here.

(*Appears.*) My daddy is grim and my mammy is gurly.
Love nor luck, there is none of it for you.
You'll awa in the rain and never come again
For you mauna come here to woo,
My dear,
You mauna come here to woo.

(*Sit hilltop.*) Go from my window, my rascal, my heartbreak.
Go from my window, my darling, my dear.
Howe'er I be fain, you must gang in the rain
For you canna get lodging here,
My heart,
You canna get lodging here.

> MACALPIN *has accompanied the last stanza on his fiddle before she notices him.*

MAIRI. Oh, are you there, Mr. MacAlpin ? I was just singing.

MACALPIN. So I was hearing.

MAIRI. I thought you would be down at the Clachan.

MACALPIN. Och, no, I thought for a time I would go ; and then I thought, what would *I* be doing at the Clachan ?

MAIRI. Donald will be out on the hill ?

MACALPIN. Aye. Maybe he will I could not say.

MAIRI. It's queer things he will be doing, they're saying, up on the hill.

MACALPIN. Indeed, now, I do not know what he would be doing.

MAIRI. They're saying that much. Queer things.

MACALPIN. There is no saying what they will be saying.

MAIRI. They're saying he's got a friend up there—in the Pass of Slochmuich.

MACALPIN. A friend, now? Well, well.

MAIRI. They're saying it's a gay queer sort of friend.

MACALPIN. Aye. No doubt he would be doing with a queer sort of friend, for he's a queer one himself whatever.

MAIRI. They say he was changed in his cradle.

MACALPIN. I would not be knowing.

MAIRI. What for would you not be knowing, and you his own father?

MACALPIN. I misremember, but I'm thinking I was playing at a Ceilidn down by Glenshernich; but I am not sure.

MAIRI. They're saying his friend's a right queer one. Daft Lachy was saying he heard him playing to her on the chanter out by Slochmuich in the still of the night.

MACALPIN. Aye, he can play, but I would not say that he can play very well the chanter. At the dancing, now, he is good, but he hasnae the hand for a chanter. If his hands had been feet it would have been better for him.

MAIRI. They're saying no one's ever seen her, but Donald and Daft Lachy. It's a queer thing that. What will you be thinking of that now Mr. MacAlpin?

MACALPIN. Och, it's many the day since I was thinking at all. What would I be doing thinking?

MAIRI. She'll not be one of the Lannan Shi? She'll no be a fairy?

MACALPIN (up). Wheesht, wheesht, now girl. We don't talk about such things. A Lannan Shi. Dear me.

MAIRI. He's not the first one in Forrigan to have a sweetheart from among the wee folk.

MACALPIN. Och now be silent you with your blethering, and

if you havena a fairing for poor old Dugald let you be going on your way. I have no time to be talking to you, look you.

MAIRI. Well now.

MACALPIN. If you was on an errand for Donald, I am telling you that he will not look twice the way you are on. A fine lad like him, and you an outlandish creature from no one knows where. Be going now (*into bothy*).

MAIRI (*through door*). I'm wondering if you would very kindly just for a wee minute be going yourself, Mr. MacAlpin. Not very far, just over the hill a wee bit. But I'm thinking she'll not be wanting to see you or to be seeing anyone forbye.

MACALPIN (*in doorway*). Who is this that will not be wanting to see me?

MAIRI. I will tell you the truth, and tell you no lie. It is Mrs. Grant of Forrigan herself.

MACALPIN. Oh, and is it herself, the poor lady? Oh indeed then, I will be going. It is not old Dugald that would be disturbing her in her affliction. And how is the poor soul? (*Into bothy.*)

MAIRI. Och she is badly, badly. She will have nothing for it but she is a clock.

MACALPIN. What is this that you are telling me?

MAIRI. She thinks that she is a clock. We had an awful job with her down at Forrigan. She was for climbing up on the mantelpiece to tell us the time, and when the fit's on her she goes wagging her head from left to right and tick-ticking with her tongue. She strikes the hour by clapping her hands. You never saw the like.

MACALPIN. Dear me, it is the strange thing that.

MAIRI. She's no been right since her father passed away so suddenly. Old Maclean of Kinarra. Man it was sudden yon.

MACALPIN. Aye aye. It is a terrible thing sudden death. It would kill a horse.

MAIRI. They're saying it's a witch put something bad on her.

MACALPIN. It might well be.

MAIRI. She was a wee thing better this morning. Maybe the witch had forgot to wind her up; but she forgot she was

a clock and was talking quite sensible. So Forrigan says—
" Mairi lass, take her for a wee walk up to MacAlpin's bothy.
She was aye fond of the view from there. He said the Mac-
Alpins will be away, and she'd have the place to herself. But
here you are. Do you think you could be going now like a
good soul and let the poor lady have the view to herself?

MACALPIN. Indeed and I will. I will take my chanter and
my fiddle down to the Glen and be playing to myself a wee
bit. *Beannachd leat.*

(5. MUSIC)   EXIT MACALPIN. MAIRI *goes out in the opposite
                  direction.*

                  DONALD *moves, stretching himself and yawning.*

(6. MUSIC)   DONALD *is a tall man of about* 40, *dressed in the
                  most extraordinary collection of variegated rags.
                  He wears a long pig-tail, a kilt, and slashed
                  brogues.*

DONALD. *Mo chridhe! Mo thruaigh!* My sorrow and my
pain! Amn't I the sleepy one!

                              He *thumps himself on the chest.*

(END OF MUSIC 6)

(7. MUSIC)

(*Contd.*) You should think shame of yourself Donald, you that
should be minding Forrigan's sheep, and you leaving it all
to a wee dog. It is not that much sun that you should be seeing
in the sky that you should be sleeping in the shadow of your
bothy. Is it there yourself you are father?

(END OF MUSIC 7)

(8. MUSIC)   He *goes into the bothy.*

                  ENTER MAIRI *and* MRS GRANT. MRS. GRANT *is
                  a comely woman of about* 30, *dressed in a visiting
                  costume of a well-to-do tacksman's wife. She
                  walks like an invalid leaning heavily on* MAIRI,
                  *staring in front of her and muttering occasionally
                  to herself.*

(END OF MUSIC 8)

MAIRI. Now be sitting down Mrs. Grant and resting yourself. 'Deed it's a long walk to be taking, and you just out of your bed. But it'll maybe do you no harm, for indeed it's a fine day whatever—if it keeps.

MRS. GRANT *sits on the cutty-stool.*

And these tinkers—the MacAlpins are away miles from here, so there's no occasion for you to be bothering yourself, no occasion at all. Just sit you down and have a wee rest. Indeed it is a view that need not be proud if the king himself was looking at it.

MRS. GRANT. Yes it's bonny enough.

MAIRI. Are you feeling a wee thing better, Mrs. Grant?

MRS. GRANT. Yes, I'm a wee thing better.

MAIRI. Mind you, I often think if they was to put the hills of Badenoch in a bottle it would do more good than all the medicines and the Doctor's shop at Inverness.

MRS. GRANT. Hoots with your nonsense. You couldna put all these big hills in a bottle.

MAIRI. Maybe not, and all the time they have been standing there. It'll be thousands of years, will it no, Mrs. Grant?

MRS. GRANT. Yes, a long time . . . time . . . time . . . time. . .

(9. MUSIC)   *She begins to move her head slowly from side to side making a clicking sound with her tongue to mark the seconds.*

MAIRI. Now don't be doing that up here, Mrs. Grant. *Mo chridhe*, you give me the shivers. Don't you now. Don't you.

(10. SONG)   MRS. GRANT.

MRS. GRANT. Time, time, time, time.
                    Like lead in my head that hums like a top
                    Slow beats; tick, tock;
                    Bing bang goes the Clock.
                    One and two and three and four, it ticks and
                        ticks and canna stop.
                    One two three four.
                    Just that, no more.
                    Back, forrit; forrit, back.

Tickety, tockety, clickety, clack.
Till we rust into dust
Like the mole in the park and the gull in the
    sky
The fox on the hill and the trout in the loch
They hear the Clock and they ken they'll die.
(*Shouting*) Forrigan, Forrigan ! What garred
    you bring me here to die ?

MAIRI. Wheesht ye now, Mum, wheesht.

ENTER DONALD *from the bothy. He gives the ladies an
elaborate bow.*

DONALD. Good day to you Lady of Forrigan, and good day
to you Mistress.

MRS. GRANT. I knew it, I knew it. It is the Devil himsel' ;
the Father of Lies, and the Prince of the Power of Darkness.

MAIRI. No, Ma'am. No indeed at all. It's just Donald
MacAlpin, Forrigan's herd. You know him fine, Mrs. Grant.
Many's the time he's been doon at the house for his bannocks
and his dram.

DONALD. Och, the poor lady.

MAIRI. Away you go, with you, Donald MacAlpin, and
don't be standing there in your ignorance frightening the poor
lady out of her seven wits.

MRS. GRANT. Are you Donald MacAlpin, the great dancer ?
Or Lucifer Son of the Morning, the great dancer too ? Or
are you the both of them ?

DONALD. Och Ma'am, I am Donald MacAlpin, and I'll have
danced a step now and again, and they're saying I am not bad.
But do you be contenting yourself now, and I'll get you a
drink of water from the well and a sup of crowdie.

MRS. GRANT. No nor crowdie. You would be buying my
immortal soul with your water and your crowdie. It is not to
you I would be selling my immortal soul, Lucifer.

MAIRI. Och Ma'am, you're making a mistake. He is not
Lucifer whatever. He is Donald MacAlpin the herd.

DONALD. And that is true indeed, and well spoken.

MRS. GRANT. I think you are Lucifer, and I never make a mistake. And if you are Lucifer there is something I will be wanting to ask you. Go you down the road lassie for it is not for you to hear.

MAIRI. Toots, toots, Mrs. Grant. You be coming down the road yourself. Forrigan will be asking for you, and it's the red face I would have if I said to him I had left you here at the bothy.

MRS. GRANT. It comes to me that you are forgetting your place. Do you what you are told this instant, or it is away packing you will go to the outlandish part where you were born. Go you like a good lass.

MAIRI. Indeed and I will not Mrs. Grant. I have my duty to Forrigan.

MRS. GRANT. You tinker's brat, you will do as I tell you, or it is not another Monday or Tuesday or Wednesday you will be seeing. Tell Forrigan I will be back in a wee while. Away with you.

> MAIRI *gives her a terror-stricken glance and is about to speak, but* MRS. GRANT *advances on her in such a menacing fashion that she is forced to flee.*

I am glad that she is gone. She is a decent girl, but foolish, foolish. Now you will tell me what I want to know.

DONALD. Yes Ma'am, if it is in my power.

MRS. GRANT. What for is it that I am made like a woman and go like a clock?

DONALD. A clock, Ma'am?

MRS. GRANT. Yes, I go tick, tick, tick, tick, back and forwards, back and forwards and never stop, and when the fit is on me I know that if I was to run down I would die. It is a terrible thing that.

DONALD. I'm sure, I'm sure.

MRS. GRANT. Sometimes I'll be going fast and sometimes I'll be going slow. I have it in my mind that I'm going fast just now.

> *She gesticulates rapidly.*

(*Slow first then accelerate to fastest possible.*) The quickerIgo
the quickerI'llrundownthequicker IgothequickerI'llrundown
the quickerIgothequickerI'llrundown.

DONALD. Is that not a terrible thing? Wait you till I cal.
my father. Father! Come you here a wee minute.

MACALPIN (*without*). I will, I will.

MRS. GRANT. The quickerIgothequickerI'llrundown.

> *She hurries back and forwards within a small compass.*

ENTER MACALPIN

DONALD. Oh dear me father. What are we to do? She's
going that fast she's feared she will run down.

MACALPIN. Well now, if I was to play her a bit of a slow
march what do you think of that?

DONALD. Och it would do no harm, whatever. None at all.
Only haste you.

(11. MUSIC)   MACALPIN *begins a slow march on his chanter.*
            MRS. GRANT *immediately walks more slowly and*
            more calmly.

Mighty me! I wouldna wonder if that was the thing. You
couldnae play MacAlpin's Farewell and maybe she will go
away and leave us in peace.

MACALPIN. I misremember the tune.

MRS. GRANT. Don't stop. Play a Strathspey.

(12. MUSIC)   *He plays a Strathspey and* MRS. GRANT *moves*
            gracefully into a dance, humming the air as she
            does so.

That is right, there is time now. They were telling me you
were the wonderful dancer Lucifer, and there you are standing
like an old cow at a gate. Be putting some life in your toes
man. And you, old fellow, stop cheeping on that chanter and
give us a spring on your fiddle.

(13. MUSIC)   MACALPIN *takes up his fiddle and plays a lively*
            reel.

That's the way of it! That's the thing! Och, it's the old
itch I have in my French heels and my ten wee toes wiggling

like a basket of eels ! Put you some smeddum in your elbow,
old fellow ! And you, you big wandered stot, shake you your
great big feet !

> *She dances.* DONALD *looks on sheepishly. She stops.*
> MACALPIN *stops.*

MRS. GRANT (*contd.*). What for do you not dance ? Am I
too ugly for you ?

DONALD. Oh, it's not that, Mem, it's not that at all.

MRS. GRANT. I'm ugly but it's not that ?

DONALD. Oh, dear me, it is not ugly you are, as well you
know, Mem.

MRS. GRANT. What is it then ?

DONALD. It is not the thing for the like of me to be dancing,
just the two of us, me and the Lady of Forrigan.

MRS. GRANT. It's a lady I was ; but it's a lady I am no more.
I'm the wife of a tacksman, and dance, you !

DONALD. Yes tacksman's a tacksman ; and who am I, I'm
asking you ?

MRS. GRANT. A tacksman's a tacksman—a tick, tock, tick,
tock tacksman. A ticksman a tocksman. With a tick and a
tock and a tack . . .

DONALD. Och, father, my sorrow she's away with it again.
Play you, man ! Play Maggie Cameron or the Drunken Piper.
It is a terrible woman this, and her a lady.

(14. MUSIC)   MACALPIN *plays.* MRS. GRANT *takes no notice at*
> *first ; but goes on ticking and wagging her head.*

Me thruaigh, me thruaigh, what are we to do now at all
at all ?

MACALPIN. Dance you, Donald, and see if she comes out of
it.

> DONALD *dances.* MRS. GRANT *stops ticking and looks*
> *at him curiously.*

DONALD. Dear me, now. She has the terrible look in her
eye !

MACALPIN. Let you her eye alone. Shake your foots, lad.
Shake your foots.

(STOP MUSIC 14)

I'll give you a wee touch of the

(15. MUSIC) Shan Trews . . .   Give a Hooch, man, give a Hooch!

DONALD. Would that be respectful, now?

MACALPIN. You can give a respectful Hooch.

DONALD (*respectfully*). Hooch!

MRS. GRANT. Hooch!

MACALPIN. Good lad, good lad! Stop you and I'll give you a tune of my own composure.

(16. MUSIC) Dance, man! Dance.

> MACALPIN *is now thoroughly enthusiastic. He stands up, playing his kit and now and again executing a few shuffling steps.* MRS. GRANT *is infected by his enthusiasm and begins to dance, discreetly, with, still a far-away, daft look on her face. She joins in the refrain of " Dirrum-dumdee-dumdaddy-oh."* DONALD *is dancing as well as he can though still with some embarrassment. He and* MRS. GRANT *begin to set to one another in a centre-danse.*

MRS. GRANT (*suddenly*).
>> Dirrum-dumdee-dumdo-dumdee
>> Dirrum-dum doo-dum daddy-oh!

(17. MUSIC)

MRS. GRANT. I'm whirring, I'm going to strike! Faster, Faster!

> MACALPIN *breaks into a very fast reel and the dancing becomes fast and furious.*

Play up, Auld Hornie, play up! Are ye sleeping, Donald, ye sturdied hogg? Dance, man!

MACALPIN. Dance, man.

DONALD. Dance, is it? I'll show you dancing, look you. I'll show you dancing you doitit hizzie. Give it your elbow, father, and your shoulder and all that is in you.

MRS. GRANT. And De'il take the hindmost.

[18]   260

DONALD. He can take what is left, whatever. Step you, my lassie. Step you.

MACALPIN. Hey! Hooch!

DONALD. Hey! Hooch!

MRS. GRANT. Hey! Hooch!

1st CURTAIN

CURTAIN *up to Moonlight scene. Full out.*

CURTAIN

Music staggers. CURTAIN *up again. Moon down.*
Just before dawn. MACALPIN *sitting playing in his sleep.*
DONALD *near death.* MRS. GRANT *fresh as ever.*

(18. MUSIC)   *The* CURTAIN *comes down to indicate a lapse of*
time. The Orchestra takes up the air con brio.
When the CURTAIN *rises again, it is bright moon-*
light and MRS. GRANT *and* DONALD *are still*
(19. MUSIC)   *dancing.* MACALPIN *is nodding over his instrument*
and only playing by fits and starts. DONALD *is*
exhausted, but still game. MRS. GRANT *is as*
fresh as a daisy.

Occasionally happy "Hoochs" from MRS. GRANT.

DONALD. *Ochanoch! Dhia gleid sinn! Tha mi Dubhachas!*
Let be, now let be. Let us be resting a wee while.

MRS. GRANT. No. No. Go on. Go on. Dance!

DONALD. *Droch caoidh ort!* The black sorrow on you, you wild cat.

MRS. GRANT. Are you beat, then? Are you beat?

DONALD. I am not. I am Donald MacAlpin, the finest dancer that ever was seen or heard of from here to the word's end. Play up, you palsied old *bodach!*

He plays. They dance.
THE DAWN BREAKS.

DONALD. Ochone and there's the breaking of the day. I have danced the sun down and the moon up. I have danced all through the night. I have danced the sun up out of the sea and over the bens. Never was there such dancing.

261   [19]

> DONALD *falls suddenly to the ground and passes out.*
> MACALPIN *drops his fiddle and goes to his assistance.*
> *After a few hesitant steps* MRS. GRANT *joins them.*

MRS. GRANT. What is the matter with the man?

MACALPIN. Indeed, you are the one to be asking. I am thinking you have ruined the poor lad entirely.

MRS. GRANT. Och, it was only a wee dance. I have no mind how it started.

MACALPIN. Away you, Mem, now, like a good lady or it will be the worse for all of us ... Is it well with you now, calf of my heart?

DONALD. I am fine. I am in fine, fine trum. Take you your fiddle and I will show you dancing.

(20. MUSIC)

> FORRIGAN *calls off.*

MRS. GRANT. Forrigan!

> *At this point* ENTER FORRIGAN, *a sturdy, middle-aged man, followed by a* LAD *with a blunderbuss.*

(21. FORRIGAN'S 1st SONG)

FORRIGAN. The hen went wandering out-owre the moor
> Out-owre the moor, out-owre the moor.
> The hen went wandering out-owre the moor,
> I canna win to my hen.
> I'd give a' the grazing in Forrigan glen
> I'd give my steading, my but and my ben
> And a' my lassies and a' my men
> To ha'e her back again.

> FORRIGAN *takes the centre of the stage. He is tired and angry and carrying a big stick. The halflin* LAD *is carrying a lantern as well as a blunderbuss.*

At last. Put out that lantern, you stupid fellow.

> *The* LAD *extinguishes the lantern.*

You would be looking for a lady with a lighted lantern and it high noonday. I never saw such a stupid fellow ... Jean, where have you been and how do you find yourself, whatever?

MRS. GRANT rises then faints suddenly.

Dear me, what is this at all?

> *He kneels down by* MRS. GRANT. *The* OTHERS *watch him silently.*

It is just a faint and I do not wonder and her wandering the moor through the night. Or was she wandering the moor? ... Here, you, Murdo, you stupid fellow, take you her head. And go you, you old creature and get some water, if you know the element by sight, which I am very much doubting.

MACALPIN. Indeed, it is a very good idea.

> EXIT MACALPIN *into the cottage.*

> FORRIGAN *advances on* DONALD *threateningly,* DONALD *stands his ground, looking stupid, because he is too tired to do anything else.*

FORRIGAN. And now what sort of a ploy is this?

DONALD. Och, it was a wee ploy. The leddy and me. Just a wee ploy. (*He lies to sleep.*)

FORRIGAN. What? You unsophisticated black tinker. I'll break the bones of you, so I will.

(22. MUSIC)

(*Repeat.*) What—caper is this? Will you be telling me or will you not?

DONALD. Be taking your hands off me, now, Mr. Grant.

> RE-ENTER MACALPIN *from the bothy.*

FORRIGAN. If I have a word out of your head!

MACALPIN. Don't be hitting him, Donald. We will have the law on him.

FORRIGAN. Will you be speaking or will you not?

> FORRIGAN *beats* DONALD. OLD MACALPIN *goes to* MRS. GRANT *with his quaich of water.*

By—speak you or I'll crack your head open on the wall o your own bothy.

(END OF MUSIC 22)

MACALPIN. Let him give it you, Donald. It is a sore lot he

263   [21]

will be paying when we take him to the Courts . . . How do you find yourself, Mem?

MRS. GRANT. Ahhh.

> FORRIGAN *turns at sound. Kneels. Donald escapes into the bothy and slams the door.*

FORRIGAN. See me that quaich.

CUE *for* CURE *music.*

MACALPIN. The poor fellow and him maimed for life, I wouldna wonder . . .

MRS. GRANT. Where am I?

MACALPIN. You're among friends, Mem.   Just that. Among friends.

> *He takes the quaich from* MACALPIN *and kneels beside* MRS. GRANT.

FORRIGAN. Take you a wee sup of this.

Very soft.

MRS. GRANT. Is that yourself, Mr. Grant?

FORRIGAN. It is, it is.

MRS. GRANT. I'm tired.

FORRIGAN. Aye, you'll be tired.

MRS. GRANT. What am I doing up here in a place the like of this?

FORRIGAN. That is what I do not know, but I will find out look *you.*

MACALPIN. Poor poor Donald. Maimed for life.

MRS. GRANT. I want to go home.

FORRIGAN. I'm sure. I'm sure.

MRS. GRANT. What in the world am I doing, sleeping up here on the tuleich?

FORRIGAN. That's what I'm asking myself.

MRS. GRANT. I had the queerest dream if I could remember it.

FORRIGAN. I'm sure.

MRS. GRANT. What time is it?

FORRIGAN. Och, don't you be fashing yourself about time.

[22]

MRS. GRANT. It's all very well for you, with no house to redd up and no cows to milk.

FORRIGAN. Wait you till I get that girl.

MRS. GRANT. What girl?

FORRIGAN. That girl Mairi. I gave you in her charge.

MRS. GRANT. It will be a funny like thing when any girl has charge of me. I do not know what you are saying.

FORRIGAN. Well, well.

MRS. GRANT. Help me up and we'll away out of this . . . Och, it will be the rheumatics I'm having, my legs are that sore.

FORRIGAN *helps her up.*

FORRIGAN. Well, well. And how do you find yourself?

MRS. GRANT. I'm fine, but for the legs and the hook of my back. What way are you looking at me like that? You would think I was daft.

FORRIGAN. Well, well.

MRS. GRANT. My goodness, it's not that, will it be? It's not queer in the head I am?

FORRIGAN. No. No. I wouldna say that. It is very strange.

MRS. GRANT. Come away home.

FORRIGAN. Yes indeed. (*To* MACALPIN.) I will be up to see you before long. And see you that you do not run away. For, by the hokay, I will hunt you down with dogs.

MACALPIN. You will find me here, Forrigan.

FORRIGAN. See that I do. And that skelly-eyed natural your son too . . . Take my stick in your hand, my dear, and I will oxter you down the path.

EXEUNT FORRIGAN, MRS. GRANT *and the* LAD. MACALPIN *looks after them.*
In a little, DONALD *puts his head round the corner of the door.*

DONALD. Are they away?

MACALPIN. They are away. And stay you where you are, my son. I have a thought or two in my head. Lie you there close like a buckie in its shell till I tell you what you are to do.

DONALD. He's a terrible man that, in his ragings.

MACALPIN. Are you hurted sore?

DONALD. No. I was sore feared, but the like of him couldna hurt the like of me.

MACALPIN. Well, well. Shut you the door and lie close. Do what I'm telling you, now.

> DONALD *disappears.* MACALPIN *in deep thought begins to hum McCrimmon's Lament.*

MACALPIN. *Cha till, cha till, cha till mi tuille* . . .

ENTER MAIRI, *cannily.*

MAIRI. Hist! . . . Mr. MacAlpin!

MACALPIN. Is that yourself Miss Mackintosh?

MAIRI. Aye.

MACALPIN. Dear me, now.

MAIRI. I'm just after a long long night in a peat hag and you will be saying that's no place for a decent young girl.

MACALPIN. It is not. And what would you be doing in a peat hag?

MAIRI. I was feart to go home . . . Oh, my grief, never have I had a night the like of that.

MACALPIN. It would not be very comfortable.

MAIRI. It was fair miraculous, dear me. The trembling on me Mr. MacAlpin was such that I near shook myself out of my shift. And the fairy fiddler was playing all night long. And the skrieching and the hooching and the stamping of the fairy horses' feet. It was fair monotonous. Imagine the terror that was on me, and me sitting in a wet ditch. Do I look terrible, Mr. MacAlpin?

MACALPIN. Aye, aye. A wee thing terrible.

MAIRI. What'll I do, dear me? What'll I do?

MACALPIN. I would away home, like a good lass.

MAIRI. I couldna do that. What would they do to me, and me deserting my post?

MACALPIN. They'll never notice you. Say you your auntie was ill.

MAIRI. I have no auntie.

MACALPIN. That is a peety. You can think of me as your
auntie and true it is that I am not feeling very grand. So
away you go.

MAIRI. I couldna.

MACALPIN. Och, the nonsense. A wise like lass like you.
They have things to think of down in Forrigan the day. Run
you down by the cottie where they canna see you and get you
the warming pan ready for the lady's bed. And mind that
you were with your auntie and she was sore distressed with
the defluxion and hard put to it to see out of her two eyes . . .
Run you like a hare. And look you. She gave you the slip
by the fir planting. She said to you, " Away to your auntie,
lassie. I am for home." Say you that and say you no more.
She will not remember what she said to you . . . And remember you have not seen the MacAlpins except the one and
he was so like your auntie, you never knew the difference.
Run, now.

MAIRI. Heavens Moses! That's wild all the gither. Can
you imagine me saying the like of that, forbye remembering
it.

MACALPIN. Och, it will come to you natural. It is natural
to a brisk young girl to be telling lies.

> MAIRI *has been gazing at the ground during the latter part*
> *of the talk.*

MAIRI (*suddenly*). Oh! ! !

MACALPIN. What's taken you now?

MAIRI. The ground. Do you see the ground?

MACALPIN. I do.

MAIRI. *An eirig m'anama !* It is trampled flat.

MACALPIN. Maybe.

MAIRI. I knew it. I knew it.

MACALPIN. Eh?

MAIRI. All night I heard the trampling and the whinnying
and the neighing of horses.

MACALPIN. Aye, you were saying so.

MAIRI. It's the fairy horses! It's the wild white horses of
the Lannan Shi.

MACALPIN (*up*). Well, I'm not saying but that it might be that.

MAIRI. Were you not hearing them yourself, and them rampaging round your very door ? (*Tail off in terror.*)

MACALPIN. I may have heard something.

MAIRI. Oh, it's the fool I am to come here ! And your son the fancy man of a woman of the Shi and you yourself as unchancy an old warlock as ever I mean. My soul and my grief, I'm away out of this !

> EXIT MAIRI, *running.* MACALPIN *looks after for a moment and then picks up his fiddle.*

MACALPIN. You be doing a wee bit thinking for me, sweetheart ; for it is not a practice I am much used to, at all, at all. Let me see, let me see.

> *He plays a few bars and then sings, if he pleases, without accompaniment,* THE WREN. (*Herd's Collection,* 1776.)

(23. SONG)

THE WREN

The wren she lies in Care's nest
In Care's nest, in Care's nest.
The wren she lies in Care's nest
Wi' muckle dole and pine, O !
When in came Robin Redbreast,
Redbreast, Redbreast.
When in came Robin Redbreast
Wi' succar saps and wine, O !

Now, maiden, will you taste o' this ?
It's succar saps and wine, O !
Na, ne'er a drap, Robin,
Though it were ne'er so fine, O !
And where's the ring that I gied ye,
My little cutty quean, O ?
I gied it till a sodjer,
A true sweetheart of mine, O !

Nae mair ye'll see the face o' me,
Ye ill-conditioned wren, O !
I'd rather nor be fashed wi' ye
Tak' a bonny wee speug for my hen, O !

CURTAIN *as he begins to play his fiddle.*

END OF SCENE I

(24. MUSIC)   INTERLUDE

ACT I

Scene II

(25. MUSIC)   SCENE : *The same.*
TIME : *Next day. Early afternoon.*
Sun and cloud alternating. MACALPIN *is sitting on the ground at his cottage door. To him,* GRANT OF FORRIGAN, MR. MACK, *an elderly lawyer with a Lowland accent, and* MAIRI. MAIRI *looks very frightened and is reluctant to appear.* MACALPIN *pays no attention to his visitors, beyond cocking an eye at them as they come on.*

FORRIGAN. Mairi Mackintosh, keep you by me, or it will be the worse for you.

MAIRI. I'm feared.

FORRIGAN. Tuts. We have Mr. Mack with us. There is nothing natural or supernatural that has the measure of a clever lawyer.

MAIRI. All the same . . .

FORRIGAN. Tuts ! Don't you be passing an insult on Mr. Mack. I thought you better knew your place.

MACK *takes snuff.*

MAIRI. I did not intend . . .

FORRIGAN. Very well then . . . MacAlpin ! Is this your Highland courtesy ?

MACALPIN. I have no inclination to exchange courtesies with Grant of Forrigan this day, whatever.

FORRIGAN. It is so, indeed ? Well then, courtesy or no courtesy, you will get to your feet or I will help you with the toe of my boot.

MACK. Easy, Mr. Grant. Easy.

MACALPIN *gets up.*

MACALPIN. I did not observe that there was a stranger.

FORRIGAN. Where is Donald ?

MACALPIN. Ah, you may ask, the poor lad. The Donald you knew and the Donald he is will never be the two of them the same to all eternity, whatever.

FORRIGAN. I want to see him.

MACALPIN. What for because?

FORRIGAN. Never you mind.

MACK. Excuse me ... You'll be Mr. Dugald MacAlpin, I'm thinking?

MACALPIN. I am, sir.

MACK. Aweel, Mr. MacAlpin, we have business with your son that would be best conducted with sweet and brotherly accord.

MACALPIN. You'll be a man of Law, maybe?

MACK. I wouldna say but you're right.

MACALPIN. Have you any knowledge of a pup of a man they call Creeping Wullie Mack in the vennels of Inverness?

MACK. I am Mr. William Mack.

MACALPIN. Then you'll be that pup of a man. Well, well.

FORRIGAN. You ill-conditioned tyke!

MACK. Canny, now, canny. The poor fellow doesna ken what he's done. It's a very chancy thing to use words like that Mr. MacAlpin. In front o' witnesses, anyway. But no doubt you meant no offence.

MACALPIN. I have not much English, but my meaning was plain in my head.

MACK. You take a high hand.

MACALPIN. It is a way of the MacAlpins.

MACK. Mphm. But there's one or two MacAlpins that might think it a wise-like thing to ask a stranger his errand before flying out on him.

MACALPIN. I care not what is your errand. You will be telling your errand to the Sheriff, or maybe to the Lord Judges in the Court of Session itself. They'll be better able to understand it than an ignorant man the like of me.

FORRIGAN. That's a true word. Ignorant.

MACK. Now, now, Mr. Grant ... Man, MacAlpin, it would save an awful lot of trouble if you werena so Heiland. Mr.

Grant and I have good news for you and here's you going on as if we carried an ejection warrant.

MACALPIN. I do not think you will be ejecting me.

FORRIGAN. I would not be too sure of that.

MACK. Man, for God's sake hold your tongue. You're as Heiland as him. There's nobody going to evict you, Mr. MacAlpin.

MACALPIN. I'm glad of that, truly.

MACK. So am I. So am I. It's a sorry business that.

MACALPIN. And you are a good judge.

MACK. That's as may be. Now listen here to what I'm telling you.

MACALPIN. My old grannie had a warrant on her in the snow of winter and her ninety years old in her stocking soles.

MACK. Aye. A hard thing that. Well, as I was saying . . .

MACALPIN. And there was my sister Lizzie that was married on a Robertson . . .

MACK. No doubt, no doubt. But that would be a long syne. Now, what I'm saying is.

MACALPIN. It may be long syne or short syne, but there is no long or short in the memory of the Gael.

MACK. Aye. I've noticed that.

MACALPIN. We'll forgive, whiles, but we never forget.

MACK. A proud boast, a proud boast.

MACALPIN. And it is no boasting forbye.

MACK. I know that. Now, haud your horses a minute and listen.

MACALPIN. When we cut our way through the Philistines on the plains of Moab and took ship from a port of Cathay . . .

MACK. I've heard tell of it. And now . . .

MACALPIN. It is in the books of History.

MACK. Aye, it's all there. Sneck up a minute, you daft cateran, and let me tell you something.

MACALPIN. What will you be knowing of the great Kings of Albian that could part two fighting rams with their naked fists ?

MACK. We could be doing with one of them here.

MACALPIN. We could.

MACK. We're agreed on that point.

MACALPIN. We are.

MACK. Man, that's fine. Now here's another point.

He sits on MACALPIN's *cutty-stool.*

Mary, lass, step forward and dinna be feared. And see that you tell the truth this time.

MACALPIN. She knows nothing, that lass. Nothing at all, at all whatever, in her ignorance.

MACK. Wheesht. Mary, you brought your mistress up the hill to the bothy?

MAIRI. It was her. She made me come.

MACK. Well, well. And you had a word with Mr. MacAlpin here and his son Donald MacAlpin.

MAIRI. Yes, sir.

MACK. And they spoke her fair and civil?

MAIRI. Yes, sir.

MACK. Then she bid you begone because she would have a word with Donald MacAlpin in private.

MAIRI. Yes, sir. She said I was a tinker's brat and . . .

MACK. Her exact expressions are immaterial.

MAIRI. Och, no indeed yes, her trouble was on her gey bad.

MACK. Aye, the poor lady.

MAIRI. She was going tick tick.

MACK. Yes. And you went as she bade you.

MAIRI. I was feared of her, her having the trouble.

MACK. Nobody's blaming you. What happened then?

MAIRI. I don't know. I ran and I ran. She had an immaterial expression in her eye.

MACK. Are you feared of her today?

MAIRI. No, sir. She's herself again.

MACK. Douce and wise?

MAIRI. What you say yourself, sir.

MACK. Mr. Grant, you would say yourself that your wife is altogether cured of her strange distemper?

FORRIGAN. I would, I would. It's miraculous. She hasna been like this for three long years.

273   [31]

MACK. Well, there it is. We made an unfortunate beginning Mr. MacAlpin. There were faults on both sides. But you'll see that we've come to you out of pure gratitude.

MACALPIN. Indeed, is that so ?

MACK. It is. Nay more, Mr. Grant is anxious that you should take a wee gift in token of the gratitude he feels. Now, would ten pound Scots be any use to you ?

MACALPIN. What we did was nothing at all, nothing. My son was glad to be of any service.

MACK. I know, I know. But Mr. Grant would feel happier in his mind if you would accept a small token. And there's another thing. In return for this small consideration, it would be an advantage to know how the cure was brought about. The lady might take a relapse, you see.

MACALPIN. No doubt it would be a great advantage.

MACK. Good. Good. So, if we could have a word with young Mr. MacAlpin . . .

MACALPIN. You will have a word with him if he is able.

MACK. Grand. Grand. Is he in bye ?

MACALPIN. He is within.

MACK. Will I go in ?

MACALPIN. No, sir. I will call him forth—if he is able.

MACALPIN *goes to the door.*

Are you hearing me, Donald ?

DONALD (*within*). Och. Och. Ochanee.

MACALPIN. Is it sore afflicted you are, Donald ?

DONALD. Aye. It is. It is.

MACALPIN. If I was giving you a hand, could you be coming out to give these gentlemans I have here a sight of their handiwork ?

DONALD. Och. I will try, whatever.

MACALPIN. Och, the poor lad !

(26. MUSIC)   MACALPIN *goes into the hut and returns immediately supporting* DONALD, *who can hardly be seen for sticking plaster, bandages and crutches. At this point a Gaelic Lament for* DONALD *is sung.*

Ah, now, would not the sight of that be drawing tears from Forrigan's bull?

(27. LAMENT)

OMNES. O, Spirits! O, Spirits!
Mend the broken bones and heal the bruises.
Heal Donald! Heal Donald!
Make him strong and well to tread the heather.

MACALPIN. Look *you*, what will the Red Lords in Edinburgh be saying to that, or is there no justice in all the land of Scotland at all?

MAIRI. Oh, my sorrow, is that not terrible!

MACALPIN. Will you be writing that down in the language of the Law, Mr. Mack. It will be a thing to fill with astonishment the generations yet unborn.

FORRIGAN. Man, it's sorry I am. I do not know my own strength. Is it sore hurted you are, Donald?

DONALD (*moans*). Ah!

MACALPIN. I do not think he will be having two bones stuck end to end in all his body.

FORRIGAN. I am terrible in my rages. Terrible!

MACK. Now, don't you be saying too much. Leave this to me.

FORRIGAN. Och, but my heart is sore! There stands the man who restored my good lady to health and strength and me to lift my hand to him in my wrath. It is a sore lesson to me . . . and a lesson to those too who anger me without cause.

MACK. Well, well. Mr. Forrigan has come forrit with a very handsome apology, as I think we will all agree; and there should be sma' difficulty in arranging the little matter of compensation . . .

MACALPIN. I'm thinking the Red Lords in Edinburgh will be as terrible in their wrath as Forrigan, when they hear what he did to the poor lad.

MACK. You'll be acquaint with those same Lords of Session?

MACALPIN. No, sir, no. But I have seen them in a picture and fearsome they are, I do assure you.

MACK. Aye. You're a bold man, Mr. MacAlpin. It's not

many a wee crofter from Slochmuich would face the Lords
on their bench, and him wi' little of the English and less
Latin, I'm thinking. *Quod Deus vult perdere prius dementat.*
Have it your own way.

MACALPIN. You were observing ?

MACK. *Prius dementat ?* If you canna construe that, you've
a poor chance wi' their Lordships. You'd be better to face
St. Peter and you no' kenning your catechism.

MACALPIN. Dear me, is that so ?

MACK. Do what you like. Away you go to Edinburgh. But
experientia docet. *Verbum sap*. You'd be better biding where
you are.

MACALPIN. And what would they be doing to me and me
not knowing their Latin ?

MACK. I wouldna say. It all depends. I've known a man
hangit because they couldna make out what he was ettling to
say.

MACALPIN. Dear me, now. That is a wild like thing.

MACK. They've little patience, their Lordships. See now.
What do you say to living here rent free for the next twelve
month and twenty pound Scots in your sporran and no
bothering their Lordships ava ?

MACALPIN. What do you think, Donald ?

DONALD. Take it, man. Take it.

MACALPIN. Well, now . . .

MACK. Right. Make your mark here.

> MACK *whips out a parchment and an inkhorn.* DONALD
> *makes his mark.* MACK *smartly pays him his money.*

MACK (*putting the paper in his pocket, after sanding it*). And
you will note, that, being the Tenant of Mr. Aeneas Grant,
Tacksman of Forrigan, half of all emoluments accruing to
you from the exercise of the Art of Healing, Comforting,
Curing etc., etc., of the Sick, Maimed, Lunatick etc., etc., will,
of right, be paid to said Aeneas and so on. Well, Mr. Grant,
we'll be stepping.

DONALD. Yes, yes. And how is the poor lady ?

FORRIGAN. Never better. Thanks to you, Donald. I know not how you achieved it, but I am content. She will be a sorry woman to learn that you are not so well.

MACK. We'll be stepping.

FORRIGAN. If there is any way in which I can repay you mind you in reason— . . .

MACK. They're weel paid. Come away man.

FORRIGAN. Well, well. Good day to you MacAlpin.

MACALPIN. ⎫
           ⎬ Good day to you, Forrigan.
DONALD.   ⎭

EXEUNT MACK *and* FORRIGAN. MAIRI *lingers*.

MACALPIN. Well, well.

DONALD. Did he give you the money?

MACALPIN. He did, now.

DONALD. That is a good thing. Although, mind you, I am not liking all this paper business at all, at all.

MACALPIN. We will conseeder.

DONALD. It is devil's work, this making marks on paper.

MACALPIN. Maybe, maybe. We will conseeder.

MAIRI (*to* DONALD). It is the great man you will be being from now to all eternity, Mr. Donald.

DONALD. It is possible. My father and I will conseeder.

MAIRI. If I could be bringing you a kebbuck or a kid up from the farm now and again, now, would you take it ill?

DONALD. No. No. I would not say.

MAIRI. There are whiles I have the fearful pain in the hook of my back—just there, see. Is there any help for that at all, would you be thinking?

DONALD. I would not say.

MAIRI. I hope you are soon well yourself.

DONALD. Indeed, I hope so.

MAIRI. It's here the pain gets me. It's like there was a partan aye grip-gripping. Och and it's sorry for you I am. Them that suffers themselves is aye the most pitiful of the woes of others. The pain of it fair gets me greeting. It is awful bad at this very moment. But, och, there's no occasion for you to be bothering and you that sore afflicted yourself.

DONALD. Aye, aye. Just that.

MACALPIN. You be going on your way, young Mistress and not be bothering the lad.

MAIRI. I was just going. Though it's that sore I would not be surprised if I was to faint by the wayside. It's here, like a red hot coulter. You could feel it if you put your hand to it. Ochanoch! It is the sore pain and sorrow to me, whatever. Here.

> *She carries* DONALD's *hand to her back and immediately becomes radiant.*

Oh, Holy Heavens! You have the Touch! It has gone like snow off a dyke! Is not that the wonderful thing?

DONALD. I would not say.

MACALPIN. Be away with you now.

MAIRI. It is a mighty miracle. Oh, it is the happy one I am! I could burst out at singing like a lintie. It is the kind, kind ones that you are, whatever.

DONALD. It is nothing. It is nothing.

MACALPIN. If it is singing you will be, sing then and be going.

MAIRI. Be singing you too.

(27a. TRIO)   MAIRI, *and the two* MACALPINS.

> Ho Ro! Naebody at home?
> Meat nor drink nor money have we none.
> For you're no love for me, my dear,
> And I'm no love for you.
> What mair is there that we can do?
> Nothing ava, nothing ava!
> So we'll up with our pack on our back
> And awa boys awa.

> EXIT MAIRI.

MACALPIN. Well, well.

DONALD. It was a queer thing, yon.

MACALPIN. Aye, aye.

DONALD. Do you think, father, that maybe I have the
healing touch?

MACALPIN. I'm conseedering.   I'm thinking that maybe
there's more you can touch than the crook of a wee lassie's
back . . . but, I'm conseedering.

DONALD. Have you conseedered what to do with the siller
the man gave you?

MACALPIN. Ach, that requires no conseederation.

(28. DUET)   MACALPINS.

We will out and we will hame
Airing dizzily and toddling lame.
Routhie, couthie, stottering and a'
Woe betide us gin we fa'.
    Eirich! We'll win hame soon
    Stotting hame with seeping shoon
    Canny takes you up and canny takes you doon,
    By the light of the cappernoytit moon.

(29. MUSIC)   DANCE.

EXEUNT to bothy.

CURTAIN

END OF ACT I

(30. INTERVAL MUSIC)

ACT II

SCENE I

(31. MUSIC)   *Two months later.* MAIRI *is discovered setting to rights a living-room at Forrigan. The* GRANTS OF FORRIGAN *are well-to-do people, and though their house is an old one and not very big, there is a sort of slovenly attempt at grace in its appointments and decoration. The garments of good Queen Anne have been drawn rather hurriedly over the nakedness of "the savages north of the Grampians."* MRS. GRANT *has been to school in Edinburgh. She can even play the spinet. There is one in the corner.*

(31a. SONG)   MAIRI.

" Och a Dhe, the sorrows on me.
    Wae is me," said the lassie said she,
" Weary be on me when the gloaming shimmers,
    For the lad that had a notion of me
    The sappy lad with his lambies and his gimmers
    Is piping a tune to his fairy limmers
    Nor wots he a button if I live or dee."
    Och a Dhe. Then farewell he.
Thou wast a bonny laddie and I did love thee.

MRS. GRANT (*without*). Mairi !

MAIRI. Yes, Mistress Grant !

        EXIT.   RE-ENTER, *carrying a clock, with* MRS. GRANT.

Are you sure, now, Mistress Grant ?

MRS. GRANT. Of course I'm sure. Put it down there and don't be letting it fall.

                  MAIRI *puts down the clock.*

MAIRI. I was just wondering.

MRS. GRANT. Would we be having visitors and not let hem see our grand clock? You are foolish, foolish.

MAIRI. You've wound it up, Ma'am.

MRS. GRANT. That's right.

MAIRI. You're sure it's all right, Ma'am.

MRS. GRANT. What has come over you, today? . . . Oh! Dear me, that's over and bye with. You have surely that confidence in the Healer to be sure that his Healing sticks for good.

MAIRI. That is a true word. There is not the washing in the whole of the world would give me a chug in my back. And it was a sore judgment to me in days gone by.

MRS. GRANT. You are an ungrateful oinseach, so you are. What are we, I'm sure, if we have no faith in those who do us good?

MAIRI. I'm sorry, Ma'am.

MRS. GRANT. There's no word of the carriage?

MAIRI. No, Ma'am. Forrigan has rode out to meet it on the roan mare. Murdo's at the gate in his new kilt.

MRS. GRANT. Well, haste you and put on a clean apron. That one's all over dust from the clock.

MAIRI. Oh dear me, so it is. And, my Heavens, I can hear the wheels.

MRS. GRANT. Run then.

> EXIT MAIRI. MRS GRANT *lays down her work and begins to set herself and her room to rights.* MAIRI *comes back changing her apron.*

MAIRI. The Healer and old MacAlpin are here.

MRS. GRANT. Oh dear me, on this day of all days. I hope they'll not be offended at me for not receiving them. You told them we were expecting visitors.

MAIRI. Aye, Ma'am. It wouldna be the thing for them to be meeting the English gentry. They have the Gift, but to speak the truth, Ma'am, they are awful looking tinkers.

MRS. GRANT. Ah, poor souls, so they are. Where are they?

MAIRI. In the kitchen, Ma'am. They are quite joco.

MRS. GRANT. Did you give them a dram?

MAIRI. They dina need asking, Ma'am.

MRS. GRANT. Well, well. Away you go to the lobby and be ready to take anything the ladies are carrying in their hands.

(32. MUSIC)   *Sound of wheels and horses' hooves.*

(33. MUSIC)

SONG OF WELCOME.   FORRIGAN.

Come, bring in your brogues to the heat o' the peat
The heat o' the peat, the heat o' the peat;
And settle your hurdies on my ingle seat
And kittle your heart with a dram.
You are kin to a king; you have naething to fear.
We are poorly for gear; and unchancy in leir.
But we'll rant and we'll sing and make Highland good cheer
When we tickle our hearts with a dram.

> EXEUNT MAIRI *and* MRS. GRANT. *The stage is empty for a little and the clock is heard ticking. It chimes the three-quarters and is drowned by the noise of the reception of* GUESTS.
>
> *The* GUESTS *are* SIR BRIAN COOKE, *a consequential little man in his late fifties;* MRS. MEARES, *his cousin and pensioner in her late fifties; and* CLARINDA COOKE—

(34. MUSIC)

> *—his daughter in her late 'teens. They are ushered in by* FORRIGAN *and* MRS. GRANT.

MRS. GRANT. Come in, come in.

FORRIGAN. Come along Mr. Phillips. The young lad will see to the horses.

SIR BRIAN. Oh, let him see to them. He likes it. He likes horses. Why, I'll be damned if I know. Stupidest beasts in the world, Ma'am.

> FORRIGAN *goes to the door.*
>
> ENTER PHILLIPS, *a young man about town. He is followed by* MR. MACK.

FORRIGAN. How are you, Mack? This is Mr. Phillips, my dear.

MRS. GRANT. We are happy to welcome you to Forrigan, Mr. Phillips.

PHILLIPS. You are most obliging, Ma'am. Your obliged and humble servant.

MRS. GRANT. And now Mrs. Meares, Sir Brian, will you partake of a little cordial? I am sure you are tired, indeed.

MAIRI ENTERS with a jug of Athole Brose.

COOKE. If you will first allow us to remove the stains of travel, Ma'am, we shall be most happy.

MRS. GRANT. Miss, here, looks poorly. Would she not be the better of a wee suppie? It's Athole Brose.

MACK. A Highland beverage, Sir Brian. Verra sustaining.

MRS. MEARES. Will you excuse us, Ma'am? My niece is a great invalid. With your permission we shall retire to our apartment.

CLARINDA smiles bravely and wanly.

MRS. GRANT. Surely, Ma'am, surely. I'll take you up myself. There's a green log fire in the room. It will help to revive her. Athole Brose is sometimes chancy on a tender stomach. Put down that pig, girl, and take Miss Cooke's other oxter. The poor wee lass . . . Take you the gentlemen, Forrigan.

FORRIGAN. I will, I will. Will you be pleased to step this way.

With some ceremony, EXEUNT OMNES.

OLD MACALPIN insinuates himself in at the door. He is carrying a set of bagpipes. He has now an air of tatter-demalion grandeur, in a patched pair of tartan trews and a bonnet with a feather. He takes off the bonnet.

(35. SONG)   MACALPIN.

THE TINKLER
(Traditional Air)

The lady she was dressing
A-dressing for a Ball

When she spied the Great Big Tinkler
Sleeping up against the wall . . .

Refrain :

Wi' his plaid and his flea-bit sporran
His whiskers flying free
And his bonnie ragged bonnet hanging low upon his bree.

The lady wrote a letter
And on it she did say
She'd rather have a Tinkler
Than her husband any day.

The Tinkler read the letter
And syne says to himsel,
" I'm six foot ten of tinkler
And I think I might as well."

" I have whiskers like a sunset.
The leddie's kind and douce.
I canna disoblige a leddie.
I'll awa into the hoose."

He kissed them in the kitchen
He kissed them in the Hall.
" Ochonorie," said the wifie,
" Is he going to kiss them all ? "

They're awa out owre the heather
They're awa oot owre the brae.
For she'd sooner hae the braw big Tinkler
Than her husband any day.

> ENTER MAIRI, *without seeing him. She tastes the Brose.*

MAIRI. Oh, Mr. MacAlpin, you shouldna have come here.
This is the best room.

MACALPIN. Is it, indeed ? (*He hiccups solemnly.*) If you came
from these parts it would not be unknown to you that a King
would be proud to receive one of the Clan Alpin in the best

parlour in the best of his hundred palaces. (*He hiccups again.*)
So he would.

MAIRI. Oh, Mr. MacAlpin, don't be telling me you've had
a drop too much and you playing for the gentry at their supper.

MACALPIN. There is not in the mighty ocean a drop too
much for old MacAlpin and him playing for the gentry.
What is that you have there?

MAIRI. Athole Brose.

MACALPIN. Do you tell me that?

> MACALPIN *picks up the jug and sits down with it on his
> knees.*

MAIRI. Be a good man, now, and put that back.

MACALPIN. I'll be putting it back in my own good time.

MAIRI. I'll get my head on my hands.

MACALPIN. It would be as useful in your hands as anywhere
else, whatever.

MAIRI. Are you out of your senses? Put it back, then.

MACALPIN. That is just what I'm going to do.

MAIRI. That is the fine manners, I promise you.

MACALPIN (*drinking*).   Slainthe.   You mind your own
manners and I'll mind my own.

MAIRI. I don't know what Forrigan will say, so I don't.

MACALPIN. He would say to me, " MacAlpin, make yourself at home." It is that I am doing.

MAIRI. Ach, it's the old ignorant drunken trash you are,
getting me into trouble.

MACALPIN. It's yourself you will be getting into trouble if
you use that language to me.

MAIRI. You Hieland thief, I have no fear of you, no indeed,
yes. Maybe except for the fleas you carry on your ragged old
carcase.

MACALPIN. It is the wicked tongue, you have, for sure, and
the great ingratitude.

> *He drinks.*

MAIRI. It's small cause I have to be grateful to the like of
you, you skelly-eyed old Satan.

MACALPIN. I will have a word with my son Donald and he will put that murdering trouble in the pit of your back would make you think you was being ridden by the old Man of Moidart himself.

MAIRI. Oh now, surely, you wouldn't be doing the like of that!

MACALPIN. Let him cast his eye on you and he'll twist the strings of your haunches till the yelling of you is heard in the Western Isles and America itself forbye.

He drinks.

MAIRI. My sorrow, not that for an idle word!

MRS. GRANT (*without*). Mairi!

ENTER MRS. GRANT.

MRS. GRANT. Where have you been, in all the world?

MAIRI. Oh, Mistress, don't let him do it!

MRS. GRANT. Dear me, the poor man can have a wee drink if he feels the want of it . . . How are you, Mr. MacAlpin?

MACALPIN *rises, fairly steadily.*

MACALPIN (*in Gaelic*). God's blessing on you, lady of the house.

MRS. GRANT. And the same to you, heartily. But maybe you would be going now to the kitchen and Mairi will be putting on for you a white pudding and a black with a cogie of usquebagh to wash it down.

MAIRI. Tell him no' to put the black witches on my back.

MRS. GRANT. What would he be doing that for, dear me?

MACALPIN. The poor young girl is a wee turned in the head with all the excitement. I will bid Donald take a look at her.

MAIRI. No! No, no! No!

MRS. GRANT. Dear me, it is very kind of Mr. MacAlpin to speak to his son about you, and him so busy these days doing his good works among the sick and ailing. Go you and get the warming pan—Miss Cooke is going to lie down for a wee —and then be putting the puddings on the fire for our good friends the MacAlpins . . . Is Donald well?

[44]

MACALPIN. Thank God, he is, Ma'am. I thank you for asking.

MAIRI *is about to speak, but thinks better of it and goes.*

MRS. GRANT. He is the great man now.

MACALPIN. We cannot complain.

MRS. GRANT. It is a wonderful gift.

MACALPIN. So they are saying.

MRS. GRANT. Did he have a look in the byre at the old white cow that was badly ?

MACALPIN. He did. It will be a matter of two pounds ; but just when you're ready.

MRS. GRANT. Forrigan will see you about it. You're playing tonight ?

MACALPIN. If it is your pleasure.

MRS. GRANT. Good. Away you go now, for I don't know whether I'm standing on my head or on my heels.

MACALPIN. Och, I can tell you that, Ma'am. You are on your heels. It would be a strange thing for a lady of your graciousness to be standing on her head. And so I will go.

ENTER FORRIGAN, COOKE *and* PHILLIPS. MACK *following.*

FORRIGAN. Ah, MacAlpin.

MACALPIN. And how is yourself, Forrigan ? I was making my way to another part of the house.

FORRIGAN. Fine, man, fine. And how is your good son ?

MACALPIN. He halts a wee on his left foot and his ribs, look you, will never be the same. But I thank you for asking.

FORRIGAN. He should cure himself.

MACALPIN. He does the great cures, but that would be the greatest—to cure himself.

COOKE. A philosopher, eh ?

MACK. Aye, Sir Brian, we have them in these parts. More of them than honest workmen, I'm thinking.

MACALPIN. I do not know whether you rank as Forrigan's guest, but I will give you the benefit of the doubt, Mr Mack, sir . . .

MACK. Thank you kindly.

MACALPIN. I was thinking, Forrigan, that I might be playing
" The Battle of the Birds " tonight.

FORRIGAN. Fine. It is a good tune.

MACALPIN. And, if you will excuse me, I will be leaving
you. My service to you, Ma'am ; and gentlemen. And to
you, yourself too, Mr. Mack.

EXIT MACALPIN.

COOKE. A character, eh ?

MRS. GRANT. An old servant, an old servant. He is very
independent. But I must be going too or that stupid lass will
be burning the skin off Miss Cooke with the warming pan.
Poor young lady, she is in a sore way. You have the jug
there, Forrigan, if there's any of it left.

EXIT MRS. GRANT.

FORRIGAN. You'll be trying some Athole Brose.

COOKE. Well I've heard of it.

FORRIGAN. It is a good poultice for the stomach. It is
honey and oatmeal and a wee drop of whisky. It'll warm you.

He pours out.

MACK. It will that. We say in Scotland that it builds bonny
bairns. I was brought up on it myself. I've changed a wee
bit, of course, but I was a handsome baby.

COOKE. I don't doubt it. Your health, sir.

PHILLIPS. I join in that.

FORRIGAN. I thank you.

COOKE. Very good.

PHILLIPS. Enchanting.

COOKE. Mrs. Meares must ask your lady for the recipe.

FORRIGAN. She will be very pleased. Mr. Mack, help yourself.

MACK. I will.

FORRIGAN. Be seated, gentlemen.

ALL sit, a short silence.

FORRIGAN. Aye, aye, she will be very pleased.

COOKE. What's your acreage of Scotch pine ? Never mind
the larch and the birch. We can come to them later.

FORRIGAN. Well, now, that would be a matter for Sir John; but I could show you what we have from here to Delbuiack and on the other side to Inverlaidnan . . .

MACK. Tuts! We cannae talk business on empty stomachs.

PHILLIPS. I agree with all my heart.

FORRIGAN. It is as you wish, gentlemen.

COOKE. We've a bit of country to cover, Walter.

PHILLIPS. We can ride round the forests tomorrow. You cannot drag Clarinda any further.

COOKE. Your countryside would be none the worse of a little money, Mr. Grant.

MACK. No countryside is any the worse for a little money.

FORRIGAN. So they are telling me.

COOKE. Pretty wild and desolate, eh?

FORRIGAN. Aye. You might find it so.

COOKE. If my plaguy bronchitis would stand it, I'd tidy it up for you in four or five years.

FORRIGAN. I'm sure, I'm sure.

PHILLIPS. You must admit, uncle, it is all vastly romantic.

COOKE. Mph.

PHILLIPS. Those mighty, frowning hills turn the mind inevitably to the supernatural, I find. What legends lurk in those gloomy glens! What singular beings have consorted in these shadows with the indigenous inhabitants! What rites have been exercised! What forgotten songs sung! What clashing of claymores! What cries of agony!

COOKE (*to* MACK. *In hushed whispers*). What the devil . . . we must give him a pill.

(36. SONG)   PHILLIPS.

The peaks and the crags of the stag and the eagle
What visions they conjure; what thoughts they inspire!
What terrors imagined their purlieus inveigle!
What substance provide for the Bard and his Lyre!
How fierce blows the blast over torrent and heather!
How wildly the Clansman employs his claymore,
Made drunk by tradition and whisky and weather;
The skirl of the bagpipes, the odour of gore!

Those threatening Bens cannot fail to concern us
In their mantle of mist and their tippet of pine.
Majestic they tower like the Hills of Avernus
While low in the valley the coronachs whine.
Ah! Feeble indeed must be his inspiration
On some rocky precipice taking his post
Who broods on the view of each wild situation
And peoples the scene with no demon or ghost.

COOKE. What the devil! We must give you a pill.

MACK. Aye, aye, queer things have happened here.

COOKE (*looking at* PHILLIPS). I don't doubt it.

MACK. It was a namely spot once for brownies and war-locks; kelpies and witches.

(37. MUSIC)

PHILLIPS. I knew it.

MACK. I would not say they have all gone with the old religion. I wouldn't say that.

PHILLIPS. You still have witches.

MACK. Aye, so they say.

FORRIGAN. A wheen of old wives' tales.

MACK. You get bitter badness in some old wives and a lot of truth in their tales.

COOKE (*turning uneasily towards the darkening window*). Witches, eh?

PHILLIPS. You interest me profoundly. Pray continue.

MACK. There is nothing for continuance. But even I—I'm an educated man, if you understand me—even I would rather be in the wynds of Auld Reekie in a dark winter night for fear of queer things coming chapping at my door.

(38. MUSIC) ENTER MRS. GRANT *with* MAIRI *and the* HALFLIN *carrying candles.*

MRS. GRANT. Bless me, you're sitting in the dark. Forrigan, indeed you should think shame of yourself . . . What in the world were you talking about?

PHILLIPS. Of goblins and ghosties, long-leggity beasties and things that go bump in the dark.

[48]

MRS. GRANT (*suddenly serious*). Preserve us ! No. I wouldn't be talking about the like of that. I thought you would be talking business.

COOKE. I wanted to, Ma'am ; but there were too many poetic gentlemen in the room.

MRS. GRANT. You will be having a hard day tomorrow, going round the forests.

COOKE. Yes.

MRS. GRANT. It's a sorrowful thing, cutting down a tree.

COOKE. Never found it so, Ma'am.

MRS. GRANT. You'll have cut down thousands in your time.

COOKE. I've given orders for it.

MRS. GRANT. Ah, then you'll be like some great general. It is not much pity you will be having.

(39. DUET)   SIR BRIAN *and* MRS. GRANT.

MRS. GRANT.   O spare the larch and spare the pine
               That shade our happy vales ;
               That stand so soldier-like and fine
               Against our cruel gales.

SIR BRIAN.   I hack and hew and saw their ranks
               To bring you wealth untold ;
               To irrigate your barren banks
                   With floods of yellow gold,
               To guard our coasts from sterner blasts
               I chop your pinetrees into masts
                   To bear Britannia's sails
                   'Gainst cannon balls and gales
               And I must say it seems to me
               A proud and glorious destiny
               For any ragged Highland tree.

MRS. GRANT.   Yet I must say it seems to me
               A sad and doleful destiny
               For any noble Highland tree
                   For any Highland tree.

PHILLIPS. It is a profound thought, Ma'am, that those to

whom are entrusted the destinies of their fellow creatures are compelled to deny themselves the luxury of pity.

MRS. GRANT. It's a comfort that you and I are little folk, Mr. Phillips—though I should not be saying that and you a grand London gentleman—for it's a great pity I feel for all of you as hungry as hawks and my useless trash in the kitchen not ready for you yet. We're not over used to visitors up in Forrigan; but we'll get better with practice, for you'll be making a good long stay now that you are here.

COOKE. We must be off tomorrow, Ma'am.

MRS. GRANT. Tomorrow? Indeed and you will not. You'll be killing the poor young lady, among you.

COOKE. She has her ups and her downs. She may be as gay as a linnet in an hour or two. But I confess that she gives us anxiety.

MRS. GRANT. Dear me, I don't wonder. The paleness of her! And she's all the time on the edge of tears. Have you had doctors to her, now?

COOKE. We have, Ma'am. Twenty solemn, rapacious blackguards who only made her worse. The most recent of them advised travel and change of scene. But I fear that has failed of its effect.

MRS. GRANT. I wonder, now . . .

COOKE. She has been bled, she has been blistered. She has swallowed a Sahara of powders and drunk gallons of sewage at dozens of Spas. And yet she is no better. We are at our wits' end.

MRS. GRANT. I was very ill myself, this very summer. Two months ago.

COOKE. Indeed, Ma'am? You look the picture of health.

PHILLIPS. There is a certain salubriety, no doubt, in the Highland air . . .

FORRIGAN. It was nothing. Nothing at all. You must not be speaking of such things to your guests.

MRS. GRANT. I would have it that I was a clock.

(39a. MUSIC)

FORRIGAN. Now, now, I forbid you to speak of it.

[50]   292

PHILLIPS. A clock, Ma'am?

FORRIGAN. It was nothing at all, nothing at all. A daft notion she had. Away you to the kitchen, woman, and see what they are doing there. You will have us all in starvation with your blethers.

MRS. GRANT. They're saying I was bewitched.

FORRIGAN. Och, what will we be hearing next? Away you go.

MRS. GRANT. Of course, I don't believe that.

MACK. There's evidence for't one way and there's evidence the tither. I wouldna go so far as to say . . .

(39a. END OF MUSIC)

MRS. GRANT. It was a queer, queer thing.

FORRIGAN. The point is, you're quite well now and we are hungered.

MRS. GRANT. Aye, I'm quite well now . . . Och, here's Mrs. Meares.

ENTER MRS. MEARES.

PHILLIPS. How is she?

MRS. MEARES. She has had another of her seizures; but she is better a little and may sleep.

COOKE *stands*.

(40. MUSIC)

MRS. GRANT. Will we send her up some supper? She'll have a tender stomach and she'll not be wanting much, but we can give her cockie-leekie and there's a bit of a salmon and a boiled trout or two and some smokies from the East Coast, and some cheese eggs, and a roastit capercailzie and a grouse or two; and there's a side of venison and a pigeon pie and a jugged hare and a plum tart seeing you're English . . . we're simple folk up here in the wilds, you will understand, Ma'am . . . and a kebbuck and some crowdie and some bread and scones of my own baking if there are any corners to fill up. But don't you be thinking you'll be faring so poorly as all that. You'll have heartier appetites than a sick lassie and I've that in mind too.

(40. END OF MUSIC)

COOKE. You are very considerate.

MRS. GRANT. It's the least we can do. But I must see to my sluts in the kitchen or it is the poor fare you will be getting. Mr. Grant!

FORRIGAN. My dear?

MRS. GRANT. Will you be stepping to the pantry and giving some fresh air and a touch of the fire to two or three bottles of claret?

FORRIGAN. Bless me! Was I not forgetting? You will excuse me, Madam and Sirs?

COOKE. Why yes, certainly.

MACK. This is a matter that will require legal assistance.

EXEUNT FORRIGAN, MACK *and* MRS. GRANT.

COOKE. I hope that their claret does not deserve of such mishandling. A touch of the fire, indeed!

PHILLIPS. Come, come, sir. It is all kindly meant. I am, indeed, in a state of continual astonishment at the good nature of the denizens of these most barbarous localities.

COOKE. You are forever in a state of continual something or other.

PHILLIPS. If I displease you, sir, I regret it heartily.

COOKE (*sitting*). When I was your age, sir, I did not care a brass farthing whether I pleased or I didn't please.

MRS. MEARES. You are hard on Walter, cousin. You must reflect that he is a young man of the most exquisite sensibility.

COOKE. Sensibility is no doubt very elegant, but I prefer a trifle more manliness.

PHILLIPS. No one, sir, has hitherto dared to impugn my manliness.

COOKE. Nor do I.

PHILLIPS. You may inquire of a certain Irishman and a certain Dutchman whether it is safe to do so. I ran the first through the lung and the second carries a bullet in his left shoulder.

COOKE. I know. I was hasty. I am three parts Irishman

myself. But I wish to Heaven you would marry my daughter
and take her off my hands.

PHILLIPS. Sir !

MRS. MEARES. I cannot sit silently and listen to such un-
endurable coarseness.

PHILLIPS. You know how ardently I wish it. But what can
I do ?

COOKE. How do I know ? It is seven long months since
you asked my permission to pay your addresses to her. You
seem to have made little progress and she grows worse and
worse.

PHILLIPS. Am I to blame for that ?

COOKE. How do I know ?

MRS. MEARES. Sir Brian, you know very well that he is not
to blame. He treats her with the most tender consideration.

COOKE. I know. I know.

MRS. MEARES. If I may hazard a poor lonely old woman's
opinion, he treats her with more consideration than her
father does.

COOKE. What do you mean ?

MRS. MEARES. Dragging a poor delicate creature like her
through a howling wilderness like this !

COOKE. Dr. Mool said she needed change of air.

MRS. MEARES. He suggested neither such a violent change
nor such a superfluity of air. Last night we slept with our
entire wardrobe piled on top of us and a damp and alpine
mattress beneath us. I awoke, however, in the night looking
into the cold calculating eye of a barnyard fowl. It was sharing
our apartment and had perched on the bed.

> COOKE. *Move to fire rubbing hands. Sit first on centre
> chair.*

COOKE. It is a wild, savage country.

MRS. MEARES. I am happy that you admit it. Perhaps you
will also admit that you did wrong in subjecting a delicate
young lady to such horrors. To say nothing of me.

COOKE. Of you—(*laugh*)—fillet and skelp me here's a pretty

change of front. Walter here, would have it we get our throats cut, and here he is poetizing about their good nature. As for you, you lashed us into the venture with prognostications of an earthly paradise. (*Laugh*.) And anyway we are not so ill off here.

MRS. MEARES. In this hovel ?

COOKE. Yes.

MRS. MEARES. It is true that a cracked veneer of gentility covers their native savagery. But they owe that to the wealth they stole from England in the shameful so-called Union of 1705.

PHILLIPS. Nay, you are ungenerous. There is a native nobility among the very poorest of this race that might well put to shame the best born among us.

MRS. MEARES. They are ragged boors, every one of them. They are vain, uncleanly and pedantic and I cannot abide them.

COOKE. Well, well. We are as God made us.

MRS. MEARES. And they have no sense of humour.

COOKE. They can't have everything.

MRS. MEARES. They are boastful liars ; they are practically atheists ; and they are constantly and persistently tipsy.

PHILLIPS. You have then little liking for them ?

MRS. MEARES. None at all.

PHILLIPS. There is truth in what you say of the Scots ; but yet I find in them some tincture of the gallantry of their rampant lion or their native stag.

MRS. MEARES. I have not noticed it. Except, what I forgot to mention, they are extremely bad-tempered. They are also mean. And thieves. I can see nothing to commend in the men of Scotland ; though there must be something. They are better than the women. O, to be in England !

COOKE. *England !*

(41. TRIO)   MRS. MEARES, PHILLIPS, COOKE.

Like doves in wilderness on weary wing
  Far from their nest in some deep shady wood,

[54]

From the sad bosoms of our wandering
We hymn the strain of our nostalgic mood.

Why hither, gods of wanderers, why hither
Fly we where tempests howl and precipices frown?
What still awaits us? By what paths and whither
Come we at last to solace and the Town?

Like doves in wilderness on weary wing
Raising sad eyes to heavens of leaden hue
From the sad bosoms of our wandering
We mourn our lot, we mourn our cot with melancholy
" Coo, coo, coo.
Roocoocoo, chuck, chuck. Coo, coo."

RE-ENTER FORRIGAN *and* MRS. GRANT.

MRS. GRANT. It was a shame to leave you like this. But you would have plenty to talk about.

COOKE (*rising*). We were talking, Madam, of the Scottish race.

MRS. GRANT. Deed and I hope you were speaking well of them.

PHILLIPS. Mrs. Meares was commending them highly.

COOKE. Especially the men.

MRS. GRANT. Listen to that, Forrigan. Are your ears not burning?

ENTER MAIRI.

MAIRI. Your supper's ready, Mrs. Grant. And O, Mrs. Grant, the table looks bonny!

MRS. GRANT. Thank you, Mairi.

FORRIGAN (*to* MRS. MEARES). Madam, will you do me the honour?

(42. PIPE MUSIC) *Bagpipes are heard tuning. They go into Supper.*

CURTAIN

END OF SCENE I

(43. PIPE MUSIC)   INTERLUDE

ACT II

Scene II

SCENE. *The same an hour or two later.*
A kettle is on the fire and a tremendous array of bottles and glasses is near at hand for the toddy.

(44. MUSIC) MRS. GRANT *is at the spinet singing a Highland song to her own accompaniment.*

SONG. MRS. GRANT *at the spinet.*

A chuid do Pharas da, mo chridhe !
His share of Heaven to the lad that's gone from me.
The song is quiet that sang in my heart.
Naught sounds there but the cry of the whaup
And the lambs that bleat for lost yowes.

Pruitcha, ladies, come to the byre.
The moor is cold, in the house is never a fire ;
And none to feel the sun in my hair ;
None to see the rowan in my mouth ;
None to hear but the cows.

> MRS. MEARES *is sitting bolt upright with a forbidding expression on her face, doing some lace work.* CLARINDA, *convalescent, is reading a book.* MRS. GRANT *finishes her song and turns round to the others.*

CLARINDA. That was beautiful. Was it your own composition ?

MRS. GRANT. Oh, dear me, no. I'm not so clever as all that. It is a song the girls sing when they are taking the cows back from the pasture.

CLARINDA. It is a very sad song.

> CLARINDA *touches her eyes with her handkerchief.*

MRS. GRANT. Oh, it is nothing to what we can do in the way of sadness. But maybe it was too much for you ?

CLARINDA. It is my wretched sensibility.

MRS. GRANT. Maybe you should not have come down.

CLARINDA. I felt so much better. And it was all so strange and lonely.

MRS. GRANT. Aye. So it would be.

The wind howls.

CLARINDA. How the wind howls.

MRS. GRANT. Aye. You will hear it howling now and again.

CLARINDA. It is like a lost soul in torment.

MRS. GRANT. I do not know that I have ever heard a lost soul in torment, but no doubt you will be right.

CLARINDA. Will you sing to us again?

MRS. GRANT. Och, it's only the daft, savage sort of songs that I know. I tried my hand at the others. Handel, and the like of that—but och! It was like a lost soul in torment.

(45. MUSIC)   DRINKING SONG   *Off.*

FORRIGAN.	I ga'ed to the gaol for a cogie of skilly.
OMNES.	Hech, boys, the cogie! And now for a dram.
FORRIGAN.	But when I got there, faith, I must have looked silly.
OMNES.	Forget it, forget it and tak' off your dram.
FORRIGAN.	I have a wee still out-bye in the heather.
OMNES.	Hey for the Devil and hey for his dam!
FORRIGAN.	And there we will drink and grow canty together.
OMNES.	For there's naething in Scotland to beat a good dram.

MRS. GRANT. Wheesht, now. Here are the gentlemen coming.

> ENTER COOKE, PHILLIPS, FORRIGAN *and* MACK. *They are solemn and dazed, as well they may be. They are not strictly speaking tipsy; but the gravity of the Englishmen betokens a recent awe-inspiring experience. They make steadily for the chairs and lower themselves into them.* FORRIGAN *takes his tone from his guests. Through* MACK'S *solemnity, some kind of devilish secret*

delight keeps breaking. He sits on the window box and rubs his hands stealthily.

COOKE (*before sitting*). A monumental repast, if I may say so.

Sit.

MRS. GRANT. You are very kind, Sir Brian.

PHILLIPS (*starting*). Clarinda ! You here ?

CLARINDA. Yes, Walter.

PHILLIPS. But is this wise ?

CLARINDA. I have never been noted for my wisdom.

PHILLIPS. Mrs. Meares . . .

MRS. MEARES. Such little influence as I have had over your cousin has gone long ago.

CLARINDA. That is unkind.

MRS. MEARES. Accuse me to your heart's content. I have learned to bear it.

FORRIGAN. Well, well, we'll say no more about it. We are glad to see you. There is great gaiety in female companionship, say you what you like. Let us do our best, there is no sparkle in the company until we join the ladies. Mr. Mack, will you lend a hand with the toddy ?

MACK. I will.

Rises.

(45a. MUSIC)   *The Toddy is prepared in a gloomy silence.* PHILLIPS *goes solicitously to* CLARINDA *and attempts to touch her hand, but she withdraws it. Even* MRS. GRANT *shows some signs of exhaustion, but she moves a table nearer to her guests.*

MRS. GRANT. Was Mr. Mack telling you any of his stories, Sir Brian ?

COOKE. Yes, Ma'am.

MRS. GRANT. He is a terrible man, Mr. Mack.

MACK (*at back*). Defamation of character, Mrs. Grant. Defamation of character.

MRS. GRANT. Dear me, we must be careful. He'd have me down before the Lords of Session as soon as look at me.

COOKE. Would he indeed ?

MRS. GRANT. The Red Lords, we call them in the north. Judges, if you understand.

COOKE. Judges, eh? I dislike litigation myself. Always avoid it if I can help it. There are other ways of going about to get one's own way.

MRS. GRANT. I'm sure, I'm sure.

MACK. Aye, there are ways and ways.

COOKE. I never go to law if I can help it.

MRS. GRANT. I'm sure you're very wise.

Cross to Clarinda.

COOKE. Yes (*to* CLARINDA) ... Do you find yourself somewhat restored, my dear?

CLARINDA. Yes, Papa.

COOKE. Good. Good.

MRS. GRANT. We'll need to teach her to take some nourishment, while she's staying up here. She picks like a wee hen. All that long journey and half a bowl of broth and a wee bit of salmon and a slice of roast venison and a spoonful of kail and the sensation of a pigeon pie at the hind end of it. And but two glasses of Madeira to wash it down with. It would break your heart. But the Highland air will change all that.

> *While she is speaking, the toddy is served and they pledge each other. Even* CLARINDA *takes a glass. She makes a wry face, but comes back for another before long.*

COOKE. I hope so ... Your respectful and obedient, Ma'am. Indeed I hope so. Alas, I sometimes think that hope only exists only to be blighted.

> CLARINDA *and* MRS. MEARES *shed a few tears unostentatiously.*

COOKE. My daughter was a healthy, happy child. She weighed nine pounds when she was born. Later, her glad cries were forever resounding through the Italian gardens of my demesne in Yorkshire. (*Cross to fire.*) Nay, as she grew to blossoming womanhood, she was still the gayest of the gay.

At balls, routs and assemblies, her laughter rang the loudest of all.

PHILLIPS (*affected*).   Nay, but a short year ago, my fair cousin was the most joyous madcap in the shire. Ah, woe the day when she began to wilt upon her stem !

(45b. SONG)   CLARINDA.

> In spring the lambs do bleat and bound.
> So bounded I, so bleated I.
> In spring the jocund warblers sound.
> So in my spring I used to sing.
> But now, alack, I bound no more.
> I am not as I was before.
> The feathered choristers in their glee
> Can find no counterpart in me.
> My Hey and my Hi and my lilly lolly o
> Have changed to accents charged with woe.
> Ah, pity me ! Ah, pity me !
> Pity a poor, disordered maid.

COOKE. Yes. Her physicians were baffled. They are still baffled.

CLARINDA (*strong after song*). I beg of you, sir, to spare me. I am indeed and indeed much, much better. Your sad words dim the evening's merriment . . . Mrs. Grant, will you sing to us once more that mournful little strain ? In some strange manner it recalls to me memories of happier days.

COOKE (*inquiringly*). You are talented, Ma'am ?

MRS. GRANT. Dear me, no.

CLARINDA. She is. She has a wild, strange talent. Pray sing, Mrs. Grant.

MRS. MEARES. You must not pester Mrs. Grant to sing if she does not wish to do so.

MRS. GRANT. It is no bother to me, no bother at all ; but I was thinking my singing did you more harm than good.

FORRIGAN. Aye, sing us a song, Jean, we'll have a cielidh.

MACK. Go on, Mrs. Grant, or I'll be singing myself.

[60]

MRS. GRANT. No, no. Sing you, Mr. Grant. I nearly had the lassie greeting when I sang to her.

FORRIGAN. Oh, well, now, I'm a wee roupy, but I'll try.

MRS. GRANT and FORRIGAN go to the spinet.

(45C. SONG)   FORRIGAN.   (Traditional)

O gin my love were yon red rose
That grows upon the castle wa',
And I mysel a drap o' dew,
Into her bonnie breast to fa'.
My love's bonnie, bonnie—bonnie,
My love's bonnie and fair to see;
And aye when I thrill on her dapperbye face,
Then in her company I would be.

CLARINDA. O !

MRS. MEARES. What is it, my precious ?

CLARINDA. Aunt, have you my smelling salts ?

COOKE. What's the matter now ?

CLARINDA. It is nothing. A brief spasm of faintness.

PHILLIPS and MRS. MEARES make a fuss of her.

MRS. GRANT. Take some more toddy. It will do you good.

CLARINDA. Thank you. A very little.

COOKE. Don't discompose yourselves. It will pass off. Won't it, my love ?

CLARINDA. I hope so.

COOKE. She doesn't like too much attention paid. Let us by all means have a song, or some cheerful anecdote or witty conversation.

PHILLIPS. Yes, yes. Believe me it would be best.

MRS. GRANT. Let it be witty conversation. We looked forward to your coming, just for that. Mr. Phillips, start you some witty conversation.

PHILLIPS. With all the pleasure in life, Ma'am. Do you choose a subject.

MRS. GRANT. There now, you have me beat. I can't think of a thing.

303   [61]

MACK. I mind when I was a wee laddie running about the Parliament House . . .

CLARINDA. Oh! Oh!

MRS. GRANT. Oh, dear me, where is it now, my lamb?

CLARINDA. I never in all my life felt so dreadfully.

MRS. GRANT. Tell Mrs. Grant, now.

(46. MUSIC)

CLARINDA. It begins round my heart which feels like a large jellyfish caught in a jogging tide-eddy in a narrow channel between barnacled rocks. It then rises up to my throat in great waves as if I had swallowed an animated feather bolster, with a huge lump of polished marble in the depths of it. All over the surface of my body I feel a sensation that is neither hot nor cold, but partakes of the unpleasant qualities of both. My limbs are enveloped in a prickling numbness. I think it is of the nature of a creeping paralysis, if you wish me to be more exact. It is as if I had been totally immersed in some heavy liquid and stung vigorously by nettles. My mouth and throat are dry and parched and I have a throbbing headache. The headache is not exactly a pain like toothache, though I have a pain like toothache just here in the upper region of my waist. The sensation in my head is exactly as if I were standing upright in a huge printing press and gigantic, invisible hands were turning the screw. In addition to this, it throbs, I cannot express to you how it throbs . . . But I am talking about myself. Do not let me interrupt the social current of the evening. I have learned to suffer in silence.

(END OF 46)

MRS. GRANT. You will go straight to your bed this minute.

MRS. MEARES. Indeed, yes.

PHILLIPS. Clarinda, if this mortal frame of mine could bring you relief by dying for you on the spot, you have but to say the word.

CLARINDA. I shall never forgive myself for having discomposed you, dear Mrs. Grant; and you, my kind friends.

FORRIGAN. I'll tell the lad to saddle the mare and ride to Grantown for the Doctor.

PHILLIPS. I shall accompany him. (*Going to door.*)

MACK. I have a better plan.

COOKE. Out with it.

MACK. It'll take an hour to get to Grantown and an hour to get back. (*He takes snuff.*) There is a Doctor in the hoose.

COOKE. Where?

MACK. Well, he's no' just exactly a Doctor.

PHILLIPS. For God's sake, man, pretermit your legal quibbles. There is no time to be lost.

MACK. You'll have heard tell that Mrs. Grant hersel' was sore afflicted for many a long month. The Doctor at Grantown and an auld billie from Edinburgh College confessed themselves baffled.

COOKE. We all know that Doctors have great facility in confessing themselves baffled. Go on. Go on.

MACK. Weel, as I was saying . . .

MRS. MEARES. Sir, the matter of Mrs. Grant's illness may be of great interest to you and to the company; but my duty is to get my young charge to bed. Will you assist me, Mrs. Grant?

MRS. GRANT. Surely, Ma'am. Surely. Come away, my precious, and we'll get the clothes off you and the warm blankets round you in a jiffy. And I've a syllabub ready that will put new life into you.

CLARINDA. Alas, what have I done that I should be so afflicted?

EXEUNT MRS. GRANT, MRS. MEARES *and* CLARINDA.

PHILLIPS. And now, sir? You were drawing, I hope, towards the point of your discourse.

MACK. There was a herd man in Forrigan—a kind of a natural, if you understand me, fell in with Mrs. Grant at the height of her distemper. It had never been suspected, but he had the Gift. By what process we know not; but he so worked upon Mrs. Grant that she fell into a refreshing sleep and awoke completely restored.

He takes snuff.

FORRIGAN. It is the truth. Between ourselves, gentlemen, it is a true word.

COOKE. And this natural—this shepherd. What became of him.

MACK. It got about. These things get about. He is in a fair way to becoming the Aesculapius of Speyside. The sick and the halt tak' their ailments, real or imaginary, to the fellow and I must say they are weel satisfied. Between ourselves, so is Forrigan here.

PHILLIPS. I can well imagine it. What a joy to have the wife of one's bosom restored to health!

MACK. It's not only that. He draws a percentage.

COOKE. What?

MACK. A pairfectly legeetimate percentage. We presairve some o' the more satisfactory elements of the feudal system, up here in the Highlands, Sir Brian.

COOKE. We have these rural magic-mongers and quack-salvers in our own part of the country; but what you say puts a more respectable complexion on it.

FORRIGAN. He's a highly respectable man. Donald Mac-Alpin.

MACK. He's all that.

COOKE. His fees, then, are high?

MACK. We'll leave that to your own loving-kindness, gratitude, and sense of your own importance, Sir Brian.

COOKE. Um. Ha.

PHILLIPS. Pray bid this man instantly be brought. In this wild country, there may well be more things than are dreamed of in our philosophy.

FORRIGAN (*to* MACK). Do you think, now . . . ?

MACK. My soul and conscience on it.

FORRIGAN. Very well. I will bring him to you.

EXIT FORRIGAN.

COOKE. I am reluctant to have any traffic with witchcraft.

MACK. Och, there's no question of that. Sit ye doon and have a rummer of toddy (*don't take toddy*). We're a' enlightened, civilised men here. Especially you, Mr. Phillips. Beelzebub would scunner at the like of us. There's still a drop in the kettle.

MACK *pours out toddy.* RE-ENTER FORRIGAN.

FORRIGAN. I have sent for him. You must not mind, Sir Brian, if his looks are a wee bit peculiar.

MACK. Nothing surprises a Sassenach north of the Grampians. You'll hae a dram, Forrigan ?

FORRIGAN. I will. I will.

(47. MUSIC)   DONALD *appears at the doorway with* OLD
MACALPIN *lurking behind him. He has acquired
a great dignity which is, at the moment, not a
little due to alcohol.*

DONALD. You have sent for me into your presence, Forrigan.

FORRIGAN. I have, Donald, I have. It was kind of you to come so quickly. Will you take a wee dram, now ?

DONALD. I will. And my father will be taking one too, also, whatever.

The MACALPINS *come into the room and are served with
drams.*

THE MACALPINS. Slainthe !

FORRIGAN. This is Sir Brian Cooke, Donald. He is a great man in his own country, which is England.

DONALD *bows.*

DONALD. I have heard of England and, no doubt, it will be a very agreeable place, whatever.

COOKE. Is this the Doctor ?

FORRIGAN. Well, they call him the Healer in these parts.

COOKE. Well, my man . . .

DONALD. You will pardon me, but I am not your man.

COOKE. Forgive me. It is a way of speaking.

DONALD. It does not seem to me to be a very good way, whatever.

MACK. Now, now. You're owre important a man to heed a foreign way of speaking.

DONALD. I was forgetting that the gentleman was foreign. Indeed, I am sorry . . . You, sir, were about to make an observe?

COOKE. I hear that you have performed some very remarkable cures.

DONALD. I wouldn't say. Maybe a wee bit, yes.

COOKE. You may have heard that my daughter is very ill.

DONALD. I may and I may not. They were telling me somewhat of it.

COOKE. Do you think you could undertake her case?

DONALD. If it is Forrigan's will, I will consult with my father and we will see. There is much that I would do for a guest of Forrigan.

FORRIGAN. It would be a great obligement, Donald, if you would help the poor lassie.

COOKE. What is your fee?

DONALD. I do not understand what is a fee.

COOKE. Rat me, you are a curious Docor.

MACK. I think, Sir Brian, it would be advisable no' to say too much about a fee. I will have a word with you apart on the topic.

COOKE. I'm not a rich man.

DONALD. You were not accused of any such and a thing, whatever.

MACALPIN. In the Highlands, riches are not a thing to be talked about between gentlemen.

PHILLIPS. Gentlemen, we are wasting time. I have confidence in this man. There is a dignity in his bearing and an imperiousness in his regard that betoken unusual gifts. Let us not haggle nor chatter. Sir, will you undertake the cure of this young lady?

DONALD. Sir, I will.

PHILLIPS. I trust in your honour that you will do your best: for, to speak truth, I hold this young lady in the tenderest esteem.

MACALPIN. Keep you your mind at ease. What can be done will be done. Where is the young damsel?

COOKE. She is in her bedchamber. Shall I conduct you.
thither ?

DONALD. O, I couldna be doing that . . . Father !

MACALPIN. My son is a wee bit bashful. It will be needful
to bring the young lady down here.

FORRIGAN. I think it would be best.

COOKE. Bid your cousin attend us here.

PHILLIPS. She was sorely afflicted, sir.   Would it not be
well . . .

COOKE. Say that it is my command.

PHILLIPS. Very well, sir.

EXIT PHILLIPS, MACALPIN *whispers to* FORRIGAN

FORRIGAN. Yes, yes . . . Sir Brian, he says it is necessary
that the gentlemen should retire and that he should see the
young lady himself and his father only.

COOKE. Eh ? Why ?

FORRIGAN. He says it is not right that you should be asking
why. It is his way of doing things.

COOKE. But, but . . .

FORRIGAN. I will pledge my honour for these men that no
ill will befall her.

COOKE. At the same time . . .

FORRIGAN. The honour of a Grant of Forrigan is no small
matter, Sir Brian Cooke, as I hope it will not be necessary
to remind you.

PHILLIPS. I have conveyed your instructions to my aunt, sir.

COOKE. Very well.

FORRIGAN.   I thank you. If you will follow me to the little
wee mean room where I do my business matters, you will
find a peat fire and a bottle of punch. Allow me.

> *He lifts a couple of candlesticks. So does* MACK.
> EXEUNT *with* COOKE.

> *The* MACALPINS *help themselves to another dram and
> converse for a moment in the Gaelic. They put out all
> remaining candles but one.*

309   [67]

MACALPIN. Now put you down your glass, Donald, and stand here in the middle of the floor with the candle to your hand. Or would you rather be sitting?

DONALD. I can stand.

MACALPIN. I wasna very sure if you would be able. But that's fine, man, fine. You'll have mind what to say?

DONALD. Aye.

MACALPIN. Do you feel the gift strong in you?

DONALD. I am feeling something strong in me anyhow, whatever.

MACALPIN. Good, good. I will be sitting back here in the dark so as no' to frighten the lassie. And if you forget what to say, there is always the Gaelic.

(48. MUSIC) MACALPIN *retires to a dark corner and plays a few melancholy chords on his fiddle.* DONALD *swaying slightly, stands in mid-stage near a candle, which throws a huge shadow on the wall.*

ENTER CLARINDA, *her hair down and wearing a bed gown.*

CLARINDA. Oh!

(49. MUSIC)

DONALD. Do not be afraid. Come here to me. Put your hand in my hand.

He lifts the candle and studies her face intently.

Aye, there is the sorrow in that face.

CLARINDA. But...

DONALD. Do not be speaking for a wee. I will be saying to you the Sian against Harm.

He chants in a low monotone.

(50. MUSIC)

DONALD. (*contd.*)

Sian a chuir Moire air Mac ort,
Sian ro' marbadh, sian ro' lot ort,
Sian eadar a' chlioch 's a' ghlun,
Sian nan Tri ann an aon ort:

[68]

Sian seachd eadar a h-aon ort,
Sian seachd eadar a dha ort,
Sian seachd eadar a tri ort,
Sian seachd eadar a ceithir ort,
Sian seachd eadar a coig ort,
Sian seachd eadar a sia ort,
Sian seachd paidir nan seachd paidir dol deisel ri diugh nrach ort,
ga do ghleidheadh bho bheud 's bho mhi-thapadh !

CLARINDA. I don't know what you're talking about ; I feel giddy ; and I want to sit down.

DONALD. You may sit down for a wee minute.

He guides her to a seat. He then, during the following speech, strides up and down. MACALPIN *has been playing the fiddle, very softly, all the time, but he stops now.*

DONALD. There is good things and there is bad things round about your head. There is black spirits sitting on you like as if you were a sheep and they crows hunting for ticks. There is more black spirits than there is white spirits. You are terrible badly, to tell you no lie. Dear me, it is hard to be telling what to do. Stand up.

CLARINDA. Indeed, I shall not.

DONALD. What did you say ?

CLARINDA. You are trying to frighten me. I am not afraid of any savage in petticoats that ever scratches himself. Go instantly and bring my father.

DONALD. I will not bring your father.

CLARINDA. Then I shall scream and that will bring him and my cousin and you will be soundly beaten.

DONALD. I do not think that there is anything the matter with you at all, at all. Forbye badness.

CLARINDA. You are quite wrong. I am very ill indeed. Now, bring my father.

DONALD. I will not. What care I for your father ?

CLARINDA. I warn you, my patience is nearly exhausted.

DONALD. Stand up. You may scream and you may yell,

but you will do as I tell you. *Dhonas's dholas ort, agus leatsa.*
Dole and sorrow to you and yours if you do not stand up on
your feet and look me in the face.

CLARINDA *stands up and faces him.*

DONALD. The best thing for you would be to take you across
my knee and give you the good and holy thrashing. But I am
a gentleman and I will not do that. Look me in the eye. Will
you tell me now what way you are so proud and wicked to
the good young man, your kinsman?

CLARINDA. No.

DONALD. You are not for telling me?

CLARINDA. No.

DONALD. Very well, then. Stand you with your left toe
pointed and your heel in the arch of your right foot. Kilt up
your coats as high as you can and tie them with your waist
band. My father and I have seen bare legs before and more.
We will not be blushing, whatever . . . *Droch caoidh ort.* Bad
moanings on you, do what I tell you!

CLARINDA, *a little dazed, obeys,* MACALPIN *begins to
play a Strathspey.*

(51. MUSIC)

CLARINDA. I'll tell my father.

DONALD. You are a clype-clash-my clever. Well I know it.
You can clype your fill when you have done as I tell you.
What you will do now is called the *Ceum Shuil,* or the pro-
menade step and I will show you how it is done.

(52. MUSIC)   *He dances a few steps.*

DONALD. Now, put you your feet as I do and try you to hold
yourself with some grace. It is like a heifer with the stomach-
ache you are! . . . There, now. That is not so bad. I will show
you now the *Ceum Coshich.* It is the footing step. It is grand
for the black vapours or the wind round the heart . . . That
is very good. I would not wonder but you had Highland
blood in your veins. You may rest now, a wee minute, and
I will reward you by showing you a step of my own. It is

[70]

the *Gruin Leum*, they call it, or MacAlpin's own leap. Play
up, you auld bodach, and we will give the lady the fine treat!

(53. MUSIC)   *He dances furiously, finishing with a prodigious
                   jump.* CLARINDA *bursts into hysterical laughter.*

CLARINDA. Hahhahhaha! Oh! Oh! OOOOO!!

          PHILLIPS *dashes in at the door with his sword drawn.*
          COOKE, FORRIGAN, MACK, MRS. MEARES, MRS.
          GRANT, MAIRI *and the* HALFLIN *follow, some of them
          with candles. The room is now brightly lighted.*

PHILLIPS. Thunder and blood! Stand back, you dog! . . .
My darling, speak to me!

CLARINDA. Hoohooohooo! Whoop!

PHILLIPS. Her dress is disordered. She is in a frenzy. Let
me at that son of perdition.

(54. MUSIC)   FORRIGAN *and* MACK *restrain him. The* MAC-
                   ALPINS *pick up poker and tongs and prepare
                   to defend themselves.* COOKE *and the three
                   women* WOMEN *cluster round* CLARINDA. MAIRI
                   *separates herself from the group and takes the
                   floor.*

MAIRI. Let me speak, for speak I must. Listen to me. It's
heard I will be or I fall down on this floor in a fit and never
again see the light of day! . . . Donald MacAlpin and Dugald
MacAlpin, I accuse you both of witchcraft and of trafficking
with the Evil One, the Cross of the Nine Angels be upon me
from my chin to my toes.

          *The force of her sincerity draws and rivets the attention
          of everybody else on the stage. She gives a short gasp
          and gets her second wind.*

(55. MUSIC)

MAIRI. Look at him where he stands with the poker in his
hand. He is not content, mind you, with carrying on with a
fairy-woman in Slochmuich Pass. No, no. There is a coven
of witches that meets at Carn Dubh and does the black rites
of the Old Religion in the bend of midsummer under the

Witches' Moon. And who is the man with the white cuff and
the hair black hand, I am asking you? And the black hound
at his heels? Donald MacAlpin, the Forrigan herd, and none
other. They touch the heel and the head and sell themselves
to immortal shame. Kate MacIntyre was there, and Annie
Carmichael was there, and Jean Dalrymple and all the old forgotten cailleachs in Speyside and Badenoch was there. And
there's things in the croft at Carn Dubh that would set your
blood running cold. And all of them with the spot where the
Auld Yin touched them that they can feel no pain in, never
forever more. Call the witch finders. Call the Minister.
You will learn then, I promise you. Put a silver crown in your
gun, Forrigan, or they will jink you yet. You said yourself,
Mrs. Grant, that he was Lucius, Son of the Morning. Go you
to the croft at Carn Dubh and you will see the grass tramped
flat with the split hooves of a legion of Devils. You saw for
yourself, Mr. Mack. (*Cross over to L.C.*) Seize them and bind
them. Seize them and bind them, before they bring ill on this
house.

(**55. END OF MUSIC**)

MRS. GRANT (*coming to herself*). Such like nonsense. You
should think shame of yourself, a decent lass like you. You'll
excuse her, Sir Brian.

COOKE (*doubtfully*). I don't know. It is very difficult. Of
course, I don't believe in these things. But, at the same time...

PHILLIPS. Take your hands off me. I will be calm. I shall not
hurt those wretches until I hear what has happened in this room.

MRS. GRANT. The wee girl can tell us that.

PHILLIPS. Clarinda. Speak to me.

CLARINDA. Don't speak to *me*. I shall never, never forgive
you. You are making a fool of yourself.

PHILLIPS. What?

CLARINDA. You are not content with delivering me into
the hands of an ignorant, half mad peasant. You must strut
and rant like one of those creatures in an opera. You make
me sick.

[72]   314

PHILLIPS. I do, do I ?

CLARINDA. Yes. Go away. I cannot bear to see you. You cut a ridiculous figure.

PHILLIPS. I hardly dare to describe the figure you cut.

CLARINDA. The figure I cut ? I am dragged from a bed of sickness to conform to your drunken whim. I . . . I hate and despise you. Mrs. Meares, lead me to my room.

PHILLIPS. Aunt Sophonisba, I forbid you to do any such thing.

CLARINDA. *You* forbid !

PHILLIPS. Yes. One short half hour ago, you gave a realistic impression of a young female at death's door. Now you fall with great energy and spirit to the agreeable task of being offensive and impertinent. You are an actress, Madam.

CLARINDA. Oh.

PHILLIPS. I might use even a stronger term.

CLARINDA. Father !

COOKE. My child ?

CLARINDA. Will you stand by and see me so affronted ? And by one who, in the past, has wearied me with his protestations of undying respect and affection ! It is too much. I cannot bear it. I shall die.

PHILLIPS. You have no intention of doing anything of the kind.

CLARINDA. Leave my presence instantly.

PHILLIPS (*sheathing his sword*). With all the pleasure in life. I shall leave you to the grotesque embraces of this monstrous mountebank, if it pleases you to imagine yourself a Circe to the swine.

DONALD. Do my ears deceive me, or did you use a word that is not suitable for the use of gentlemen ?

PHILLIPS. I am not responsible for your ears. They are very large and I observe that heather is growing out of them. But if you desire it, I shall cut them off with the greatest pleasure.

DONALD. You will be cutting off my ears, my gracious ! I tell you this and I tell you no more, I will be cracking you on my thumbnail, you shilpit creature that you are !

315

CLARINDA. Oh! Oh! I cannot bear it! My heart! My heart!

She rapidly develops signs of hysterics.

PHILLIPS. Be silent.

CLARINDA. Oh! Oh! You call yourself a man! Is it for this I have borne for all those years your intolerable society—the cringing attentions forced upon me? A pretty metamorphosis, from a fawning cur to a snarling tyke.

She stands up and faces him like a fury.

PHILLIPS. And I lavished the tender affection of an honest heart on this fishwife! You are a slut and you can take that!

> PHILLIPS *hits* CLARINDA *a hearty smack on the cheek. There is a gasp of horror from the assembly.* CLARINDA *stands, holding her cheek and staring at* PHILLIPS *with a peculiar expression on her face.*

COOKE. Wat! You are beside yourself!

MACALPIN. Dear me! To strike a woman and them no' married.

DONALD. If there was an excuse for that act, you have the excuse. But there is no excuse. Prepare to take a trup to the Golden Gates of Heaven or the Red Hot Gates of Hell! Royal's my race, and be damned to you.

MACALPIN. Stop you. Look at the lassie.

> CLARINDA *is wreathed in smiles.*

CLARINDA (*rapt*). I am conscious of a strange sensation. It astonished and perplexed me till I realised that I had felt it before. I have not felt it since I went galloping on my pony across the moor to Skipton with the wind in my hair. I am feeling WELL!

COOKE. You certainly look different.

CLARINDA. Walter, it was not I who spoke to you those harsh and wicked words. It was a simulacrum of your Clarinda. And now you have rescued me by that sacred, sacred blow from the Shadows as Orpheus rescued his Euridike, as Perseus rescued the other young person from the clutches of the horrid Dragon ...

[74]

PHILLIPS. It was Andromache, my darling.

CLARINDA. Was it? How clever of you to know! But you know everything, my dearest.

PHILLIPS. My life! My own!

(56. MUSIC DUET)

CLARINDA and PHILLIPS.

> As Orpheus from the realms of light
> In trembling ardour took his way
> To caves of black Cimmerian night
> To rescue his Euridike,
>
> So came you to me,
> So came I to you.
>
> And merrily we two shall reunited be,
> With a fol-lol the day
> And a tirra-lirra lee,
> Hey, so jolly we shall reunited be,
> With a fol-lol tirra-lirra lee.
>
> I lay in troubled slumber tied
> Like princess pent in leafy cell.
> You to my pale, pale cheek applied
> Th' awaking blow that made me well.
>
> So smacked I you,
> So smacked you me.

Chorus.   As before.

THEY *embrace.*

MAIRI. Oh, dear me, is that not beautiful!

She bursts into tears.

MACK (*taking snuff*). A highly satisfactory outcome. At the same time, I respectfully suggest that credit should go where credit is due. Mr. Phillips's skelp on the lug was no doubt very efficacious, but it followed the conscientious labours of our good friend Donald. I merely state the fact for purposes of record, Sir Brian.

COOKE. Eh? Yes. Remarkable. Remarkable.

CLARINDA. That is true. It was a lovely treatment and I began to get better at once—though perhaps I didn't realise it. Father, will you take Donald with us to Skipton. When I think of the poor sick people there . . . !

COOKE. There might be money in it.

PHILLIPS. We shall take him to London.

MRS. GRANT. The folk here would have something to say about that.

MACK. It might be arranged, though. It might be arranged. On a suitable monetary basis, of course.

FORRIGAN. What would you have to say to that, MacAlpin?

DONALD. Oh, I couldna be leaving you wanting a herd.

FORRIGAN. It's the poor herd you have been to me these last weeks.

DONALD. Indeed, and do you say so? There is not a finer herd than herself in all the Land of Scotland, I am telling you.

MACALPIN. Donald, Donald, remember your place!

DONALD. Nor a finer dancer nor a better doctor, forbye.

MACALPIN. Yes, yes. But the gentlemen understand these things better nor you.

DONALD. Give me another dram within me and I will show you dancing, aye, and doctoring.

MRS. GRANT. Toots, it's getting late. It's time we were all in our beds.

DONALD. Ladies and gentlemans, take your partners for the Reel of Tulloch!

COOKE. For what?

DONALD. Take you the Lady of Forrigan, gentlemans, and stand you there. Forrigan, take you the old gentlewoman and stand you there. You young ones, take your places here. Come by me, Mairi, and we will show them how to dance.

MAIRI. But I canna dance for the pain you put in my back.

DONALD (*smacking her on the behind*). Foosh! It's away now

forever more and all eternity forbye.   Play you your fiddle, father, as if it was the Duvvle himself that was in you . . . Hooach !

(57. MUSIC)   *They dance the first act of a Reel, the* HALFLIN *and the ad lib.* SERVANTS, *clapping their hands in time to the music.*

CURTAIN

As soon as the Curtain falls, MRS. GRANT *appears in front of it, laughing and breathless, and speaks—The Epilogue.*

EPILOGUE TO THE FORRIGAN REEL

SPOKEN BY MRS. GRANT.

Well, there you are. By way of aftermath
I bring soft answers to the righteous wrath
Of those who feel this kind of Lowland Fling
Crude and impertinent and no' the thing.
We have no wish to set the heath on fire
From far Loch Eirebo to near Kintyre.
Nor do we seek to boil the simmering pots
Of dour, pragmatical, sermon tasting Scots.
The most ingenious of them can't but fail
To point a moral to our crazy tale :
Unless it be that every now and then
Women go daft from dullness—like their men.
The dreary seconds go, " Tick-tock, tick-tock,"
Till they grow skeerie and run up the clock.

So cheer us up whenever you've a mind.
Kiss us or skelp us as you feel inclined ;
But keep in mind that half of our camsteeriness
Is just pure, simple, undiluted weariness.

The author chose, tonight, to light his Stage
With simple humours of a by-gone age.
You find his capers creak, his tapers dim ?
Don't boo the actors—lay the blame on him.
To cheer you up a bit was all he meant.
If he has done it, he is well content.
Go out, then, to the thoroughfare and say :
" In parts, amusing ; not what I call a play."
But say of us (and we can stand the test),
" They're decent poor souls ; and they did their best."

[*The Curtain rises again and* SHE *joins the* DANCERS.

FINIS